28TH EDITION

THE HACHETTE LEARNING GUIDE TO

Preparatory Schools 2025

A guide to 1300 independent preparatory and junior schools in the United Kingdom providing education for 2 to 13-year-olds

Together we unlock every learner's unique potential

At Hachette Learning (formerly Hodder Education), there's one thing we're certain about. No two students learn the same way. That's why our approach to teaching begins by recognising the needs of individuals first.

Our mission is to allow every learner to fulfil their unique potential by empowering those who teach them. From our expert teaching and learning resources to our digital educational tools that make learning easier and more accessible for all, we provide solutions designed to maximise the impact of learning for every teacher, parent and student.

Aligned to our parent company, Hachette Livre, founded in 1826, we pride ourselves on being a learning solutions provider with a global footprint.

www.hachettelearning.com

Every effort has been made to trace all copyright holders, but if any have been inadvertently overlooked, the Publishers will be pleased to make the necessary arrangements at the first opportunity

Although every effort has been made to ensure that website addresses are correct at time of going to press, Hachette Learning cannot be held responsible for the content of any website mentioned in this book. It is sometimes possible to find a relocated web page by typing in the address of the home page for a website in the URL window of your browser

Hachette UK's policy is to use papers that are natural, renewable and recyclable products and made from wood grown in well-managed forests and other controlled sources. The logging and manufacturing processes are expected to conform to the environmental regulations of the country of origin

To order, please visit www.HachetteLearning.com or contact Customer Service at education@hachette.co.uk / +44 (0)1235 827827.

ISBN: 9781036011420

© Hachette Learning 2025

First published in 2025 by
Hachette Learning,
An Hachette UK Company
Carmelite House
50 Victoria Embankment
London EC4Y 0DZ
www.HachetteLearning.com

The authorised representative in the EEA is Hachette Ireland, 8 Castlecourt Centre, Dublin 15, D15 XTP3, Ireland (email: info@hbgi.ie)

All rights reserved. Apart from any use permitted under UK copyright law, no part of this publication may be reproduced or transmitted in any form or by any means, electronic or mechanical, including photocopying and recording, or held within any information storage and retrieval system, without permission in writing from the publisher or under licence from the Copyright Licensing Agency Limited. Further details of such licences (for reprographic reproduction) may be obtained from the Copyright Licensing Agency Limited, www.cla.co.u

A catalogue record for this title is available from the British Library

Typeset in the UK
Printed in the UK

MIX
Paper | Supporting responsible forestry
FSC™ C104740

Contents

Editorial

Foreword – Giving our children the best start in life, Dominic Norrish, IAPS 5
How to use this guidebook 7
Choosing a school – what to consider 8
The secrets of success: beyond grades, Ballard School 10
'Into the Trees' at Barrow Hills School 12
How Kodály-inspired learning has revolutionised music at Feltonfleet 14
Cool to be kind, Hanford School 16
The benefits of scholarships, Highfield and Brookham School 18
Find your song and sing it – the importance of learning through experience, Kent College Junior School 20
Rediscovering the joy of hands-on learning in primary education, Merchiston Castle School 22
Top 5 tips for choosing a prep school, Millfield Preparatory School 24
The school taking the classroom outdoors, Moor Park 26
Initial advice 28
Help in funding the fees, *Chris Procter* 35

Profiles

Schools in the UK
England   *Central & West* 40
          East 44
          East Midlands 53
          Greater London 54
          London 61
          North-West 63
          South-East 66
          South-West 84
          West Midlands 88
          Yorkshire & Humberside 89
Scotland 93
Wales 97

Geographical directory of schools in the United Kingdom D101
Channel Islands D103
England   *Central & West* D105
          East D109
          East Midlands D115
          Greater London D119
          London D125
          North-East D133
          North-West (including Isle of Man) D135
          South-East D141
          South-West D151
          West Midlands D155
          Yorkshire & Humberside D159
Northern Ireland D163
Scotland D165
Wales D169

Index 171

BACK-TO-SCHOOL
TUCK BOXES AND TRUNKS

T: 01702 216222 | 07768 364726
info@storagetrunks.co.uk
www.storagetrunks.co.uk

IN A VARIETY OF COLOURS, DESIGNS AND SIZES

LOGICLINE TRUNKS
HANDMADE IN ENGLAND

Giving our children the best start in life

Dominic Norrish, Chief Executive of IAPS, writes the foreword to the 2025 edition of John Catt's Preparatory Schools

Having taken the decision to offer your child the many potential benefits that an independent education can bestow, you as parents should be praised for having had the foresight, responsibility and bravery to give them priority over the many other needs competing for your time and resources.

Identifying the right school for your children is perhaps the most impactful decision you will make this year – a place where they can flourish academically, have their natural talents nurtured from the start and are encouraged and developed by empathetic, supportive teachers within a secure educational environment.

Unless money really is no object – and statistics suggest that there are few who fall into the category – then choosing an independent education will not have been a decision lightly taken. You won't have failed to notice that the affordability slope has been further steepened by decisions made by the current government.

For some parents, the overwhelming desire to provide for their child, affording them the opportunities that they themselves may not have had, is a huge motivation. For this group, choosing a more frugal personal lifestyle in order to afford school fees just makes logical sense. These parents have decided that an independent education for their children takes precedence over some of the benefits of their hard work and sound financial management – a larger home, new cars, overseas holidays – which society holds up as the hallmarks of success. This is the 'bravery' referred to above: the acceptance that having identified your child's needs and the best solution for them, you are committing to 'eat last', as the management literature would phrase it.

What will have helped persuade these parents to take this path is the knowledge they are accessing something very special for their child – not only the benefits of studying a broad curriculum that every pupil needs and is entitled to, but also the opportunity and space to spend time exploring the things they enjoy and excel in. As well as being encouraged to have their heads buried in books, reading and writing at length, independent school pupils can participate in the activities they love, whether that is a particular sport, creating art, playing an instrument, dancing, performing or cooking healthy and creative food. It is a rich experience and the quality of the school chosen bestows significant benefits on the child. They are, above all, developmental environments that draw out and nurture talent.

I am privileged in my role to visit so many truly wonderful prep schools in IAPS membership, to see the facilities and meet the passionate, caring people who make an independent education such a special thing. The headteachers who give such inspiring, learned leadership to their talented staff of expert teachers and classroom assistants will provide many parents with their first and most enduring impression of the school. As you might expect in my role, I know hundreds of them and am consistently awed by the sheer scope of their expertise and unfailing commitment to, and knowledge of, the pupils in their care.

When I visit an IAPS school, I am always struck by the obvious and unmistakable happiness of the children. Whether studying in classrooms that are purpose-designed to help them thrive and flourish, or playing sport on expansive fields and in top-quality indoor facilities, or just enjoying themselves at play in thoughtfully created outdoor spaces, there is palpable joy in the growth taking place.

The politeness, respect for others and sense of personal pride that emerge in these children through their experience of success in a place that treats them as individuals are also remarkable. Great schools have always been engines of socialisation, key institutions in the creation of a positive, respectful world, and independent schools are notable for the way in which they help children to develop their character. Crucial to this is the availability of an impressive range of structured co-curricular activities by which children

> Great schools have always been engines of socialisation, key institutions in the creation of a positive, respectful world, and independent schools are notable for the way in which they help children to develop their character.

Foreword

Hanford School - see editorial on page 16

are afforded the opportunity to explore, to excel, to struggle with difficult things and to deal with failure, in essence, to learn what it is to grow up well.

None of this happens by accident. The prep and junior heads who lead these wonderful schools have built careers over years of inspirational classroom teaching, expert subject specialism and various senior leadership roles. They, and none better, know what makes a great school and are well aware of the responsibility you are granting them.

Choosing the right school for the first few years of your child's development ensures the very best foundation for their educational success in senior school and beyond and you have in this publication all the information you will need to help you make your decision.

For more information about IAPS, see page 31

Independent Association of Prep Schools

How to use this guidebook

Are you looking for...

Help and advice?
If so, take a look at our editorial section (pages 5 to 36). Here you will find articles written by experts in their field covering issues you may well come across when choosing a school for your child.

A school or college in a certain geographical region?
Then you need to go to the map on D102 to find the directory page reference to a particular region. We suggest that you look first in the directory for basic information about all the schools in each region, complete with contact details, so that you will be better informed about the choices available to you. From this section you will be directed to more detailed information in the profile section, where this is available.

A certain type of school or college in a particular area?
Look in the directories for the area you want (again, you can find a directory page reference from the regional map on D102). Underneath each school listed you will find icons that denote different types of schools or qualifications that they offer. You can find a key to these icons on the following page; this key is repeated at the front of each section of the directory.

A specific school or college?
If you know the name of the school or college but are unsure of its location, simply go to the index at the back of the guide where you will find all the schools listed alphabetically. You will find that some page numbers are prefixed with the letter D, this denotes that the school appears in the directory section. Page numbers not prefixed by the letter D denote schools that have chosen to include a fuller school profile, which will provide you with much more extensive information.

More information on relevant educational organisations and examinations?
In the editorial section you will find 'Initial advice', a helpful explanation of the various educational organisations relevant to preparatory schools. There are articles from the Boarding Schools Association (BSA), Girls' Schools Association (GSA), Headmasters' and Headmistresses' Conference (HMC), Independent Association of Preparatory Schools (IAPS), Independent Schools Association (ISA), Independent Schools Council (ISC) and the Society of Heads.

Keys to directory information
The diagrams below explain what the different icons used in the directory mean, and indicate the type of information given for each school in the directory.

Key to directory

- County
- Name of school or college
- Address and contact number
- Head's name
- Age range
- Number of pupils. B = boys G = girls
- Fees per annum.
  Day = fees for day pupils.
  WB = fees for weekly boarders.
  FB = fees for full boarders.

Wherefordshire

College Academy
For further details see p. 00

Which Street, Whosville,
Wherefordshire AB12 3CD

Tel: 01000 000000
Head Master: Dr A Person
Age range: 11–18
No. of pupils: 660 B330 G330
Fees: Day £11,000 WB £16,000 FB £20,000

Key to icons (abridged)

Key to symbols:
- Boys' school
- Girls' school
- International school

Schools offering:
- Boarding accommodation
- Bursaries
- A levels
- International Baccalaureate
- Learning support

Moor Park - see editorial on page 26

Choosing a school – what to consider

However much a school may appeal at first sight, you still need sound information to form your judgement

Schools attract pupils by their reputations, so most go to considerable lengths to ensure that parents are presented with an attractive image. Modern marketing techniques try to promote good points and play down (without totally obscuring) bad ones. But every Head knows that, however good the school prospectus is, it only serves to attract parents through the school gates. Thereafter the decision depends on what they see and hear. Research we have carried out over the years suggests that in many cases the most important factor in choosing a school is the impression given by the Head. As well as finding out what goes on in a school, parents need to be reassured by the aura of confidence that they expect from a Head. How they judge the latter may help them form their opinion of the former. In other words, how a Head answers questions is important in itself and, to get you started, we have drawn up a list of points that you may like to consider. Some can be posed as questions and some are points you'll only want to check in your mind. They are not listed in any particular order and their significance will vary from family to family, but they should be useful in helping you to form an opinion.

Before visiting and asking questions, **check the facts** – such as which association the school belongs to, how big it is, how many staff *etc*. Is there any form of financial pie chart showing how the school's resources are used? The answers to questions like these should be in the promotional material you've been sent. If they aren't, you've already got a good question to ask!

Check the website. Is it up-to-date? Look at the school's social media feeds and videos. What type of tone do they set? That first impression is very important.

When you get to the school you will want to judge the overall atmosphere and decide whether it will suit you and your child. Are any other members of the family going to help to pay the fees? If so, their views are important and the school's attitude towards them may be instructive.

When you make it to the inner sanctum, **what do you make of the Head as a person?** Age? Family? Staying? Moving on? Retiring? Busted flush? Accessible to children, parents and staff? If you never get to see the Head, but deal

Academic priorities – attitude towards league tables? This is a forked question. If the answer is 'We're most concerned with doing the best for the child', you pitch them a late-developer; if the answer is, 'Well, frankly, we have a very high entry threshold', then you say 'So we have to give you a foolproof academic winner, do we?'

Choosing a school

Supplementary questions:

- What is the ratio of teachers to pupils?
- What are the professional qualifications of the teaching staff?
- What is the school's retention rate? In prep schools this means how many pupils do they lose at 11 when the school goes on to 13.
- How long is the school day – and week?
- What are the school's exam results?
- What are the criteria for presenting them?
- Were they consistent over the years?
- Is progress accelerated for the academically bright?
- How does the school cope with pupils who do not work?
- Where do pupils go when they leave?
- How important and well resourced are sports, extra-curricular and after school activities, music and drama?
- What cultural or other visits are arranged away from the school?

Other topics to cover:

- What is the school's mission?
- What is its attitude to religion?
- How well is the school integrated into the local community?
- How have they responded to the Charities Act initiatives?
- What are the responsibilities and obligations at weekends for parents, pupils and the school?
- Does the school keep a watching brief or reserve the option to get involved after a weekend incident?
- What is the school's attitude to discipline?
- Have there been problems with drugs, drink or sex? How have they been dealt with?
- What is the school's policy on bullying?
- How does the school cope with pupils' problems?
- What sort of academic and pastoral advice is available?
- What positive steps are taken to encourage good manners, behaviour and sportsmanship?
- What is the uniform?
- What steps are taken to ensure that pupils take pride in their personal appearance?
- How often does the school communicate with parents through reports, parent/teacher meetings or other visits?
- What level of parental involvement is encouraged both in terms of keeping in touch with staff about your own child and more generally, eg a Parents' Association?

And finally – and perhaps most importantly – what does your child make of the school, the adults met, the other children met, pupils at the school in other contexts, and the website?

The secrets of success: beyond grades

In today's fast-paced and ever-changing world, parents are increasingly concerned about ensuring their children are not only academically successful but also well prepared for the future. It's a common misconception that a successful school is solely defined by its ability to produce high grades and exam results. However, the true measure of success lies in the holistic development of pupils, equipping them with essential life skills such as teamwork, leadership, adaptability and resilience. Independent schools are leading the way in providing a well-rounded education that goes beyond the classroom.

Research emphasises the importance of fostering a growth mindset in pupils. According to the Education Endowment Foundation, pupils who understand that intelligence can be developed are more likely to persevere through challenges and achieve higher academic success[1]. Ballard (Independent Co-educational School of the Year) empowers its pupils by encouraging them to seize opportunities, leading them to significant personal and academic growth.

Co-curricular activities and holistic development
Research shows that busy, happy children do well in the classroom. Independent schools, with their fantastic facilities, specialist staff and opportunities to enable extensive co-curricular activities, excel in this area. The Social Mobility Commission reports that co-curricular activities lead to numerous benefits, including a sense of belonging, increased confidence and enhanced social skills, which are invaluable to employers[2]. Schools offering a variety of activities help children learn and play together, developing strong social bonds and a sense of community.

At Ballard, pupils have access to over 150 activities each week, including experimental archaeology, Mandarin, citizenship, orchestra, theatre productions and a range of sports. These opportunities not only enrich the academic experience but also help pupils build essential life skills such as creativity, resilience and teamwork.

Proactive pastoral care also plays a crucial role in supporting pupils. Programmes like 'Ballard on Board' help them navigate the complexities of friendship, encouraging them to find their own solutions, having a positive impact on mental wellbeing and academic performance[3]. By fostering a supportive and caring environment, schools like Ballard ensure that every pupil feels valued and understood, paving the way for personal and academic growth. Research underscores the importance of student leadership opportunities in promoting resilience and self-efficacy among young people[4]. Ballard's Student Council has impacted all areas of the school including uniform, food, values and driving the Eco Agenda.

Ballard School

Academic excellence and beyond

Academic success is still important and the gap between independent and comprehensive schools is widening to 29 percentage points in 2024 for top grades (7–9). Schools like Ballard ensure that pupils are stretched, challenged and supported to be the best that they can be, which may be straight nines or a 100% pass rate. At Ballard, all pupils achieved an average of 0.79 of a grade higher, across all papers, than their baseline assessment (GCSE results, 2024).

Research also shows that these approaches directly impact GCSE results. A study found that students participating in co-curricular activities, such as sports and debates, showed improved academic performance, with logical thinking and time-management skills positively influencing their GCSE outcomes. As mentioned earlier, pupils who embrace a growth mindset tend to perform better academically and exhibit greater wellbeing.

Values such as positivity, kindness, curiosity, respect, responsibility, honesty and safety resonate with parents who see their children flourish in multiple aspects of their lives. Schools that nurture the whole person ensure that success is not just about academic achievement but also about fostering well-rounded, happy individuals prepared to face future challenges.

Early years and holistic education

It's never too early. Holistic education starts from the early years, combining cognitive and physical development, language, literacy and numerical skills with social and emotional growth. This approach helps children grow into well-rounded, confident and capable individuals. Inclusive environments foster a sense of belonging and community where every child feels valued and respected. At Ballard, staff view themselves as an extension of the family, supporting pupils at every stage of their development.

Investing in the best education for children at a young age is an investment in their future. Research has shown that high-quality early years education can lead to better academic performance, improved social skills and greater emotional resilience. Schools like Ballard are committed to providing education that goes beyond the classroom, preparing pupils from the earliest age for future challenges and opportunities.

Ballard's beautiful grounds and state-of-the-art facilities provide a balanced and nurturing atmosphere with an ever-expanding curriculum. From Nursery, pupils are taught cookery, dance, music, PE and gymnastics by specialist teachers. In Kindergarten, pupils embark on exciting adventures with Forest School and Beach School, enhancing their understanding of the environment and promoting physical health and wellbeing. By Year 1, children begin learning French; in Year 3 there are specialist science, art, ICT and DT lessons, with Spanish from Year 4.

In conclusion, the secrets of success for pupils go beyond mere academic prowess. By nurturing essential life skills such as teamwork, leadership, adaptability and resilience, and providing strong pastoral support and a wealth of co-curricular opportunities, independent schools like Ballard ensure that every pupil has the chance to thrive. As a parent, there is no greater joy than seeing your child flourish in all aspects of life.

Success at Ballard is not just about academic achievement but also about fostering well-rounded, happy individuals who are prepared to face the challenges of the future. The school's holistic approach ensures that new pupils quickly feel that they belong and leave in Year 11 with a powerful sense of self, equipped to build a bright future in our fast-changing world.

Footnotes:
1. Education Endowment Foundation (2021) 'Growth Mindset Intervention'.
2. Social Mobility Commission (2019) 'An Unequal Playing Field'.
3. National Institute for Health and Care Excellence (2019) 'Pastoral Support in Schools'.
4. Department for Education (2018) 'Student Leadership and Resilience'.

For more information about Ballard School, see page 68

'Into the Trees' at Barrow Hills School

Barrow Hills, one of the three historic Bridewell Royal Hospital schools, is fortunate to be located within an extensive woodland setting, giving us much natural space to work with. Over the years, we have made consistent efforts to ensure this magical environment is a key part of our educational provision. Recently we have built on this foundation, partly as a conscious response to the pandemic and the freedoms curtailed for many children. Additionally, considering the increasingly pervasive influence of smartphones, gaming and social media on our pupils' lives, we strive for more green and less screen. Our primary motivation, though, is simply the desire to embrace outdoor learning as much as possible. With our all-school 'Into the Trees' project, we aim to foster a deeper immersion in nature. Our objectives include:

- integrating outdoor learning purposefully into the curriculum, encompassing art, design, adventurous play, ecology and environmental awareness
- engaging all pupils with their environment in hands-on, meaningful ways
- nurturing 'soft skills' through outdoor activities, such as collaboration, problem-solving, teamwork, joy and safe risk-taking
- creating a unique and material impact on our local natural environment.

With these goals in mind, and informed by pupil feedback, we have invested in a wide range of ecological actions to deepen connections with the natural world.

At the outset of the project, we upskilled cohorts of pupil 'Ecology Captains' in sustainability, biodiversity, and local and wider ecology. These young leaders were incredibly enthusiastic to have this agency and stewardship. We have onboarded cohorts of Ecology Captains in waves, eventually reaching our tipping point where at least 25% of the school have received additional environmental knowledge and had opportunities for direct action. This has included construction projects and a broad range of other environmental activities. Peer-to-peer knowledge sharing is now substantial; younger pupils look up to their older peers and being an eco-warrior is viewed as pretty cool.

'Farm to Table' is an example of an accessible activity. We created vegetable, fruit and herb beds and ensured time for cookery lessons within our design and technology curriculum, focusing on dishes we can grow ourselves. Even with limited space, items such as tomatoes, squash and

Barrow Hills School

In a world where smartphones, gaming, and social media increasingly dominate our pupils' lives, we strive to create more green and less screen, encouraging them to embrace the natural world and the countless benefits of outdoor learning.

herbs are easy to grow and prepare. Schools often love a competition – be it the Primary Maths Challenge or the IAPS Hockey Tournament – and gardening competitions can also inspire effort and enthusiasm. We have become avid dahlia growers (top tip: dig the root ball out, wrap it up and store it for winter; they thrive with some horse manure if available). Pupils have been thrilled to see their flowers win first prizes in a regional flower show. Such competitions can bring energy to areas where schools may not typically focus.

Our pupils also wanted more quality outdoor play that was both accessible and challenging. We have created two woodland play and learning areas. The first, built with pupil input, is a sustainable woodland adventure playground for younger pupils, a standard in many schools. However, the next, our creation of 'living willow domes', which serve as outdoor classrooms and play spaces, is very unusual. Built by children, these domes apply concepts from maths, science, art and design. Willow branches, when planted in soil and watered, have grown well and have been woven together. We now have three domes; additionally, a fallen tree trunk became a canvas to carve and paint a totem pole, adding character to the area, with this hands-on work connecting pupils to natural materials and inspiring creativity. We have also tried pyrography – using soldering irons to intricately decorate wood – allowing pupils to upcycle fallen wood into art, fostering sustainability.

Underlying all these activities, we have strengthened the skills and knowledge for responsible environmental stewardship. Forest School is now part of our regular timetable, rather than an add-on. Adventure Club, as a co-curricular activity, teaches 'bush skills' and risk management, from campfire cooking to whittling sticks. Staff have been constantly inspired by the environment. Each week, our Head, John Towers, takes his mountain bike club to a nearby National Trust common, a short ride away. At our school, grazed knees are viewed as badges of honour, valued by all stakeholders for the healthy risk they represent.

'Into the Trees' has profoundly impacted our pupils' appreciation of, and commitment to, a sustainable future. More than a quarter of our pupils have gained additional knowledge and skills that lay the foundation for environmental stewardship. All pupils have experienced Forest School, gained confidence with bush skills and learned to navigate and appreciate local flora and fauna.

They have developed resilience, soft skills and a deep appreciation for nature. The integration of outdoor learning has enriched various subjects – for example, in maths, Year 7 pupils have planned and measured the layout of the willow dome, while in art, Year 5 pupils have woven the roof. Our Ecology Captains helped us achieve Green Flag accreditation in 2023 and we earned a distinction in 2024.

Through wide-ranging projects like 'Into The Trees' across our school, Barrow Hills will continue to encourage our kids to get out there. For as we say here in Witley, 'There is no such thing as bad weather, just bad clothing choices.'

For more information about Barrow Hills School, see page 67

How Kodály-inspired learning has revolutionised music at Feltonfleet

Chris Andrews MA, BMus (Hons), PGCE, LTCL – Director of Music at Feltonfleet

As a younger teacher, I knew my pupils enjoyed music class, but something felt amiss. Those who played instruments gained something tangible, but for others the learning felt less permanent. Even choir members in Years 7 and 8, who could learn songs beautifully by ear, were slowed by an inability to read music from the page. I wanted more for all my pupils: not just a love for music but a solid foundation of musical literacy they could carry with them for life.

The turning point came when I observed a new colleague's lesson. Her approach was unlike anything I had ever seen. It was playful and joyful, yet deeply rigorous, with a structure that covered multiple skills in a single lesson. Inspired by the philosophies of Hungarian musician Zoltán Kodály, this approach transformed my understanding of what music education could be. It was thorough, accessible and entirely child-friendly – a revelation.

A new approach to music education

Kodály's philosophies shifted Feltonfleet's music curriculum from topic-based learning to a cumulative skill tree. Pitch is taught using solfege (e.g. do, re, mi) and rhythm using time names (e.g. ta, ti-ti), with each new concept introduced in a carefully sequenced order that is logical for children. Each new pitch and rhythm are then practised through performing, reading, writing, dictation, part-work, composing and improvising. This skill development is interspersed with singing games that subconsciously prepare pupils for the next concept. To the casual observer, lessons are full of songs and games, but they are underpinned by an intentional progression of skills.

The result? Every child develops musical literacy, not just those taking instrumental lessons. This approach ensures that children build a strong foundation in music and become competent musicians.

Feltonfleet School

The impact on pupils

Joy

Kodály advocated that music learning should be 'a joy […] and not a torture!' Time is made in every lesson for play and laughter. Singing games give everyone a break – including the teacher – and make singing fun. For students, this is both powerful and essential. Joyful singing breeds comfort with their own voice, helping them embrace mistakes and feel safe to explore.

The progressive steps of a Kodály programme mean all students are successful. This is a more profound type of joy: singing a pitch pattern correctly, mastering a clapping game or simply offering to sing on their own for the first time – these small successes build intrinsic motivation and are empowering, especially for those who do not play instruments. No iPads or gimmicks required – just a child's voice and the realisation that music can belong to them too.

This philosophy has fostered genuine enthusiasm and long-term commitment to music at Feltonfleet. It saw the choirs become so large that we had to split them into four groups.

Long-term, usable skill

By Year 8, Feltonfleet pupils possess an exciting level of musical skill. This includes sight-singing, recognising tonalities and intervals by ear, notating songs in different keys and rhythm dictation at post-GCSE level, to name a few.

The tools of a Kodály-inspired programme make complex musical ideas easy to explain. The approach has empowered our students with skills that – as a younger teacher – I could only dream of.

Removing barriers and improving retention

There are two big challenges for the beginner instrumentalist: the physicality of the instrument itself and reading music. At Feltonfleet, specialist Kodály teaching begins in pre-prep, so by the time children start learning an instrument, they already have a grounding in notation. This reduces one of the hurdles, making the process less overwhelming and more enjoyable.

Since we implemented a Kodály-inspired approach, the retention rate for instrumental lessons has soared. Over 2–3 years, we saw such significant growth that we increased the number of visiting music teachers from 10 to 16.

Upskilling

A misconception in music education is that this approach is only for young children, but the progression extends to adulthood. As a postgraduate pianist, I considered myself a competent musician, but attending my first summer school with the British Kodály Academy (BKA) showed how many holes there were in my own abilities. A decade later, I enjoy the enormous privilege of working as one of those tutors myself, both with the BKA and NYCOS (National Youth Choirs of Scotland), which both provide excellent training.

Beyond music: wider benefits of Kodály-inspired learning

The benefits of this approach extend far beyond music. Research collated by Susan Hallam shows that children who engage with a structured music programme gain advantages across all subjects, even after accounting for general intelligence. Music training enhances the brain's encoding of sound, improving auditory processing and memory. The benefits for dyslexic students are well-documented by Professor Usha Goswami (Cambridge University) - notably in the way rhythm is taught by breaking down word patterns.

Furthermore, children with musical training exhibit better verbal learning and retention abilities, a critical skill for success in literacy and communication. Group music-making also fosters social inclusion, with frequent participation in musical activities contributing to a strong sense of community and belonging.

At Feltonfleet, these benefits are not just theoretical. Singing assemblies, for instance, have become a highlight of the week, with staff often attending even when they don't need to. The joy of collective music-making is infectious, creating an uplifting and cohesive school atmosphere.

A revolution in music education

The Kodály-inspired approach has revolutionised music at Feltonfleet. It equips pupils with robust and transferable skills, instils a deep understanding of music and cultivates a love for the subject that lasts a lifetime. More importantly, it makes music accessible to every child.

> The Kodály-inspired approach has revolutionised music at Feltonfleet, making music accessible to every child.

For more information about Feltonfleet School, see page 73

Cool to be kind

Hilary Phillips, Head of Hanford School

We are very pleased at Hanford this month. We have won an award! But more of that later.

Spring is in the air and certainly we hope it will be bringing kinder weather. We had a discussion in morning chapel at the beginning of March about the wind which, at the time, was making itself known with gusto. The girls talked about how the wind can cause all sorts of problems, blowing off roof tiles, uprooting trees and spreading rubbish, to name but a few. They also came up with several ways in which the wind has a positive effect. How would seeds disperse, they asked, if not for the wind? They talked about energy from the wind and this led to them doing some useful research. Of course, it being Hanford, the girls also talked about how riding up a hill then cantering over the top allows the wind to blow right through you, leaving you exhilarated, breathless, laughing. It's a personal spring clean!

Spring cleaning is a marvellous thing. Getting rid of clutter is so satisfying and the pleasure from clear surfaces is deep. However, if you are anything like me, it doesn't take long for them to clutter up again. Back to that morning chapel discussion and I asked the girls what they could fill themselves up with once the wind had cleared out any internal clutter. They came to an agreement that filling themselves up with kindness would be a great plan. This was music to my ears as, like all schools, we want everyone to be kind to each other, to show compassion. Confucius said that being kind to others makes us wise and we could do with a bit more wisdom in the world, couldn't we? Kindness also makes us strong and resolute, too. Kindness isn't the same as niceness. It's actively seeking to do the right thing.

As adults, we all know and hopefully have experienced how random acts of kindness really can make a difference to someone's day. It really is cool to be kind. However, it's easy to forget to be kind when you are worrying over something and our kindness muscle can very easily get out of shape or atrophy from lack of use. It's important, therefore, to exercise that muscle and try to be a little kinder than necessary.

Can you teach kindness? There was a fad a few years ago of schools teaching 'happiness', which I felt was rather missing the point. Surely creating an environment where

Hanford School

happiness can blossom is more effective. Maybe there are schools where right now pupils are sitting down to a 'kindness' lesson. I prefer a more holistic approach where we try to lead by example. A good school will make kindness central to everything their pupils are taught. Over the years traditions have developed at Hanford which help keep that 'kindness muscle' in shape. There are no Head Girls or Prefects, rather all senior girls are members of committees which help the school run smoothly and a key committee is the 'Undercover Agents'. Their sole remit is to make sure they know how all girls are getting on, find out if anyone is having a difficult time and make sure she is scooped up and looked after. A reward system of 'Hands Up' is a favourite tradition – girls who have been kind or thoughtful are given a yellow 'Hands Up' sticker which they then stick on a Kindness Tree. Recent stickers were awarded for 'Being kind and thoughtful', 'Being brave before riding' and 'Being kind to new pupils'.

There can be little doubt that being kind isn't only the right thing, but that it makes us feel good, too. Literature is full of miserable 'baddies' – just think of poor old Scrooge. However, I don't know how much research there is about how hard it is to be kind. I can't pretend that kindness comes easily to us all, at all times, children and adults alike. It can be so much easier to say the wrong thing, to ignore the problems of others, to join in with the gang and that is why

schools in particular should focus as much on the curriculum of being kind as it does on maths, English and all the rest.

And so back to our award. We have been recognised by a national magazine as being 'Best of the Best at Kindness'. We are really pleased about this because, to us, the most important thing we can teach our pupils here at Hanford is to be kind to each other, to be honest about assessing when something isn't right and to work towards rectifying the situation. That's what will fit our girls for the future.

For more information about Hanford School, see page 84

The benefits of scholarships

Scholarship programmes in UK prep and senior schools offer a range of benefits, both for the students who receive the scholarships and for the schools themselves.

These benefits go beyond mere financial assistance and extend into the academic, social and cultural aspects of education. As such, scholarship schemes play a significant role in promoting academic excellence, diversity and the holistic development of students.

Pupils at Highfield and Brookham School have a strong record when it comes to securing senior school scholarships, particularly Year 6 and Year 8 leavers.

Last year alone, 22 pupils from the thriving nursery, pre-prep and prep school on the rural borders of Hampshire, Surrey and West Sussex secured an incredible 29 scholarships between them to ten different senior schools, including Wellington College, Charterhouse, Marlborough College, Cranleigh and Benenden.

And the prized awards covered nine different subjects, including academia, music, sport, dance, DT, art and drama, underlining the school's quality and strength right across the curriculum.

While 24 scholarships were awarded to children leaving Year 8, the most common exit point at Highfield and Brookham, five were also awarded to children leaving at the end of Year 6, showing that the school is successful in tailoring the journey to senior school for each child.

The latest batch of sought-after senior school scholarships takes the co-ed day and boarding school's tally to an astonishing 166 in the past decade alone, a key reason why many parents choose a Highfield and Brookham education for their children.

The scholarships are also a big vote of confidence for the school's progressive curriculum, which blends the stepping stones for academic achievement with the development of essential life skills.

So, having recently unveiled Year 3 and Year 5 all-rounder scholarships, which are designed to recognise exceptional children who demonstrate a passion for learning and a commitment to personal growth, why do we place such value on the scholarship programme?

Academic benefits
The most obvious and immediate benefit of scholarship programmes in prep schools is the financial support they provide. Scholarships can enable pupils from a wide range of financial backgrounds to access high-quality education

Highfield and Brookham School

that they might not otherwise afford. For talented pupils, the opportunity to attend a prep school without the burden of tuition fees or other financial constraints is invaluable.

However, the academic benefits extend beyond just financial relief. Scholarship recipients often bring exceptional talents or academic achievements to the school environment. Many prep schools offer scholarships in specific areas such as music, sport, art or academic performance. These pupils often push the boundaries of academic rigour, raising the standard of achievement for their peers. Their presence in the classroom and extracurricular activities can encourage a culture of excellence that benefits all students. Additionally, for pupils receiving academic scholarships, the recognition of their achievements can serve as a motivator to excel even further.

Social and cultural benefits
Scholarship programmes also contribute to fostering a more diverse and inclusive school community. UK prep schools, which are often perceived as exclusive or elitist, can benefit from having a more diverse student body in terms of socio-economic background, ethnicity and geographical location. By offering scholarships, schools can attract bright pupils from a wide range of backgrounds, enriching the school's social and cultural environment.

Diversity is crucial in preparing young people for the globalised world they will eventually work in. Exposure to different perspectives, cultures and ways of thinking within the school helps pupils develop important life skills such as empathy, respect and open-mindedness. Pupils from different backgrounds have the opportunity to engage in meaningful dialogue and collaboration, which can significantly broaden their worldview.

Furthermore, scholarship programmes enable talented pupils who might otherwise be excluded from prestigious academic settings to experience environments where they can thrive.

Personal development
For students who receive scholarships, there are significant personal development benefits. Often, scholarship programmes are not simply about academic performance but also about potential, character and leadership qualities. This approach means that students selected for scholarships are typically encouraged to take on leadership roles, whether in academic settings, sports teams or extracurricular activities. These responsibilities contribute to the development of confidence, resilience and interpersonal skills.

Additionally, scholarship recipients are often given the opportunity to engage in advanced learning experiences. For example, they might participate in special projects, receive additional mentoring or access resources that would otherwise be unavailable to them. These opportunities encourage students to step outside their comfort zones, develop their intellectual curiosity and pursue passions that may have been dormant in a less stimulating environment. Moreover, being a scholarship recipient can foster a sense of pride and accomplishment. The scholarship is a recognition of the pupil's abilities and potential and it can serve as a motivator to work harder and achieve even more.

Long-term career benefits
The long-term benefits of scholarship programmes extend into a pupil's career. Attending a top-tier prep school provides access to high-calibre teaching, facilities and networks that can significantly enhance future prospects. Scholarship recipients often benefit from strong alumni networks and valuable connections within the broader educational and professional worlds.

Furthermore, scholarship recipients often carry with them a sense of pride and recognition that can serve them well in their future endeavours. The discipline, perseverance and ambition required to earn a scholarship can translate into a strong work ethic and determination in their future academic and professional pursuits.

Benefits to schools
Scholarship programmes benefit schools not only by bringing in bright and talented pupils but also by helping schools uphold their reputation for excellence. Schools that offer scholarships to deserving pupils attract attention from prospective families and the wider public. This can enhance the school's status and reputation, drawing in more applicants for future years.

Ultimately, scholarship programmes play a vital role in shaping the future of both students and schools.

For more information about Highfield and Brookham School, see page 76

Find your song and sing it – the importance of learning through experience

'Respect your elders was a phrase I often heard and did my utmost to adhere to when growing up. Those older in our communities have had the opportunity to see, feel and hear, for instance, many more things than those in a younger demographic.' – Mr Simon James (Head of Kent College Junior and previous Head of Economics and Senior House Parent)

Wisdom is the ability to draw conclusions and make judgements, consciously or subconsciously, from an accumulation of information, most often obtained by experiences. As we get older, more opportunities arrive to gain these experiences. This suggests that age is likely to be a key determinant of wisdom. As educators, we can accelerate this process of learning through the opportunities we provide. Children have a significant capacity to absorb information from a variety of contexts by observation and participation. Without a variety of experiences, children miss opportunities to acquire information to build their own form of wisdom appropriate to the context and challenge of growing up.

At our school, we want children to 'find their song and sing it'. It's essential to provide an abundance of metaphorical songs through many experiences. A breadth of extracurricular/co-curricular activities is as important to stretch the highest abilities and to support and develop the self-belief and esteem of those less academically able. In short, children's participation in an extracurricular programme is fundamental and a significant determinant for educational outcomes and wellbeing.

The purpose is not 'wraparound care', a buzzword in independent education as parents' work commitments increase to afford rising fees. The purpose of the extracurricular programme should be education, education, education.

A breadth of experiences can facilitate confidence and resilience

We live in an interventionist society. Information can be found at the touch of a button or the swipe of a screen. When a child has a gap in learning, we naturally want to fill that gap with a direct response or intervention, targeting that area for development. This focused provision will not always work with young children. They lack the maturity and patience to decode all the discreet tuition, perhaps more appropriate for an older pupil targeting national examinations. Demand for one-to-one tuition outside of school has grown significantly over the years, which indicates its value. However, the correlation to improved education outcomes is often linked to the confidence and self-belief that the one-to-one tuition brings to a child through undivided attention, rather than solely the skills and discrete knowledge they have obtained through that tuition. Is this confidence acquired through one-to-one attention sustainable? Is it applicable to a variety of contexts such as group learning? Is it developing the necessary independence and resilience to operate in contexts when the one-to-one tutor is not present?

When a child decides to attend more extracurricular activities, they might improve in maths, for instance, as they find confidence in a fencing, basketball or journalism club. They gain self-belief and carry this confidence into a subject or area they were previously less secure in. They feel recognised and valued by others and thus more comfortable making mistakes, which in turn prepares them to develop and learn. The environments created through different extracurricular activities require children to adapt to different personalities within peers, teachers and coaches. They learn to work with new faces, often in different year groups and, most importantly, they learn how to cope with failure: feeling comfortable being uncomfortable. This is even more relevant when they have large variety in their programme of activities, not just choosing where they believe their strengths lie. Children who have particular interests can find and engage in activities they enjoy, which in turn will stimulate and multiply interests they didn't know they had or perhaps refused to participate in. Schools should be bold with their choices, offering a balance with sport, arts, and STEM, for instance, including those more eccentric choices, tapping into the skills, interests and hobbies of the staff.

The challenges of maintaining children's participation

At our school 80% of all children regularly stay at school until 6pm; the excitement to remain and participate in our clubs programme is huge. However, as a child reaches their teens, the hormones kick in, the distraction of screens and lure of social media will cause barriers to this extracurricular philosophy. As a parent, you might hear: 'I don't want to go. No one else does it', 'I don't want to get up so early' – it's likely there will be some conflict at home! This doesn't mean they don't love these experiences anymore. Quite the opposite in most situations. The mid-teens bring more anxiety, self-awareness, inhibitions and sensitivity to trends, more so than ever with companies such as TikTok spreading consumerism into our homes.

Schools and families should hold the line, keep the experiences wide, take advantage of all the school offers and clubs outside that fit your family schedule, and make it a non-negotiable and a positive habit. If we do, children are likely to be more well-rounded, ambitious and resilient.

For more information about Kent College Junior School, see page 77

Rediscovering the joy of hands-on learning in primary education

In today's digital age, children are growing up with screens as constant companions. While technology undoubtedly offers educational benefits, excessive screen time has been linked to attention deficits, reduced creativity and diminished social skills in young children. As primary teachers, it's time to reclaim the lost art of hands-on learning and provide children with the real-world experiences they need to thrive. Hands-on learning experiences offer a unique and irreplaceable form of development. Whether it's digging in the dirt, building with blocks or conducting real experiments, these tactile activities engage all the senses and foster deep, meaningful learning. Studies have shown that spending time in nature improves children's cognitive function, attention span and emotional wellbeing (Louv, 2005). From developing fine motor skills to sparking curiosity and imagination, hands-on experiences lay the foundation for lifelong success.

In our rush to embrace technology, we risk disconnecting children from the natural world – the original and most enriching classroom of all. Outdoor exploration, coupled with curriculum-based activities, provides endless opportunities for discovery and wonder. By immersing children in the sights, sounds and textures of nature, we awaken their innate sense of curiosity and instil a deep appreciation for the world around them, allowing them to apply abstract classroom learning to real-life situations.

As teachers, it's our responsibility to resist the overuse of screens and prioritise real, hands-on learning experiences in the classroom. By limiting screen time and incorporating more tactile activities into the curriculum, we can nurture children's cognitive, social and emotional development

Merchiston Castle School

in a holistic manner. Let's reclaim the joy of childhood exploration and rediscover the magic of learning through real-life experiences.

Creating a hands-on learning environment requires a shift in mindset and practice. From setting up sensory stations to incorporating experiential learning activities into daily routines, there are countless ways to infuse the curriculum with real-world experiences. By fostering a culture of curiosity, experimentation and discovery, we empower children to become active participants in their own education, teaching them invaluable skills of patience, determination and problem-solving.

In a world inundated with screens, let's not forget the unparalleled value of hands-on learning. From sparking creativity to fostering resilience and problem-solving skills, real-world activities offer children a depth of understanding that screens simply cannot replicate. While technology and computer literacy are vital skills, IT should be taught as a dedicated subject. Through this, children can gain technological skills and an understanding of the technological and online world. By equipping them with these skills in focused lessons rather than relying on devices like iPads for every activity, we ensure that technology enhances rather than diminishes their overall learning experience.

Are you interested in outdoor education for your child? Explore our Edinburgh-based Forest Nursery and Forest Junior School here: merchiston.co.uk/the-forest.

For more information about Merchiston Castle School, see page 94

Top 5 tips for choosing a prep school

There are a number of different factors that make choosing a school a difficult task. We've summarised our top five tips for questions to ask when choosing the right preparatory day or boarding school for you and your family.

What do they mean by boarding?
Many schools brand themselves as a full-boarding school when, in reality, the school closes at weekends or is home to only a handful of pupils. Some schools offer flexi, weekly and full boarding or just one or two of those options, so it's important to check what provision works for you, how many pupils are there at the weekend and what happens at weekends.

Millfield Prep School offers full boarding from age 7+ and the school is alive at weekends. With lessons on Saturday morning and fixtures in the afternoons, Saturday evenings and Sundays are vibrant with over 100 boarders enjoying a full weekend programme of activities and trips. The school only has four fixed exeats a year when the school closes and these dates are available far in advance so you can plan when your children will be home.

Is the range of facilities broad enough to capture your child's passions?
Facilities are an important part of school life and the quality of the facilities on offer can really affect a pupil's school experience. Prep school is the perfect age for pupils to explore new interests while they are still young and find out what they are good at, so make sure there is a wide range on offer for them to try out all sorts of different things. It's also worth checking if all facilities are onsite. Some may say they have access to a pool, when in fact, it's a 20-minute drive away so it's best to check before committing. You also want the facilities open regularly for new pupils to explore and experience a new sport or hobby or learn a new skill.

Millfield Prep offers a diverse range of academic subjects, sports, creative arts and activities, supported by outstanding facilities including an equestrian centre, 25-metre swimming pool, golf courses, science centre, music halls, tennis bubble and numerous sports pitches. Pupils also regularly use Millfield's outstanding facilities, only a 7-minute drive away.

Millfield Preparatory School

> *Many schools brand themselves as full-boarding when, in reality, the school closes at weekends or is home to only a handful of pupils.*

What are the school's values?
When choosing a school, it is important to know and understand their ethos and values. Ask yourself what they mean and if they align with your personal and family values. A set of values should be the bedrock of a community and should be embedded into schools through the staff and students, curriculum and extracurricular opportunities. If you support and believe in their values, it's a good indication that this may be the school for you.

Millfield's values of 'Be Kind, Be You, Be Challengers, Be Curious and Be Brilliant' have been embedded across all areas of school life, including pupils presenting to their peers about them in assemblies and in staff inductions. The values are understood by everyone, but everyone's interpretation of the values is slightly different.

Is there a wellbeing and pastoral focus?
With wellbeing ever prominent in the world we live in today, it's important to look at the pastoral care and systems in place to support and nurture your child, especially for boarders. There should be a vigilant pastoral team and rigorous systems in place for reporting concerns that everyone in the school is fully aware of.

Millfield Prep launched the innovative Wellbeing Curriculum, with the aim of teaching young people how to recognise poor wellbeing and give them the tools to improve it through a series of activities including yoga, mindful walk and talk, soul food and alfresco pursuits. With pupils from the UK and 25+ other countries, Millfield Prep's pastoral team strive to make it a home from home for all.

How far are you prepared to travel for the right school?
Location can often be a dealbreaker when it comes to choosing a school. More often than not, your dream school could be a 4-hour drive away and those nearby are just not quite right. Look for a school that is far away enough to give your child independence, but accessible for drop-offs if they are a day pupil or for visits if you choose boarding. You might currently be driving from one after-school club to another and spending a large amount of your day in the car or in traffic attending a school nearby, when you could choose a school that offers all the clubs to suit your child's interests in one place that is further away. You will all save a lot of time, and fuel! In today's climate, it's important that the school has green open space, fresh air and room to run around and enjoy the countryside.

Being in the Somerset countryside, Millfield Prep benefits from a 250-acre rural campus, with large expanses of green open space. The school is situated in the medieval town of Glastonbury, which is only a 20-minute drive to Castle Cary, with trains to London taking under 2 hours. Bristol airport is only an hour drive and London airports are a couple of hours away.

You may visit one school or you may visit several, but if you are confident in the answers you receive to the five questions above, you'll be that bit closer to making the right decision for the next stage in your child's education.

Visit our campus, meet Head Dan Thornburn and staff, and learn more about life at Millfield Prep at our next Open Days on Saturday 10 May and 4 October 2025. Book online at millfieldschool.com/admissions/open-days

For more information about Millfield Prep School, see page 87

The school taking the classroom outdoors

Moor Park is a welcoming and hugely inspiring co-educational preparatory school located just outside the historic market town of Ludlow in south Shropshire. Nature and the great outdoors in which Moor Park School proudly sits are intrinsically woven into day-to-day life there.

The school has the rare joy of being set among 85 acres of beautiful countryside that is bordered by Mortimer Forest and shared with a magnificent herd of fallow deer native to the forest that can often be seen roaming the grounds.

Last year the school celebrated its 60th anniversary and also welcomed new Headmaster, former pupil James Duffield. As Duffield embarks on his new role taking the school into its next chapter, he is passionate about building upon the school's already strong outdoor ethos to further challenge the traditional perceptions of classroom teaching and setting a benchmark for a truly outdoor education.

Core subjects are traditionally taught within the confines of a classroom, but recent studies evidence huge benefits in taking lessons outdoors into a far more dynamic environment to stimulate creativity and literally widen horizons. Duffield is eager to create opportunities for outdoor lessons and inspire this passion throughout the school wherever possible. Aside from the many and varied health benefits offered by physical activity and fresh air, Moor Park teachers find that there's a tangible impact upon behaviour – with improvements to communication, concentration, resilience and problem-solving skills.

Duffield reflects on his vision for learning: 'Children aren't meant to sit at a desk for hours on end – they need to move, they need space and they need unstructured activities for creative learning and spontaneous play. We couldn't envisage a childhood without plenty of outdoor immersion. A Moor Park child is rarely seen without evidence of the outdoors on their person – usually a precious stone in the pocket, feather tucked into a plait or muddy knees! We encourage our children to develop a love of the great outdoors from the moment they join us and throughout their time here. Aside from sports and break times, we are now increasingly taking lessons outdoors in more formal subjects where children can fully explore concepts as wide-ranging as fractions, map skills, area, patterns, weather and the joy of speaking poetry out loud from a stage in the woods.'

Research suggests that outdoor learning can enhance academic performance, particularly in subjects like science, geography and maths, where real-world observation and hands-on learning can deepen understanding.

Katie Donaldson, Head of Science, shares how this new approach is shaping lessons in her department: 'Practical learning is at heart of science at Moor Park and we now treat the outdoors like an extension to our classroom. This week alone, we have sequenced electricity production, made paper aeroplanes and looked at how far apart objects need to be for a total eclipse – all in the grounds of the schools

To cement the school's renewed dedication to outdoor education it has welcomed the Moor Park Outdoor Education Programme, which has been woven into the curriculum and will be undertaken by all children from Early Years through to Year 8. The programme's focus is to introduce and cement a love, appreciation and respect of the natural landscape using a range of activities that complement the Moor Park mindsets, allowing the children the space and freedom to play, create, discover and collaborate.

A new purpose-made Forest School area has been created along with dedicated outdoor classrooms that further facilitate the school's passion for this style of holistic learning. The school hopes that these facilities will give the children the opportunity and backdrop to start naturally assessing and managing risk – harnessing lifelong skills – as well as encourage them to simultaneously engage with nature and reap the myriad benefits to their physical and mental health that this has been proven to provide.

Outdoor settings can inspire imaginative play and creative thinking. Without the constraints of a traditional classroom, children are free to explore ideas and solutions in a more flexible, open-ended manner.

Teacher Glyn Harrhy, who leads the programme, has seen already the results it's having: 'For those children for whom sitting still is a challenge, they often find that they thrive outdoors in a more inclusive and engaging setting where their movement is less restricted. Many children are visual learners and taking a theory outdoors allows us to take that concept and make it real for them.'

'This new summer term promises to be just as exciting, with planned activities including fire building, den making and storytelling in our amazing teepee with hot chocolate! Outdoor education has become a keenly anticipated favourite lesson for our pupils, from the Tick Tock nursery through to Year 8, and we know that the connections with one another and with nature will last a lifetime. We all know that a stick is never "just a stick" in the hands of a child!'

It is clear Moor Park is entering its next decade with a renewed sense of identity and passion, leading the way for other educational providers to follow. A school that lets its children revel in childhood – in all its muddy, adventurous, cartwheeling glory – is a rare find!

www.moorpark.org.uk

For more information about Moor Park, see page 88

Initial advice

Educational institutions often belong to organisations that guarantee their standards. Here we give a brief alphabetical guide to what the initials mean

BSA

The Boarding Schools' Association

The Boarding Schools' Association (BSA) is part of the BSA Group. BSA Group supports excellence in boarding, safeguarding, inclusion and health education, serving more than 1,700 organisations and people in 40 countries worldwide. Since its foundation in 1965-6, BSA has promoted boarding education and the development of quality boarding through high standards of pastoral care and boarding accommodation. BSA Group encompasses the following:

- SACPA (Safeguarding and Child Protection Association)
- BAISIS (British Association of Independent Schools with International Students)
- HIEDA (Heath in Education Association)
- TIOB (The Institute of Boarding)
- IELA (The Inclusion and Equity Leadership Association)

A UK boarding school can only be a full member of the BSA if it is also a member of one of the Independent Schools Council (ISC) constituent associations, or in membership of the BSA State Boarding Forum (SBF). These two bodies require member schools to be regularly inspected by the Independent Schools' Inspectorate (ISI), Care Inspectorate (Scotland), Care Inspectorate Wales or Ofsted. Other boarding schools who are not members of these organisations can apply to be affiliate members. Similar arrangements are in place for international members. In England, boarding inspection of ISC-accredited independent schools has been conducted by ISI since September 2012. Ofsted retains responsibility for the inspection of boarding in state schools and non-association independent schools.

Boarding inspections must be conducted every three years. Boarding in England is judged against the National Minimum Standards for Boarding Schools which were last updated in September 2022. There are similar standards in Wales (2003) and a separate quality framework in Scotland.

Relationship with government

BSA is in regular communication with the Department for Education (DfE) on all boarding matters in England and with devolved governments for other parts of the UK. The Children Act (1989) and the Care Standards Act (2001) require boarding schools in England to conform to national legislation. The promotion of this legislation and the training required to carry it out are matters on which the DfE and BSA work together. Other governmental departments BSA work with are the Home Office, Ministry of Defence and the Foreign, Commonwealth & Development Office.

Boarding training

BSA delivers the world's largest professional development programme for boarding staff. It offers:

- Two-year courses for graduate and non-graduate boarding staff
- A Diploma course for senior experienced boarding staff
- MA in residential education
- A broad range of day seminars and webinars
- Specialist conferences for all state and independent boarding roles
- A course for new and aspiring boarding Heads
- Certificates in Mental Health. Safeguarding, Inclusion, School Nurses, Coaching and Mentoring
- Basic training for those new to boarding.

State Boarding Forum (SBF)

BSA support state boarding school members through the State Boarding Forum. There are a total of 35 state boarding schools across England, Scotland and Northern Ireland. At these schools, parents pay for boarding but not for education, so fees are substantially lower than in an independent boarding school. The latest BSA State Boarding Forum Census was published in January 2024.

Legal Services

BSA Group Legal is the trading name of BSA Group Legal Services Ltd, a law firm authorised and regulated by the Solicitors Regulation Authority of England and Wales. The BSA Group Legal team works closely with the Home Office to support members with UK immigration matters relating to independent schools. In 2023 the BSA also partnered with Verisio to provide a Due Diligence service to support schools carrying out background checks on future students and their families.

Contact details:

Boarding Schools' Association,
167-169 Great Portland Street, 5th Floor, London, W1W 5PF
Tel: 020 7798 1580 Email: bsa@boarding.org.uk
Website: www.boarding.org.uk

GSA

The Girls' Schools Association

The Girls' Schools Association champions girls' schools, girls' education, girls, and their teachers. An expert in girls' education, GSA promotes girls' best interests and regularly commissions research to show the modern relevance, proven benefits, and enduring power of girls' schools.

The Association represents the head teachers of 152 of the UK's top performing girls' schools, a diverse collection of day and boarding schools, Junior and Senior, rural and city, made up of independent and state schools. Altogether GSA schools educate over 100,000 girls. GSA schools are internationally respected and have a global reputation for excellence. Their innovative practice and academic rigour attract pupils from around the world, and abundant extra- and co-curricular activities nourish the whole student in a complete education.

The Association aims to inform and influence national and international educational debate and is a powerful and well-respected voice within the educational establishment, easing dialogue with policy makers on vital educational issues as well as those relating to girls' schools and the education of girls. The Association has strong links with the Department for Education, OFQUAL, Awarding Bodies and Higher Education institutions.

In addition to acting as advocate, GSA provides its members and their whole school communities with expert-led professional development courses, conferences, and a unique network that provides opportunities for debate and sharing of best practice with colleagues. It also offers a vibrant and popular student events programme 'Go Bold' designed to spark courage, curiosity, delight and self-belief in every GSA girl beyond the classroom.

Modern girls' schools come in different shapes and sizes. Some cater for 100% girls; others provide a girls-only environment with boys in the nursery and/or sixth form. Some follow a diamond model, with equal numbers of boys but separate classrooms between the ages of 11 to 16. Educational provision across the Association offers a choice of day, boarding, weekly, and flexi-boarding education. Schools range in type from large urban schools of 1000 pupils to small rural schools of around 200. Many schools have junior and pre-prep departments and can offer a complete education from age 3/4 to 18. Some also have religious affiliations. Heads of schools in the Girls' Day School Trust (GDST) are members of the GSA.

Girls' schools and girls' education achieve transformative outcomes for young women. With recent Department for Education data revealing that in girls' schools: girls are 2.7 times as likely to take Further Maths and more than twice as likely to take Physics and Computer Science A level compared with girls in co-ed schools; uptake in sciences is higher, Biology is 40% higher, Chemistry is 85% higher and Maths is 88% higher; Computer Science has seen the largest growth in uptake for girls, with the percentage of girls taking Computer Science doubling in girls' schools and 68% higher than in co-ed schools; girls continue to outperform students in co-ed schools in KS5; girls perform better in girls' schools than in co-ed schools in KS4, looking at all subjects as a whole, and also for Maths and English separately. The data also show that the gap between girls in girls' school and girls in other types of schools is further widening in Further Maths, Chemistry and Computer Science, with girls' schools acting as stewards and guardians of these subjects for young women today.

The international benefits of educating girls are life changing for society; the education of girls lifts people out of poverty, grows economies, and saves lives; a child whose mother can read is 50% more likely to live beyond the age of five, and twice as likely to attend school themselves.

The GSA is one of the constituent bodies that make up the Independent Schools' Council (ISC), and its schools undergo a regular cycle of inspections to ensure rigorous educational standards are kept. Most GSA schools also belong to the Association of Governing Bodies of Independent Schools, and Heads must be in membership of the Association of School and College Leaders (ASCL) or the National Association of Headteachers (NAHT). Early Career Teachers take part in the Induction Programme overseen by ISTIP.

The Association's secretariat is based in Leicester.
Suite 105, 108 New Walk, Leicester LE1 7EA
Tel: 0116 254 1619
Email: office@gsa.uk.com
Website: www.gsa.uk.com
X @GSAUK

Chief Executive: Donna Stevens

Search for girls' schools on the dedicated www.schoolsearch.co.uk page.

Initial advice

HMC

HMC (The Heads' Conference) – Collective heads of world-leading independent schools

Founded in 1869 the HMC exists to enable members to discuss matters of common interest and to influence important developments in education. It looks after the professional interests of members, central to which is their wish to provide the best possible educational opportunities for their pupils. The Heads of some 388 leading independent schools are members of The Heads' Conference, whose membership now includes Heads of boys', girls' and coeducational schools. International membership includes the Heads of around 60 schools throughout the world.

The great variety of these schools is one of the strengths of HMC, but all must exhibit high quality in the education provided.

All schools are noted for their academic excellence and achieve good results, including those with pupils from a broad ability band. Members believe that good education consists of more than academic results and schools provide pupils with a wide range of educational co-curricular activities and with strong pastoral support.

Only those schools that meet with the rigorous membership criteria are admitted and this helps ensure that HMC is synonymous with high quality in education. There is a set of membership requirements and a Code of Practice to which members must subscribe. Those who want the intimate atmosphere of a small school will find some with around 350 pupils. Others who want a wide range of facilities and specialisations will find these offered in large day or boarding schools. Many have over 1000 pupils. About 33 schools are for boys only, others are co-educational throughout or only in the sixth form. The first girls-only schools joined HMC in 2006. There are now about 52 girls-only schools.

Within HMC there are schools with continuous histories as long as any in the world and many others trace their origins to Tudor times, but HMC continues to admit to membership recently founded schools that have achieved great success. The facilities in all HMC schools will be good but some have magnificent buildings and grounds that are the result of the generosity of benefactors over many years. Some have attractive rural settings; others are sited in the centres of cities.

Pupils come from all sorts of backgrounds. Bursaries and scholarships provided by the schools give about a third of the 294,000 pupils in HMC schools help with their fees.

Entry into some schools is highly selective but others are well-suited to a wide ability range. Senior boarding schools usually admit pupils after the Common Entrance examination taken when they are 13.

Most day schools select their pupils by 11+ examination. Many HMC schools have junior schools, some with nursery and pre-prep departments. The growing number of boarders from overseas is evidence of the high reputation of the schools worldwide.

The independent sector has always been fortunate in attracting very good teachers. Higher salary scales, excellent conditions of employment, exciting educational opportunities and good pupil/teacher ratios bring rewards commensurate with the demanding expectations. Schools expect teachers to have a good education culminating in a good honours degree and a professional qualification, though some do not insist on the latter especially if relevant experience is offered. Willingness to participate in the whole life of the school is essential.

Parents expect the school to provide not only good teaching that helps their children achieve the best possible examination results, but also the dedicated pastoral care and valuable educational experiences outside the classroom in music, drama, games, outdoor pursuits and community service. Over 92% of pupils go on to higher education, many of them winning places on the most highly-subscribed university courses.

All members attend the Autumn Conference, usually held in a large conference centre in September/October. There are ten divisions covering England, Wales, Scotland and Ireland where members meet once a term on a regional basis, and a distinctive international division.

The HMC Board and Council make decisions on matters referred by membership-led committees, steering groups and working parties.

General Secretary: Dr Simon Hyde
Tel: 01858 469059

12 The Point
Rockingham Road
Market Harborough
Leicestershire
LE16 7QU
Email: office@hmc.org.uk
Website: www.hmc.org.uk

IAPS

IAPS (Independent Association of Prep Schools) is a membership association representing leading heads in prep schools in the UK and overseas

With more than 660 members, IAPS schools educate almost 200,000 pupils worldwide with more than 162,000 attending schools in the UK. As the voice of independent prep school education, IAPS actively supports and promotes the interests of its members.

IAPS schools must reach a very high standard to be eligible for membership, with strict criteria on teaching a broad curriculum, maintaining excellent standards of pastoral care and keeping staff members' professional development training up-to-date. The head must be suitably qualified and schools must be accredited through a satisfactory inspection. IAPS offers its members and their staff a comprehensive and up-to-date programme of professional development courses to ensure that these high professional standards are maintained.

Member schools offer an all-round, values-led broad education which produces confident, adaptable, motivated children with a passion for learning. The targets of the National Curriculum are regarded as a basic foundation which is greatly extended by the wider programmes of study offered. Specialist teaching begins at an early age and pupils are offered a range of cultural and sporting opportunities.

IAPS organises a successful sports programme where member schools compete against each other in a variety of sports. In 2023-24, over 120,000 competitors took part in 160 events across 20 sports.

Schools offer pupils the choice of day, boarding, weekly and flexible boarding, in both singe sex and co-educational schools. Most schools are charitable trusts, some are limited companies and a few are proprietary. There are also junior schools attached to senior schools, choir schools, those with a particular religious affiliation and those that offer specialist provision, as well as some with an age range extending to age 16 or above.

Although each member school is independent and has its own ethos, they are all committed to delivering an excellent, well-rounded education to the pupils in their care, preparing them for their future.

IAPS
Bishop's House
Artemis Drive
Tachbrook Park
CV34 6UD
Tel: 01926 887833
Email: iaps@iaps.uk
Website: iaps.uk

Initial advice

ISA

The Independent Schools Association (ISA) brings the Headteachers of over 650 independent schools together, representing the diverse range of independent education practised across the UK and overseas.

Established in 1878, ISA is an association of headteachers of independent schools. It is one of the oldest of the associations that make up the Independent Schools Council (ISC).

ISA exists to provide professional support, fellowship and opportunity to their 674 Members who nurture and develop over 130,000 pupils within their schools. Promoting best practice and fellowship remains at the core of ISA, as it did when it began over 145 years ago.

ISA supports headteachers using their independence to meet the specific needs of their pupils. At ISA there are schools with different approaches to the curriculum, schools with different religious characters, and none, and schools with different ways of operating. This all contributes to a wide-ranging membership, not confined to any one type of school, but including all: nursery, pre-preparatory, junior and senior, all-through schools, coeducational, single-sex, boarding, day, bilingual, performing arts and specialist provision.

As well as the support and specialist professional development opportunities for ISA Members through their programme of courses and conferences, pupils in ISA schools benefit through their Head's membership with access to the extensive ISA Sport and Arts programmes. ISA Sport champions inclusion in physical activity through positive experiences for young people across a programme of 54 national (and over 150 regional) events at venues such as the Olympic Park's London Aquatics Centre.

ISA Arts helps schools inspire creativity, expression and individuality across the arts through both virtual and in-person events.

Membership is open to any Head or Proprietor, provided they meet the necessary accreditation criteria, including inspection of their school by a government-approved inspectorate.

ISA is supported by a number of committees, comprised of serving Heads and Honorary Members, who meet regularly to consider the issues that affect independent education. Some committee areas include education, monitoring developments and formulating responses to Government, also developing and promoting the principles of inclusion within the Association and supporting Members in promoting Equality, Diversity and Inclusion (EDI) in their schools.

President: Lord Lexden
Chief Executive Officer: Rudolf Eliott Lockhart

ISA House, 5-7 Great Chesterford Court, Great Chesterford, Essex CB10 1PF
Tel: 01799 523619
Email: isa@isaschools.org.uk
Website: www.isaschools.org.uk

At ISA there are schools with different approaches to the curriculum, schools with different religious characters, and none, and schools with different ways of operating.

Initial advice

The Society of Heads

The Society is an Association of Heads of approximately 150 well-established independent schools

The Society is an Association of Heads of approximately 150 well-established independent schools. It was founded in 1961 when a group of Heads decided they needed a forum in which to share ideas and experience. Since then the Society has grown substantially in size, reputation and effectiveness and represents a vibrant community of independent schools throughout England and Wales with some additional overseas members.

TThe Society's policy is to maintain high standards in member schools, to promote independent education, to provide an opportunity for the sharing of ideas and common concerns, to foster links with the wider sphere of higher education and to strengthen relations with the maintained sector by promoting partnerships.

Within the membership there is a wide variety of educational experience. Some schools are young, some have evolved from older foundations, some have behind them a long tradition of pioneer and specialist education; a number are at the leading edge of education in music, dance and the arts; and several are well known for their effective support for those with specific learning difficulties. The great majority are co-educational but we also have some all-boys and all-girls schools. Many have a strong boarding element; others are day only. All offer a stimulating sixth-form experience and give a sound and balanced education to pupils of widely varying abilities and interests.

The Society is one of the constituent Associations of the Independent Schools Council. Every Full Member school has been accredited through inspection by the Independent Schools Inspectorate (or Estyn in Wales and HMIE in Scotland) and is subject to regular visits to monitor standards and ensure that good practice and sound academic results are maintained. The Society is also represented on many other educational bodies.

All members are in membership of the Association of School and College Leaders (ASCL) or other union for school leaders and Full Member schools belong to AGBIS or an equivalent professional body supporting governance.

> The Society has grown substantially in size, reputation and effectiveness and represents a vibrant community of independent schools throughout England and Wales with some additional overseas members.

The Society hosts the autumn meeting, summer meeting and the annual conference for members. The Society also provides an extensive professional development programme.

The Society of Heads Office,
Office 101B, Harborough Enterprise Centre,
Compass Point Business Park,
Market Harborough,
Leicestershire LE16 9HW
Tel: 01858 433760
Email: info@thesocietyofheads.org.uk
Website: www.thesocietyofheads.org.uk

Initial advice

The Independent Schools Council

The Independent Schools Council (ISC) works with its members to promote and preserve the quality, diversity and excellence of UK independent education both at home and abroad

What is the ISC?
The ISC brings together seven associations of independent schools, their heads, bursars and governors. Through our member associations we represent approximately 1,400 independent schools in the UK and overseas, which educate more than half a million children.

The ISC's work is carried out by a small team of dedicated professionals in central London. We are assisted by contributions from expert advisory groups in specialist areas. Our priorities are set by the board of directors led by our chairman, Barnaby Lenon.

ISC schools
Schools in membership of the ISC's constituent associations offer a high-quality, rounded education. Whilst our schools are very academically successful, their strength also lies in the extra-curricular activities offered, helping to nurture pupils' soft skills. There are independent schools to suit every need, whether you want a day or boarding school, single-sex or co-education, a large or a small school, or schools offering specialisms, such as in the arts.

Our schools are very diverse: some are selective and highly academic, while others have very strong drama or music departments full of creative opportunities. For children with special needs there are many outstanding independent schools that offer some of the best provision in the country.

Many schools have high levels of achievement in sport, offering a wide range of facilities and excellent coaches. Independent schools excel at traditional sports like football and rugby, but also offer more unusual sports like rowing and fencing.

There is also a wealth of co-curricular opportunities available. Whether your child is into debating, sailing, or the Model United Nations, most schools offer numerous clubs and activities.

Fee assistance
Schools take affordability very seriously and are acutely aware of the sacrifices families make when choosing an independent education. Schools work hard to remain competitive whilst facing pressures on salaries, pensions and maintenance and utility costs. They are strongly committed to widening access and many schools have extended their bursary provision – this year, schools provided more than £500m in means-tested fee assistance. Over 180,000 pupils currently benefit from reduced fees, representing over a third of pupils at our schools.

School partnerships
Independent and state schools have been engaged in partnership activity for many years, with the majority of ISC schools currently involved in important cross-sector initiatives. These collaborations involve the sharing of expertise, best practice and facilities, and unlock exciting new opportunities for all involved. To learn more about these valuable partnerships, visit the Schools Together website: www.schoolstogether.org

ISC Associations
There are seven member associations of the ISC, each with a distinctive ethos in their respective entrance criteria and quality assurance:
Girls' Schools Association (GSA)
The Heads' Conference (HMC)
Independent Association of Prep Schools (IAPS)
Independent Schools Association (ISA)
The Society of Heads
Association of Governing Bodies of Independent Schools (AGBIS)
Independent Schools' Bursars Association (ISBA)

Further organisations that are affiliated to the ISC: Boarding Schools' Association (BSA), Council of British International Schools (COBIS), Scottish Council of Independent Schools (SCIS) and Welsh Independent Schools Council (WISC).

The Independent Schools Council can be contacted at:
First Floor,
27 Queen Anne's Gate,
London,
SW1H 9BU
Telephone: 020 7766 7070
Website: www.isc.co.uk

Help in funding the fees

Chris Procter, Managing Director of SFIA Wealth Management, outlines a planned approach to funding your child's school fees

Over the last year there has been greater pressure on families due to rising interest rates and an increase in the cost of living. Despite this the independent education sector remains resilient, according to the latest Independent Schools Council (ISC) survey, conducted in January 2023. The number of pupils in ISC schools stood at 554,243, a new record high.

Average school fee increases were 5.6% between the 2021/22 and 2022/23 school years, this is consistent with the higher than normal inflation that the UK economy has experienced. The average day school fees were £5,552 which is an increase of 5.8%. The average boarding school fees were £13,002 per term, an increase of 5.2%.

Fees charged by schools vary by region – for example, the average day school fees per term ranged from £4,000 in the North West to £6,676 in London.

Over £1.2bn of fee assistance was provided in the 2022/23 school year, of which 80% came from schools themselves. Over a third of pupils in ISC schools received at least one type of fee support.

£483m of means-tested fee assistance was provided, an increase of £3m on the previous year. The average means-tested bursary stood at over £11,807. Nearly half of all pupils on means-tested bursaries had more than half of their fees remitted.

The overall cost of school fees (including university fees) might seem daunting: the cost of educating one child privately could well be very similar to that of buying a house but, as with house buying, the school fees commitment for the majority of parents can be made possible by spreading it over a long period rather than funding it all from current resources.

It is vital that parents do their financial homework, plan ahead and start to save early. Grandparents who have access to capital could help out; by contributing to school fees they could also help to reduce any potential future inheritance tax liability.

Parents would be well-advised to consult a specialist financial adviser as early as possible, since a long-term plan for the payment of fees – possibly university as well – can prove very advantageous from a financial point of view and offer greater peace of mind. Funding fees is neither science, nor magic, nor is there any panacea. It is quite simply a question of planning and using whatever resources are available, such as income, capital, or tax plan planning opportunities.

The fundamental point to recognise is that you, your circumstances and your wishes or ambitions, for your children, or grandchildren are unique. They might well appear similar to those of other people but they will still be uniquely different. There will be no single solution to your problem. In fact, after a review of all your circumstances, there might not be a problem at all.

So, what are the reasons for seeking advice about education expenses?
- To reduce the overall cost
- To get some tax benefit
- To reduce your cash outflow
- To invest capital to ensure that future fees are paid
- To set aside money now for future fees
- To provide protection for school fees
- Or just to make sure that, as well as educating your children, you can still have a life

Any, some, or all of the above – or others not listed – could be on your agenda, the important thing is to develop a strategy.

At this stage, it really does not help to get hung up on which financial 'product' is the most suitable. The composition of a school fees plan will differ for each family depending on a number of factors. That is why there is no one school fees plan on offer.

The simplest strategy but in most cases, the most expensive option, is to write out a cheque for the whole bill when it arrives and post it back to the school. Like most simple plans, that can work well, if you have the money. Even if you do have the money, is that really the best way of doing things? Do you know that to fund £1,000 of school fees as a higher rate taxpayer paying 40% income tax, you currently need to earn £1,667, this rises to £1,818 if you are an additional rate taxpayer where the rate is 45%.

How then do you start to develop your strategy? As with most things in life, if you can define your objective, then you will know what you are aiming at. Your objective in this case will be to determine how much money is needed and when.

You need to draw up a school fees schedule or what others may term a cash flow forecast. So, you need to identify:
- How many children?
- Which schools and therefore what are the fees? (or you could use an average school fee)
- When are they due?
- Any special educational needs?
- Inflation estimate?
- Include university costs?

With this basic information, the school fees schedule/cash flow forecast can be prepared and you will have defined what it is you are trying to achieve.

Remember though, that senior school fees are typically more than prep school fees – this needs to be factored in. Also, be aware that the cost of university is not restricted to the fees alone; there are a lot of maintenance and other costs involved: accommodation, books, food, to name a few. Don't forget to build in inflation, I refer you back to the data at the beginning of this article.

Help in funding the fees

You now have one element of the equation, the relatively simple element. The other side is the resources you have available to achieve the objective. This also needs to be identified, but this is a much more difficult exercise. The reason that it is more difficult, of course, is that school fees are not the only drain on your resources. You probably have a mortgage, you want to have holidays, you need to buy food and clothes, you may be concerned that you should be funding a pension.

This is a key area of expertise, since your financial commitments are unique. A specialist in the area of school fees planning can help identify these commitments, to record them and help you to distribute your resources according to your priorities.

The options open to you as parents depend completely upon your adviser's knowledge of these complex personal financial issues. (Did I forget to mention your tax position, capital gains tax allowance, other tax allowances, including those of your children and a lower or zero rate tax paying spouse or partner? These could well be used to your advantage.)

A typical school fees plan can incorporate many elements to fund short, medium and long-term fees. Each plan is designed according to individual circumstances and usually there is a special emphasis on what parents are looking to achieve, for example, to maximise overall savings and to minimise the outflow of cash.

Additionally, it is possible to protect the payment of the fees in the event of unforeseen circumstances that could lead to a significant or total loss of earnings.

Short-term fees

Short-term fees are typically the termly amounts needed within five years: these are usually funded from such things as guaranteed investments, liquid capital, loan plans (if no savings are available) or maturing insurance policies, investments etc. Alternatively, they can be funded from disposable income.

Medium-term fees

Once the short-term plan expires, the medium-term funding is invoked to fund the education costs for a further five to ten years. Monthly amounts can be invested in a low-risk, regular premium investment ranging from a building society account to a friendly society savings plan to equity ISAs. It is important to understand the pattern of the future fees and to be aware of the timing of withdrawals.

Long-term fees

Longer term funding can incorporate a higher element of risk (as long as this is acceptable to the investor), which will offer higher potential returns. Investing in UK and overseas equities could be considered. Solutions may be the same as those for medium-term fees, but will have the flexibility to utilise investments that may have an increased 'equity based' content.

Finally, it is important to remember that most investments, or financial products either mature with a single payment or provide for regular withdrawals; rarely do they provide timed termly payments.

Additionally, the overall risk profile of the portfolio should lean towards the side of caution (for obvious reasons).

There are any number of advisers in the country, but few who specialise in the area of planning to meet school and university fees. SFIA is the largest organisation specialising in school fees planning in the UK.

This article has been contributed by SFIA and edited by Chris Procter, Managing Director.

Chris can be contacted at:
SFIA, 27 Moorbridge Road,
Maidenhead,
Berkshire, SL6 8LT
Tel: 01628 566777
Email: enquiries@sfia.co.uk
Web: www.sfia.co.uk

UK region map – Profiles

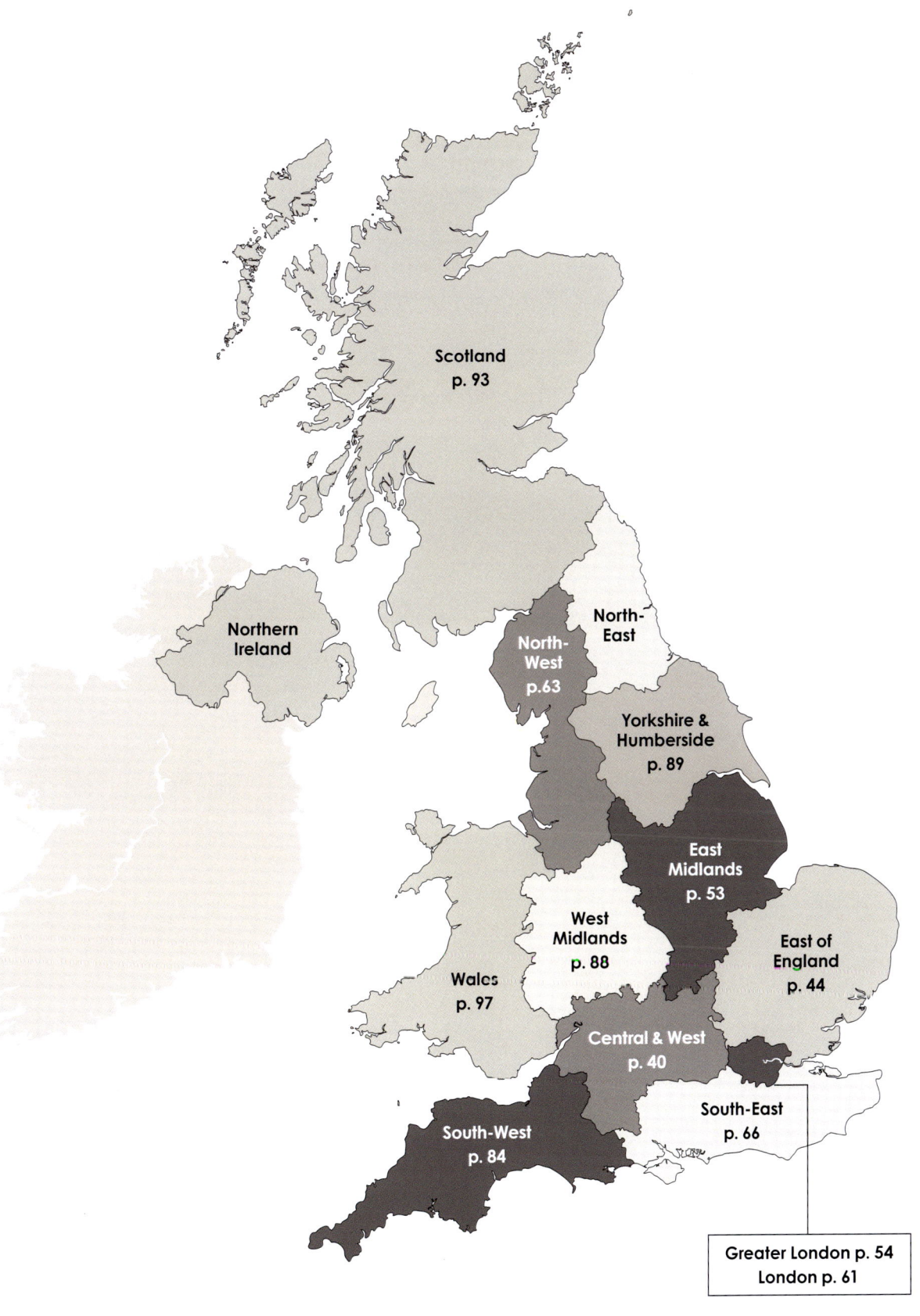

Prep schools in England

Please note that, to facilitate the use of this guide, we have introduced the geographical region 'Central & West' (see map opposite). This is not an officially designated region, and has been created solely for the purposes of this publication.

Central & West

Cranford School

(Founded 1931)

Moulsford, Wallingford,
Oxfordshire OX10 9HT
Tel: 01491 651218
Email: admissions@cranfordschool.co.uk
Website: www.cranfordschool.co.uk
Headmaster: Dr James Raymond
Appointed: 2014

School type: Co-educational Day Preparatory & Senior, Nursery & Sixth Form
Age range of pupils: 3–18 years
No. of pupils enrolled as at 01/01/2025: 575
Fees as at 01/01/2025:
Day: £4,000–£7,125 per term

Regarded as one of the UK's leading small independent co-educational schools, Cranford is renowned for its strong focus on pastoral care and consistently attaining high academic results. As an established fully co-educational school, pupils thrive where the attention to each pupil and their teaching and learning needs is second to none. Academic attainment at Cranford is outstanding, GCSE results typically see over 60% of all grades achieved at 9–7 (A*–A). The school consistently achieves a value-added score of +1.3 showing that pupils at Cranford can expect to achieve over a grade higher per subject than they would elsewhere.

With unbeatable pastoral care and superb facilities for sport and the performing arts, Cranford's pupils enjoy educational excellence. Regarded among families as one of Oxfordshire's best kept little secrets, the school rated 'Excellent' in all areas by the Independent Schools Inspectorate, is a warmly welcoming, independent day school for boys and girls aged 3–18.

'Cranford enjoys a strong reputation for both teaching excellence and for maintaining a focus on each individual pupil's progress that ensures everyone achieves their full potential. An atmosphere of academic endeavour is at the heart of school life, but a Cranford education offers much more than simple academic success. Ensuring each child feels safe and supported is key to building their growing confidence in their own abilities. Visitors to our school comment on the happy atmosphere, while our students describe Cranford as a family community where everyone knows and supports each other. Our aim is to ignite every individual's curiosity and interest and I am delighted to say that the scope of our students' accomplishments is exceptional.' – Headmaster Dr James Raymond.

The excellent quality of education on offer for each and every Cranford pupil is a hallmark, where academic pursuits are supported by an opportunity rich extra-curricular programme. Beyond the classroom, with over a hundred different engaging, fun and inclusive clubs on offer, these opportunities offer pupils ways to expand learning, build confidence and explore their sense of curiosity. To discover first-hand what a Cranford education can offer your child, open events and personal tours are available throughout the year. Welcome.

Central & West

Dair House School

(Founded 1932)

Bishops Blake, Beaconsfield Road, Farnham Royal, Buckinghamshire SL2 3BY
Tel: 01753 643964
Email: admissions@dairhouse.school
Website: www.dairhouseschool.co.uk
Head of School: Mrs Janine Bull

School type: Co-educational Day Preparatory & Nursery
Age range of pupils: 3–11 years
No. of pupils enrolled as at 01/01/2025: 125
Fees as at 01/01/2025:
Day: £2,975–£5,555 per term

Happiness is central to the aims of Dair House School. We believe that when a child is happy and looks forward to coming to school every day, they will learn far more successfully.

We pride ourselves in offering each pupil a unique education that gives pupils a wide variety of opportunities inside and outside the classroom, producing confident, independent pupils well prepared for the next steps in their journey.

Both staff and pupils live by our core values, the three C's:

Courageous: encouraging pupils to be resilient; learn from their mistakes; and challenge themselves beyond their comfort zones.

Committed: promoting persistence and dedication in the classroom, on the sports field and through the Arts. Dedicated to both academic and personal progress we believe there is no ceiling on any child's potential.

Caring: nurturing pupils to find their own strengths and strongly believing that pupils should learn to be respectful, courteous, kind and empathetic. Our school is a happy school with kindness at the heart of everything we do.

The curriculum is vibrant and varied, with small classes, personalised care and expectations that every child will excel. We are a fully inclusive school, in which each child is encouraged to try every activity and every child feels a sense of belonging.

Academic rigour drives our teaching and we tailor our teaching and learning programmes to the abilities of our children. We celebrate our children's achievements both in school and outside in weekly assemblies, where we also uphold the tradition of the Kindness Cup.

Our warm, friendly school prides itself in individual care and attention and we warmly invite you to visit the school and experience why both our staff and pupils are proud to be part of the Dair House family.

Central & West

Godstowe Preparatory School

(Founded 1900)
Shrubbery Road, High Wycombe,
Buckinghamshire HP13 6PR
Tel: 01494 529273
Email: schooloffice@godstowe.org
Website: www.godstowe.org

Headmistress: Ms Kate Bailey
School type: Girls' Day & Boarding Preparatory, Co-ed Pre-Prep & Nursery
Age range of boys: 3–7 years
Age range of girls:
3–13 years (boarding from 7)

"Something Special is happening at Godstowe"

Godstowe was founded by two strong, progressive women, originally in fact as a school whose purpose would be to prepare girls for the move down the hill to Wycombe Abbey School. Their vision was for an innovative, academic and broad education for girls and, without a doubt, this continues to live on in today's school.

Our ethos is simple. All we want is for our girls and boys to be Confident, Happy and Successful. Indeed, if the first two are true, the third will almost certainly follow. Success is defined in many ways, and we mean successful in the broadest sense: successfully kind, successfully courteous as well as successful in achieving a wide range of goals. We keep our pupils busy and engaged, we entertain and intrigue them, encourage them, and excite them.

Happy children are easy to teach. With outstanding, highly qualified teaching staff as well as a strong and experienced pastoral team, excellent facilities, wonderful surroundings, a non-selective intake policy and a more positive, exuberant and industrious atmosphere than you will find in other schools, it is likely that most of our children will be happy to learn, happy to stretch themselves, happy to support each other, and happy to do whatever they can to take an active part in their own education.

Why push children through the curriculum when they can be inspired to make their own journey, choose their own routes and arrive at their destination under their own steam?

Our pupils love their time at school. It never ceases to amaze me just how much highly motivated and enthusiastic people can willingly contribute, and we don't just mean the girls and boys, we mean the staff and the parents too!

Godstowe is alive with opportunity. Remember, to learn a lesson you need to live it.

Moulsford Preparatory School

(Founded 1961)
Moulsford-on-Thames,
Oxfordshire OX10 9HR
Tel: 01491 651438

Email: admissions@moulsford.com
Website: www.moulsford.com
Headmaster: Mr B. Beardmore-Gray
Appointed: September 2014
School type: Boys' Day & Boarding Preparatory, Co-ed Pre-Prep
Age range of boys: 3–13 years
Age range of girls: 3–7 years

No. of pupils enrolled as at 01/01/2025: 360
Fees as at 01/01/2025:
Full Boarding: £10,298
Prep Day Fee: £8,232 per term (incl. VAT)
Pre-Prep: £5,510 per term (incl. VAT)
Pre-School: £4,190 per term
Average class size: 16
Teacher/pupil ratio: 1:9

Moulsford is a thriving, independent day and boarding school of 360 pupils aged 3–13 in south Oxfordshire, set in picturesque grounds on the banks of the River Thames. Our co-educational Pre-Prep runs from Pre-School to Year 2 and is housed in a purpose-designed new building. The Prep School (Years 3–8) currently delivers an outstanding all-boys education and will be welcoming girls to Year 3 in 2026. By 2031 the school will be fully co-educational.

Moulsford's curriculum prepares pupils for senior schools, but also ensures they develop skills for life. Striving for excellent academic achievement, with foundations laid in the Pre-School to promote curiosity and a love of learning, the school's down-to-earth, focused approach embraces the fact that children of this age should be having fun at the same time as learning. The school's values of Kindness, Courage and Curiosity are at the heart of everything we do.

Moulsford's comprehensive extra-curricular programme includes many and varied opportunities for the pupils to try out new activities and discover and develop their own individual abilities and talents outside of the classroom. Pupils can try bike maintenance, cookery, photography, climbing, drama, chess, parkour and much more.

Moulsford's reputation for sport remains extremely strong with all pupils from Year 3 in teams A to F regularly playing competitive matches. Major sports are football, rugby, hockey, cricket and athletics. Music and drama remain popular with three quarters of pupils from Years 3–8 playing an instrument.

In Year 8, pupils progress to the UK's leading independent day and boarding schools at 13+ including Abingdon, Eton, Harrow, Magdalen College School, Radley, St Edward's Oxford, Bradfield, Marlborough, Wellington, Shiplake and Pangbourne.

The riverside setting provides a different dimension to prep school life with kayaks, canoes and stand-up paddleboards all put to use. At Forest School there are opportunities for fire building and making bows and arrows.

Our aim is to ensure that every child is listened to, supported, encouraged and given the opportunity to flourish.

East

Brentwood Preparatory School

(Founded 1892)
Shenfield Road, Brentwood, Essex CM15 8BD

Tel: +44 (0)1277 243300
Email: prepadmissions@brentwood.essex.sch.uk
Website: www.brentwoodschool.co.uk
Head of School: Mrs Alice Goodfellow
Appointed: 2024
School type: Co-educational Day Preparatory

Religious denomination: Multifaith school with Christian foundation
Age range of pupils: 3–11 years
No. of pupils enrolled as at 01/01/2025: 564
Fees as at 01/01/2025:
Day: £7,077
Average class size: 19
Teacher/pupil ratio: 1:6

From the age of three, we welcome children into a community that is small enough to feel secure, but large enough to offer a huge breadth of experiences. Whether in our well-equipped Foundation playground, Forest School, or our cutting edge Futures Room, pupils are encouraged to think for themselves and develop their own ideas. Whether they are taking part in the School Council or joining in one of the many clubs, sports, music and drama activities, our pupils soon develop their own sense of responsibility. They learn to care about their work, to value their contribution to the wider school community and through many pupil-led fundraising initiatives, their eyes are opened to the world beyond school.

Our curriculum has been evolving, and we are excited to be part of the global community of schools delivering the Primary Years Programme (PYP) as part of the International Baccalaureate. The PYP places children at the centre of their learning, encouraging them to be active creators of transdisciplinary knowledge. It nurtures curious and driven learners who ask thought-provoking questions and aspire to make the world a better place for everyone.

It is really important that every child is known and valued. Although the Form teachers play a significant role in caring for their class, it is the small, regular interactions between all staff and pupils that make Brentwood such a welcoming and friendly school. With the familiarity the pupils and staff feel, it helps to create a more cohesive rapport, aiding in their learning.

Our award-winning facilities are something that we are very proud of, the kind that one would expect to see at secondary level. Highlights include a Futures Room – a place for experimentation – which can be transformed from the solar system to the bottom of the ocean or the chaos of a battlefield by the switch of a button.

Eight specialist classrooms include a music room, with cutting-edge music technology, two science rooms, an IT suite, a light and airy art loft, a design technology classroom with laser cutter and 3D printer, and a food technology suite with mini hotplates, ovens and child-height workstations.

Academically, our pupils are high achievers: they are consistently at the top of the field at age 11 and a large proportion achieve scholarships at the same age. We encourage all pupils to have the confidence to stretch themselves, to celebrate their own achievements and to be generous about the success of others.

Much has changed since we were founded in 1892, but our motto of Virtue, Learning, Manners remains and you will see that in droves when you visit us.

Edge Grove School

High Cross, Aldenham Village,
Hertfordshire WD25 8NL

Tel: 01923 855724
Email: admissions@edgegrove.com
Website: www.edgegrove.com
Headmaster: Mr Richard Stanley
School type: Co-educational Day Preparatory & Nursery
Age range of pupils: 2–13 years
No. of pupils enrolled as at 01/01/2025: 397
Fees as at 01/01/2025:

Nursery: five mornings only (optional afternoons are available every day):
£3,035 per term (incl. VAT)
Reception–Year 2:
£6,310–£6,340 per term (incl. VAT)
Year 3–Year 4:
£7,150–£7,279 per term (incl. VAT)
Year 5–Year 8:
£8,394–£8,446 per term (incl. VAT)

Edge Grove is a warm, welcoming and diverse co-educational community of 2–13-year-old boys and girls who, through a strong sense of belonging, across a broad range of educational experiences, develop integrity, independence, inspiration and a lifelong love of learning.

We are a busy school with a thriving community, situated in 48 acres of Hertfordshire parkland, only 15 miles from central London and conveniently located close to the M1 and M25 motorways. Our wonderful setting and facilities ensure our children are exposed to a wide range of experiences and develop confidence in a challenging, fun and inspirational environment. Our pupils are happy, motivated, articulate and intellectually curious with the confidence and enthusiasm to make the most of every opportunity presented to them.

We are a friendly and dynamic community and a school with lots of tradition but one that is embracing 21st-century learning and are very much forward thinking and looking. Edge Grove is more than just a school which is open for the business of educating children between 8am and 4pm, it is a way of life. We are a busy and productive school in which everyone is expected to be involved and play their part, and a community that enjoys celebrating everyone's successes and is keen to help others too.

We are unique in our approach and clearly and proudly stand apart from the competition. Our teaching and learning is based on the best possible practice and innovation rather than on what our competitors do or what has been done in the past. Our pupils move on at 11+ and 13+ to a range of academically selective senior schools, frequently with scholarships.

East

Fairstead House School

FAIRSTEAD HOUSE
(Founded 1950)

Fairstead House, Fordham Road, Newmarket, Suffolk CB8 7AA
Tel: 01638 662318
Email: secretary@fairsteadhouse.org
Website: www.fairsteadhouse.org
Head of School: Mr Michael Radford

School type: Co-educational Day Preparatory & Nursery
Age range of pupils: 1–11 years
No. of pupils enrolled as at 01/01/2025: 216
Fees as at 01/01/2025:
Day: £14,508–£16,170 per annum
Average class size: 13

"Since my children started at Fairstead House, it has been wonderful to see how much the school prioritises not just their academic achievements, but also their personal and emotional development. A truly wonderful place for children to learn and grow."

A member of the King's Ely Family of Schools, Fairstead House is located in the heart of the horseracing town of Newmarket on the Suffolk/Cambridgeshire border.

We are an excellent choice for families who are looking for an independent Nursery and School in a rural setting but with the rich cultural resources of Cambridge, Ely, and Bury St Edmunds a short distance away.

Fairstead House will provide your child with a unique introduction into the world of learning and discovery. We are extremely proud of our high academic standards, our superb pastoral care, and the happy and enriching environment that we provide for our pupils.

Physical Education plays a very important part in the life of our school. Children are encouraged to achieve their full potential, to understand what is involved in being part of a team, and to learn the values of good sportsmanship.

Residential trips and outings contribute to the broad, balanced and creative education that Fairstead House provides.

Music and Drama are also a great strength and play an integral part in school life, under the direction of a specialist teacher. All children are given opportunities to sing, perform, compose and play a selection of instruments. Specialist private tuition is available in a wide range of instruments.

A whole host of clubs and activities are available. These include sports, art, music, crafts, drama, languages, storytelling, and many more. Children have the opportunity to choose their activities at the beginning of each term. A Breakfast Club is available each day from 7.30am and we have a well-established and popular After-School Care Club until 6pm.

Please phone 01638 662318 or email registrar@fairsteadhouse.org to arrange a visit!

Ipswich Prep School

(Founded 1878)

3 Ivry Street, Ipswich,
Suffolk IP1 3QW
Tel: 01473 282800
Email: prepenquiries@ipswich.school
Website: www.ipswich.school
Headmistress: Ms Claire Jackson

School type: Co-educational Day Preparatory
Age range of pupils: 4–11 years
No. of pupils enrolled as at 01/01/2025: 214
Fees as at 01/01/2025:
Day: £13,827–£18,288 per annum
Teacher/pupil ratio: 1:11

Ipswich Preparatory School is a happy school where we create extraordinary futures. Children grow in confidence, develop a love of learning and experience a plethora of opportunities.

Children develop knowledge, skills, behaviours and character as they progress through the school, benefiting from excellent resources, a broad curriculum and highly supportive teaching. Our Prep School is divided into three sections: Early Years (ages 4 & 5), Lower Prep (ages 5–7), and Upper Prep (ages 7–11).

Children at Ipswich Prep are happy because they genuinely enjoy their lessons. They have access to a dynamic and engaging programme of lessons and activities, all delivered by staff who truly care about them and understand their individual needs. Our ethos revolves around the core values of care, passion, potential and communication, creating a sense of excitement and joy that you will immediately feel when you visit.

Our curriculum is intentionally broad and delivered by specialist teachers. Prep children follow a dedicated STEAM Programme, learn languages including French, German, Spanish and Latin and take part in a wide range of lessons dedicated to Sports, Music and the Arts. Children find their passion and are taken to the limits of their potential. As they journey through the rigorous core academic curriculum and extensive co-curricular programmes, Prep children become increasingly self aware and discover their own gifts and talents.

At Ipswich Prep we have incredible facilities including dedicated Art, Music, Computing and Science Suites. Our facilities for sport are exceptional with Prep children having access to an indoor swimming pool, cricket nets, Etons fives courts, astroturf hockey pitches and netball courts. Ipswich School Sports Centre at nearby Rushmere is the centrepiece of our sporting facilities and a familiar venue for many of our sporting fixtures.

The extensive co-curricular programme at Ipswich Prep provides every child the opportunity to explore a wide range of interests beyond the classroom. With so many clubs to choose from including robotics, 'fun with food', maths master class, judo, skiing, drama, dance, LAMDA and so many more, there is something to excite every child at Ipswich Prep.

Come and take a look around Ipswich Prep. See how we turn potential into reality. We love our school and we hope you will too.

East

King's Ely Prep

(Founded 970 AD)

Ely, Cambridgeshire CB7 4DB
Tel: 01353 660707
Email: admissions@kingsely.org
Website: www.kingsely.org
Head: Mr Simon Kibler
School type: Co-educational Day & Boarding Preparatory

Age range of pupils: 7–13 years
No. of pupils enrolled as at 01/01/2025: 412
Fees as at 01/01/2025:
Day: £20,721–£23,103 per annum
Full Boarding: £32,976–£35,313 per annum
Average class size: 16
Teacher/pupil ratio: 1:12

"Within the first week of our sons joining King's Ely Prep, we simply could not believe the change in both their happiness and their commitment to learning. We think King's Ely must sprinkle some magic dust when it comes to children's enthusiasm to learn and their emotional wellbeing!" Mr and Mrs Golding, whose sons, Benjamin and Edward, joined our Prep School recently.

King's Ely is a leading independent, co-educational, day and boarding school, which serves the academic and pastoral needs of around 1,100 pupils from the age of 2 through to 18, with boarders from 8 years old. Our Prep School (ages 7–13) is filled with the same contagious energy and excitement that the whole of King's Ely is renowned for.

King's Ely is steeped in history – one which stretches back to 970 AD – making us one of the oldest schools in the country. Our beautiful 75-acre campus is just 20 minutes from Cambridge and one hour from London, with direct rail links to both. Our privately-run school buses stop at key locations around Cambridgeshire, Suffolk, and Norfolk.

King's Ely stands in the shadow of Ely's magnificent cathedral, which makes the perfect setting for concerts and performances, and serves as our school chapel. But it is not just our awe-inspiring environment that makes us unique. So too does our innovative approach to teaching and learning, our extensive extra-curricular programme, our outstanding pastoral care, and our quirky, historic traditions! We are proud to have received an 'excellent' rating in all areas following our latest Independent Schools Inspectorate (ISI) Inspection, recognising the highest levels of pastoral care, academic rigour, and opportunities outside the classroom.

King's Ely pupils are renowned for their energy, their courage, and their integrity. Whether a student shines in a classroom, in a laboratory, on a stage, on a pitch, or on a mountainside, we promise an abundance of opportunity for personal development, both academically and socially.

As reported in the Good Schools Guide, King's Ely *"turns out well rounded, likeable individuals who attain academically but who also realise there is more to life than just results."* Only by visiting King's Ely and meeting our students and staff, can you feel the warmth of our community. We look forward to welcoming you!

Notre Dame Preparatory School

(Founded 1864)

147 Dereham Road, Norwich,
Norfolk NR2 3TA
Tel: 01603 625593
Email:
admissions@notredameprepschool.co.uk
Website:
www.notredameprepschool.co.uk

Headteachers: Mrs K. Laudan & Dr L. Campbell
School type: Co-educational Day Preparatory & Nursery
Religious denomination: Roman Catholic
Age range of pupils: 2–11 years

Nestled in the Norwich Golden Triangle, Notre Dame Prep is a hidden gem where children are happy and supported in their learning. Catering for children aged 2–11, our Nursery and main school welcome children from all backgrounds and faiths – or indeed none at all. Our school prides itself on feeling like family and our Catholic ethos fully supports this. With small class sizes, our teachers and support staff really get to know the children and families in our school community, and children (and parents) form close friendships as they grow through the years.

Our school curriculum, designed to build skills and creativity, embraces modern teaching methods to foster a warm and supportive learning environment. Our academic results are excellent, but this doesn't tell you everything about our school. Our children are also artists, musicians, historians and athletes, and we are committed to delivering expert teaching across all of these curriculum areas. Our after-school clubs let students dive further into their hobbies and interests after the bell rings.

Families at Notre Dame Prep can feel good knowing our dedicated staff truly care about helping every child grow academically, socially and emotionally. You can see this commitment in our school motto: 'Ahead in education, a heart in community.'

At the heart of everything we do is our commitment to pastoral care. At Notre Dame Prep, our holistic approach gives our children a safe and nurturing foundation, allowing them to focus on what matters most. Our primary goal is for our children to be happy, caring individuals who are engaged in their learning. This promotes the academic progress and success which we see so clearly as our children transition to high school as confident, well-rounded young people.

East

St John's College School

73 Grange Road, Cambridge,
Cambridgeshire CB3 9AB
Tel: 01223 353652

Email: admissions@sjcs.co.uk
Website: www.sjcs.co.uk
Headmaster:
Mr N. Chippington MA(Cantab), FRCO
Headmistress (from September 2025):
Mrs Sarah Wright
School type: Co-educational Day
& Boarding Preparatory

Age range of pupils: 4–13 years
No. of pupils enrolled as at 01/01/2025: 409
Fees as at 01/01/2025:
Reception and Year 1: £6,558 per term
Year 2: £6,768 per term
Year 3–Year 8: £8,108 per term
Boarders: £12,776 per term
Choristers: £4,259 per term

St John's College School is a leading independent co-educational day and boarding school, set in the heart of Cambridge, which offers an exceptional educational experience to boys and girls aged 4–13. It is described by *The Good Schools Guide* as 'a joyous place that's buzzing'.

We believe in a childhood filled with affection, in which children know that they are known and valued, in which they learn to trust themselves and each other, in which they find and express their voices, discover the differences they can make for themselves and others, learn to think for themselves, to question, to collaborate, to be independent, and to own and take charge of their learning and their lives.

A St John's education is about the whole child. At its core is our focus on pastoral care and wellbeing, starting with our Emotions for Learning programme, which is at the very foundation of what we do and how we are as a school. We believe that education at its best is a profound act of care. If we care, then we will notice. If we notice, then we will act on a child's behalf. If we act for each child, then each of our children will achieve their best and become their best selves. To be known, to be noticed, to be valued, to be cared for – fundamental things for all of us, these are the essentials of a good childhood, and they are at the heart of the St John's way.

Our children become independent learners and creative thinkers prepared to question, with their curiosity very much alive. They get the best from themselves and achieve very highly within and beyond the classroom. We aim for our children to develop a real generosity of spirit, to know and care about how to get the best from others and to do well when they are with us and when they are long beyond our walls.

We focus on creativity throughout the school, both in the way we teach and the way children learn. We prefer to enable children to develop the skills they will need to succeed in the future rather than concentrate purely on gaining knowledge, gathering facts and passing exams, although these have their place in any educational environment. This different approach creates the right environment for our pupils to find their true voice and realise their potential, secure in the knowledge that they are cared for and supported by the community around them and equipped with the skills to problem-solve, collaborate and adapt.

Our youngest children are full of questions, rich with curiosity. We work to preserve and strengthen their questioning and thinking skills. From the earliest age we give them the essential tools, knowledge and understanding, but we also aim to give them more.

In the Pre-Prep a play-based approach to learning is adopted, reflecting and supporting the way children of this age learn. Play-based learning encourages skills of independence, collaboration, problem-solving, creativity and communication. Child-led independent learning, creative and critical thinking, digitally enhanced learning, executive functions, philosophy, study skills, compassion and loving kindness, as well as outdoor learning (which benefits from the addition of a landscaped forest garden) are all part of our aim to enable our children to 'learn how to learn' and become inquisitive and independent learners. An Enrichment programme has been implemented with our 9–13-year olds every Thursday afternoon to explore the development of sustainability projects, as well as cross-curricular work in computing, the arts, design technology, maths and

science, and to give space to My Mind (incorporating mindfulness, study skills, tai chi, PSHE and philosophy, as a foundation for the skills necessary for critical thinking, self-management of learning and management of self). The aim is to foster children's ability to possess their own learning, to engage their innate curiosity and creativity, and to encourage them to connect with their feelings about themselves and the world.

It is from this strong foundation that, despite being non-selective at our main 4+ intake, our pupils go on to achieve at the highest levels. This is confirmed by the results of our last inspection report where the quality of pupils' academic and other achievements and the quality of their personal development were graded 'Excellent'. Our exam results are outstanding and, on average, nearly half of our leavers gain scholarships to the strongest day and boarding schools each year.

Find out more

Visit our school and get to know us, as we are, during the normal school day on an Open Morning or an individually arranged tour. It is important to us that you should have an opportunity to see the school in action, tour each of the school's sites (usually with the children) and experience its atmosphere, as well as meet us to discuss the school's educational approach and ask any questions. To find out more and to arrange your visit or book a place on one of our Open Mornings, please contact the Registrar, Mrs Maria Mosher on 01223 353652 or email admissions@sjcs.co.uk.

St Cedd's School

(Founded 1931)

178a New London Road, Chelmsford, Essex CM2 0AR
Tel: 01245 392810
Email: info@stcedds.org.uk
Website: www.stcedds.org.uk
Head: Mr Matthew Clarke
Appointed: September 2018
School type: Co-educational Day Preparatory & Nursery

Age range of pupils: 3–11 years
No. of pupils enrolled as at 01/01/2025: 400
Boys: 200 **Girls:** 200
Fees as at 01/01/2025:
Day: £3,700–£5,432 per term (inclusive of any applicable taxes)
Average class size: 23; maximum 24

St Cedd's School is a co-educational 3–11 Charitable Trust School offering pupils the opportunity to aspire and achieve in a caring environment that nurtures talent and supports individual endeavour. This is a school in which every child matters. We value and celebrate their many diverse talents and qualities, and the grounded confidence the pupils develop results in great personal achievement.

Individual pupil progress
The progress of pupils, of all abilities, throughout the school is rapid. Our internal assessment results and 11+ scores far exceed national averages, and annually we celebrate an unrivalled success rate to selective grammar and independent senior schools with an impressive track record of scholarship awards. This level of achievement is significant given that the school is academically non-selective. Assessments on entry are designed to capture the strengths and areas for development of each child so that the education is tailored to the needs of the individual.

Centre of excellence
The Independent Schools Inspectorate (ISI) put St Cedd's School at the top level in every category of inspection in March 2022, when we were last inspected, which places the school among the very best 3–11 preparatory schools in the country. The accolade confirms what we witness every day: high academic achievement, outstanding records of attainment in music, an inclusive sporting ethos and successes at national tournaments, a sense of purpose and ambition that shows itself in the attitude and actions of the pupils and staff, and a very effective pastoral care system.

The academic excellence of the school, and our provision for the most able, is recognised by the National Association for Able Children in Education through our NACE Challenge Award accreditation.

Broad and balanced curriculum
With over 80 clubs and activities to choose from, extracurricular opportunities are balanced with a firm focus on academic work. This synergy supports the development of confident, self-assured pupils ready for the challenges ahead. PE, music, art, French and science are taught by specialists, with the teaching of PE, music and French starting in Pre-School. Acknowledging the breadth of talents of our pupils is an important aspect of life at St Cedd's School. To this end, our baccalaureate-style Year 6 curriculum, HOLDFAST, leads to awards in recognition of 'Holistic Opportunities to Learn and Develop, Furthering Achievement, Service and Talent'.

As a member of the Choir Schools' Association, our choristers sing in the Cathedral Choir and the Junior and Senior Chamber Choirs sing at evensong in Chelmsford Cathedral.

Nurturing the future
For over 90 years, boys and girls at St Cedd's School have been enjoying a quality of education that is among the very best you will find. We provide the best start in our vibrant Pre-School where the children thrive in a colourful and nurturing environment that widens their horizons and instils in them a love of learning.

Breakfast Club operates from 7.30am to 8.00am and a wrap-around care programme is open until 6.00pm. Fees include curriculum-linked extracurricular activities, lunch and the majority of after-school clubs.

To attend an open day or to arrange an individual tour, please contact our Admissions Registrar on 01245 392810 or email admissions@stcedds.org.uk.

East Midlands

Spratton Hall

SPRATTON HALL

(Founded 1951)

Smith Street, Spratton, Northamptonshire NN6 8HP
Tel: 01604 847292
Email: registrar@sprattonhall.com
Website: www.sprattonhall.com
Head Master: Mr Simon Clarke
Appointed: January 2014
School type: Co-educational Day Preparatory

Religious denomination: Church of England
Age range of pupils: 4–13 years
No. of pupils enrolled as at 01/01/2025: 390
Fees as at 01/01/2025:
Reception, Year 1, Year 2:
£13,842 per annum
Years 3, 4 & 5: £18,630 per annum
Years 6, 7 & 8: £21,672 per annum
Average class size: 15.5

Spratton Hall embodies the values of a traditional prep school, as academic achievement is always encouraged and rewarded. However, we are not an academic hot house and as such, we help children develop their strengths wherever they lie, be they in sport, drama, art, STEM or music.

We have 50 acres of first-rate facilities, including a purpose-built theatre, art studios, Forest School, science labs, an indoor sports dome, floodlit AstroTurf and multiple sports courts, tracks, pitches and nets. Combined with our 65 extracurricular activities, we definitely have something to delight and inspire every child.

In our Pre-prep, determination and kindness are woven into all areas of the curriculum, and children receive daily individual support from highly-experienced Early Years teachers. To complement their classroom-based learning, they also enjoy regular PE, dance, music, art, drama and Forest School sessions.

With a 100% pass rate at Common Entrance and multiple annual scholarships to top public schools, the rigorous academic curriculum is balanced with fun inter-house competitions, school trips and exceptional pastoral care.

Our dedicated Head of Pastoral Care oversees the wellbeing and welfare of all pupils, and a well-resourced learning support team are always on hand to help children overcome any academic obstacles they may meet. Meanwhile parents are supported with extended school days, free wraparound care, and local minibus routes.

To experience a typical school day, we hold Open Mornings in May and October. There are also termly Discovery Days for pre-school children aged 2–4. Open Mornings and private tours can be booked at www.sprattonhall.com.

Greater London

Chigwell School

(Founded 1629)
High Road, Chigwell, Essex IG7 6QF

Tel: 020 8501 5700
Email: admissions@chigwell-school.org
Website: www.chigwell-school.org
Head Teacher: Mr Damian King
School type: Co-educational Day & Boarding Preparatory, Senior & Sixth Form
Religious denomination: Anglican
Age range of pupils: 4–18 years

No. of pupils enrolled as at 01/01/2025: 1,111
Boys: 597 **Girls:** 514
No. of boarders: 27
Fees as at 01/01/2025:
Reception to Year 4: £6,492–£6,948 per term
Year 5 to Year 13: £7,680–£9,210 per term
Full Boarding: £15,978 per term

Welcome

Nestled in the outskirts of London in leafy Essex, Chigwell is a co-educational school for 4–18-year-olds with boarding available at Sixth Form. The school was founded in 1629 and for nearly four centuries we have been preparing pupils to go out into the world. Clearly that world has evolved a great deal since then and, while we are conscious of our long heritage, we are always looking to innovate so that Chigwellians are well prepared to contribute positively, to inspire change for the better and to continue learning throughout their lives.

Facilities

We benefit from a unique blend of listed historic buildings, modern facilities and extensive 100-acre grounds. We have a newly opened state-of-the-art Sport & Wellness Centre, dedicated Drama Centre for those aspiring thespians, and Music School that houses many ensembles and our prestigious Choir. We have dedicated buildings for art, science, wodern foreign languages, English and maths, and even a self-contained Prep School building with its own library for our Year 3 to Year 6 pupils. The Swallow library, situated in the oldest part of the school, has some wonderful architectural features and is of historical significance.

Our self-contained Pre-Prep school was built in 2013 to house Reception, Year 1 and Year 2 pupils. It benefits from its own library, multipurpose hall and dining room, an ICT suite, science and music rooms, spacious playgrounds, a woodland classroom, a fairy garden and an adventure play area.

In 2016 we opened our dedicated Sixth Form Centre, which is home to our A-level pupils. It has six classrooms, study and social spaces, and a centre for careers and university advice, as well as a coffee shop and a large seating area.

Our sporting facilities are second to none and we have recently opened our new Sport & Wellness Centre. It is home to a six-lane 25-metre swimming pool, five-court multipurpose sports hall, gym, individual studios, climbing wall and café.

Boarding

Our boarding provision and care have been classified as excellent by ISI. Our three boarding houses are homes from home for approximately 30 Sixth Form international pupils, who come from a range of countries both within Europe and overseas. Our boarders benefit from a homely close-knit and caring support network of houseparents.

Entry requirements

At 4+ the assessment consists of pupil participation in a range of activities based around numeracy, literacy, listening and responding to stories/songs and joining in with a range of activities centred on the EYFS curriculum. At 7+ and 11+ one can expect a meeting followed by an English and a maths examination. At 13+ candidates will sit an English and maths paper as well as a modern foreign language of their choice, followed by an interview for successful candidates. Entrance to Sixth Form typically requires 8s and 9s in the subjects being studied at A-level along with an interview and a school report.

Path to success

Chigwell School is a happy, mutually supportive, family-orientated community in which parents and staff work in partnership to help pupils reach their full potential and where friendships formed often last a lifetime. You will find that we are a busy

school where pupils of all ages work closely with each other and their teachers. In Chigwell pupils we look for academic ambition and a genuine eagerness to be involved in all that the school has to offer. Through the curriculum and the wide range of opportunities available to them beyond the classroom, each becomes the very best they can be: independent in spirit, adventurous in approach and empathetic in how they treat others. Ultimately, our aim is that each and every pupil will forge their own path to success, true to our motto: Find a way or make a way.

There is a special warmth about the nurturing Chigwell community, with excellent facilities set in a beautiful open site of 100 acres, within view of the City of London.

Greater London

Holy Cross Preparatory School

(Founded 1931)
George Road, Kingston upon Thames, Surrey KT2 7NU
Tel: 020 8942 0729
Email: secretary@holycrossprep.com
Website: www.holycrossprepschool.co.uk

Headteacher: Mrs S. Hair BEd(Hons)
School type: Girls' Day Preparatory & Nursery
Religious denomination: Catholic
Age range of girls: 3–11 years

Igniting the spark that shapes the life

Holy Cross Preparatory is an independent school for girls aged 3–11 located on 8 acres of beautiful grounds off Kingston Hill.

At Holy Cross Prep School, you will notice immediately that we identify and nurture your daughter's talents from the very start. Our emphasis on understanding the strengths and personal make-up of each individual girl has, their parents say, become the hallmark of a Holy Cross Prep education.

'We ignite the spark that shapes the life at Holy Cross Prep, nurturing our girls to develop their curiosity, discover a love of learning and aspire to be the best they can be academically, spiritually, personally and physically.' – Sarah Hair, Headteacher

The two-form entry benefits from small class sizes and provides a warm, nurturing and stimulating environment where a dynamic, highly motivating and relevant curriculum is taught by a team of excellent teachers. The school promotes a growth mindset in STEAM subjects, empowering their girls to be responsible citizens who are confident, independent, well-rounded and fully prepared to face the challenges of any selective senior school. The dedicated teaching team ensure that high academic standards are upheld across every subject, as well as the many specialist subjects, which include sport, music, drama, computing, art and French.

Mrs Hair states *'It is of great importance to me to maintain the balance between the goal-oriented side and the formation of character and development of those life skills that do indeed last a lifetime. We recognise that the signposts for travelling along the journey of life are clearly visible even in early childhood. At Holy Cross Prep we identify strengths and talents from the very start. In short, we ignite a spark; the spark that will shape the life of your daughter.'*

Greater London

Merton Court Preparatory School

(Founded 1899)

38 Knoll Road, Sidcup, Kent DA14 4QU
Tel: 020 8300 2112
Email: office@mertoncourtprep.co.uk
Website: mertoncourtprep.co.uk
Headmaster: Mr Dominic Price BEd, MBA

School type: Co-educational Day Preparatory & Nursery
Age range of pupils: 3–11 years
No. of pupils enrolled as at 01/01/2025: 315
Fees as at 01/01/2025:
Day: £3,700–£5,625

An 'excellent' school where opportunities make all the difference

Merton Court Prep, Sidcup, which combines academic excellence with a healthy holistic approach, has celebrated 125 years since its foundation, in 1899.

This ISI 'Excellent' co-educational, proprietorial school teaches 320 boys and girls from the age of three to those taking their 11+.

'We encourage pupils to achieve their best and learn the key skills that will help them through life, in an exciting environment. It takes hard graft and effort, but we shouldn't be afraid of that and, whilst schools can easily be turned into "exam factories", we have always pushed for a holistic approach that allows a child to discover what they are really good at', says Dominic Price, the school's Headmaster and Proprietor.

Merton Court's academic success sees pupils gain places at local well-regarded Grammar and Independent Schools. Smooth transition to Senior school is helped by the fact that, like at Secondary school, Merton Court pupils move classrooms, from an early age, for different subjects, which are taught by teachers with specialist knowledge, instead of staying put with just one teacher. From Early Years Foundation Stage upwards, the school is determined to inspire a real passion for learning and a 'go for it' attitude.

With a unique family ethos, and the highest quality of pastoral care, what really sets Merton Court apart is the opportunity to enjoy grass and Astro pitches, forest school, a sports hall, a swimming pool and dedicated science, music, art, dance and IT facilities all on site. All of these things give pupils the best possible start to their life story.

The school's most recent Independent Schools Inspectorate report judged Merton Court as 'Excellent' (equivalent to Ofsted 'Outstanding') in all areas of academic and pastoral development. For further details of this report and information about the school, please do visit our website: www.mertoncourtprep.co.uk

Greater London

St Catherine's School

(Founded 1914)

Cross Deep, Twickenham, TW1 4QJ
Tel: 020 8891 2898
Email: info@stcatherineschool.co.uk
Website: www.stcatherineschool.co.uk
Headmistress: Mrs Johneen McPherson MA
Appointed: September 2018

School type: Girls' Day Preparatory, Senior & Sixth Form
Age range of girls: 7–18 years
No. of pupils enrolled as at 01/01/2025: 405
Fees as at 01/01/2025:
Day: 15,285–£18,513 per annum
Average class size: 15–20
Teacher/pupil ratio: 1:9

St Catherine's is a vibrant and caring Catholic school that welcomes girls of all faiths and backgrounds. Our friendly community helps each pupil develop confidence as she explores her gifts and talents, and is inspired to meet challenges creatively. The school proudly combines excellent pastoral care with an innovative and ambitious curriculum that prepares girls for the 21st century.

Our recent excellent inspection reports from the Independent Schools Inspectorate note that 'teaching at St Catherine's is more than the sum of its classroom parts... pupils have a wrap-around experience that leads them to learn exceptionally well' and that 'pupils flourish because of the secure, caring ethos of the school'. We see these features in the achievements of our girls and in their readiness to learn.

In the Prep Department, we are moving toward an exclusively key stage two structure, and investing in a rich and varied curriculum and co-curricular programme for girls in Year 3-6. The emphasis on curiosity and discovery establishes firm foundations that later lead to success in the Senior School. Prospective families may like to know that St Catherine's Prep girls automatically move on to the Senior School, which can mean less worry at the 11+ stage, for pupils and parents alike.

St Catherine's girls enjoy a wide range of subjects and benefit from passionate and experienced teachers who know them well, offer support and challenge at all stages, and are in regular contact with parents.

The Senior School girls certainly rise to the challenges posed by public examinations. St Catherine's is proud of its value added at GCSE and A Level, and we enjoy seeing our young women go on to university courses and careers of their choice, and to bright futures.

Greater London

Those who visit St Catherine's often remark on the warm and genuine enthusiasm of our pupils. The school's Christian ethos and emphasis on values helps girls to engage with the world around them, while open discussion, time for reflection, pupil-led committees and a wide range of opportunities create a lively environment where they can feel a sense of belonging. Our emphasis on character, and on the deeper values of compassion, integrity and resilience, is also developed through a comprehensive co-curricular programme.

St Catherine's is committed to developing its facilities and over recent years we have been pleased to see girls enjoying new buildings and refurbishments, like the Science Block and Sixth Form Centre, which are designed to enhance their curriculum and social experiences. We also provide exciting trips, competitions and school events throughout the year; whether it is a trip to Iceland, regional athletics finals or a part in the latest school musical, there are plenty of opportunities for girls to develop their skills and their friendships within the school community.

Information about public examination results, co-curricular opportunities and wrap-around care can all be found on the school website: www.stcatherineschool.co.uk

Greater London

Woodford Green Preparatory School

(Founded 1932)
Glengall Road, Woodford Green,
Essex IG8 0BZ

Tel: 020 8504 5045
Email: admissions@wgprep.co.uk
Website: www.wgprep.co.uk
Head of School: Miss Jenny Maslen
Appointed: January 2025
School type: Co-educational Day Preparatory & Nursery
Age range of pupils: 3–11 years

No. of pupils enrolled as at 01/01/2025: 381
Fees as at 01/01/2025:
Foundation 1: £4,440 per term (VAT exempt)
Foundation 2 to Year 2: £5,106 per term (incl. VAT)
Year 3 to Year 6: £5,451 per term (incl. VAT)
Average class size: 24
Teacher/pupil ratio: 1:12

Established in 1932 as a Christian, co-educational school, we are proud to have been entrusted with delivering a first-class education for generations of pupils. We are a forward-thinking, diverse and inclusive community, welcoming children of all faiths and none; our approach is to enable children to learn with curiosity, enthusiasm and flair. We aim to equip children with the skills and knowledge that will prepare them for the next phase of their education and beyond.

We are quietly ambitious for every pupil in our school; our curriculum is broad, creative, and designed to adapt to the ever-changing world. We encourage all our pupils to have a 'can-do' attitude and place great emphasis on developing intellectual curiosity, depth of thought and scholarship. At the heart of the school is a strong commitment to personal development and pastoral care, for we recognise that happiness, confidence and high levels of involvement and wellbeing are the linchpins of academic success.

In May 2023, the school underwent a full inspection by the Independent Schools Inspectorate. The results of the evaluation were excellent, with the school receiving the highest commendation across all assessed areas.

Specialist teachers for art, music, modern foreign languages and sports, along with dedicated spaces like the music room, science lab, library and art studio, contribute to a comprehensive learning environment.

The school has an outstanding record of success in 11+ examinations, with a high number of scholarships consistently awarded. This is testament to both the academic rigour of our curriculum and the breadth of opportunity available.

Parents are encouraged to apply early via the website, and attend Open Events. Means-tested assisted places, of up to 100% of the full fees, are available for 7+ entry or above.

Our school crest reminds us that we are here to ignite a passion for learning and to 'let each flame burn brighter'.

London

Blackheath Prep

(Founded 1998)
4 St Germans Place, Blackheath,
London SE3 0NJ

Tel: 020 8858 0692
Email: info@blackheathprep.co.uk
Website: www.blackheathprep.co.uk
Head: Mr Alex Matthews
Head (from September 2025): Ms Vikki Lloyd
School type: Co-educational Day Preparatory & Nursery

Age range of pupils: 3–11 years
No. of pupils enrolled as at 01/01/2025: 388
Fees as at 01/01/2025:
Nursery: £5,285 per term
Pre-Preparatory (Reception–Year 2):
£6,813 per term (incl. VAT)
Preparatory (Years 3–6):
£7,249 per annum (incl. VAT)

Blackheath Prep is an outstanding, co-educational prep school for children aged 3–11. Located in an idyllic setting on the edge of the heath close to Blackheath Village, our 5-acre site offers superb specialist facilities and plenty of space for our pupils to have the freedom to learn and play in our large playgrounds, forest school areas and 2.5-acre playing field.

Our seven core values of kindness, curiosity, freedom, ambition, courage, community and joy inform all that we do and how we behave as a school community. They guide our approach to teaching and learning, to pastoral care and to wellbeing, and our engagement with those around us.

At Blackheath Prep we are ambitious for your child and who they can become. We're committed to achieving academic excellence within an ethos of strong pastoral care. We deliver this through a balanced and challenging curriculum that captures children's imagination and encourages their creativity. We nurture our pupils both academically and pastorally, enabling them to be happy, confident and inquisitive children.

Through a broad range of subjects, inspiring teaching and plenty of extra-curricular activities, we ensure that our school is a really exciting place to be, where curiosity is stimulated and a love of learning is encouraged.

We provide opportunities for our pupils to engage with every aspect of school life; in the arts, on the sports field and in the classroom as well as excellent wraparound care activities. We encourage our pupils to develop long-held passions, to try new things, to succeed and fail, to lead and serve, to play and explore, to give and give generously.

Above all, we are a kind, friendly and joyful school.

London

St Benedict's School

(Founded 1902)
54 Eaton Rise, Ealing, London W5 2ES
Tel: 020 8862 2000
Email: admissions@stbenedicts.org.uk
Website: www.stbenedicts.org.uk

Headmaster: Mr Joe Smith
Appointed: September 2023
Junior School Headmaster: Mr Rob Simmons
School type: Co-educational Day Preparatory & Nursery, Senior, & Sixth Form
Religious Denomination: Catholic
Age range of pupils: 3–18 years
No. of pupils enrolled as at 01/01/2025: 1,135
Junior School: Total: 305
Senior School: Total: 830

Fees as at 01/01/2025:
Nursery: £4,061–£6,107 per term
Pre-Prep (aged 4–7 years):
£5,614 per term
Junior School (aged 7–11 years):
£6,239 per term
Senior School (aged 11–18 years):
£7,387 per term
Average class size: Junior School: 17; Senior School: 17; Sixth Form: 7
Teacher/pupil ratio: 1:10

St Benedict's is a leading independent co-educational Catholic school, in leafy Ealing, West London.

The Junior School and Nursery provide a supportive and vibrant environment in which to learn. Sharing excellent facilities with the Senior School and a programme of cross-curricular activities help ease the transition at 11+ to the Senior School, which is on the same site.

Combining strong academic standards with outstanding personal development, within a nurturing and happy community, our aim is to enable all children to develop their full potential.

St Benedict's has the distinct advantage of offering a seamless education from Nursery to Sixth Form, meaning that children can make firm and lasting friendships and enjoy familiar surroundings and facilities, which helps ease their transition to our Senior School.

From the age of three, children can begin their very first educational steps at Nursery through to Year 6 in our Junior School. We encourage our pupils to be excited by their learning, to follow their natural curiosity and to have the confidence in their ability to make progress within a supportive, friendly and vibrant environment in which to learn.

Our Nursery offers a carefully planned development programme, while the Junior School provides a broad and balanced curriculum based on a rigorous academic core.

We boast a strong sporting tradition, where a wholesome approach to sport is encouraged in all our pupils from a very young age. Here they learn the value of teamwork, leadership, commitment, respect and discipline.

Our thriving arts programme in music, drama, dance and art provides students with opportunities to express themselves creatively. Performances and exhibitions are of the highest standard, with students of all ages actively participating with passion and energy.

Co-curricular activities are also firmly embedded in life at St Benedict's and our extensive programme of clubs offers pupils the opportunity to develop their personal interests or explore new activities.

At St Benedict's, we cultivate principled leadership, resilience and strong character, underpinned by values of integrity, kindness and generosity. Our goal is to equip young people with the skills and qualities they need to thrive – both in the classroom and in life.

Bridgewater School

(Founded 1950)
Drywood Hall, Worsley Road, Worsley, Manchester, Greater Manchester M28 2WQ

Tel: 0161 794 1463
Email: admin@bwslive.co.uk
Website: www.bridgewater-school.co.uk
Head Teacher: Mrs J. A. T. Nairn CertEd(Distinction)
School type: Co-educational Day Preparatory & Senior, Nursery & Sixth Form

Age range of pupils: 3–18 years
No. of pupils enrolled as at 01/01/2025: 471
Fees as at 01/01/2025:
Prep School (Kindergarten to Year 6):
£4,291 per term (inclusive of VAT)
Senior School (Years 7–13):
£5,777 per term (inclusive of VAT)

At Bridgewater School, we celebrate, support and nurture individuality.

We provide independent education for girls and boys aged 3–18 years in an inspirational setting that is inclusive, stimulating, supportive and totally focused on helping your child to be everything they can be.

We are proud of our family ethos, our consistently outstanding results and our forward-thinking academic environment. But most of all, we are proud to be part of each child's individual journey.

Ever since the school's inception in 1950, our family ethos has ensured that every child is known and recognised throughout their own unique learning journey. Although the scale and stature of the school have grown alongside our new buildings and facilities, we are still small enough to know each young person by name and develop a true understanding of their specific needs and abilities.

Whether your child joins us at the very start of their learning journey, as a Prep School pupil or at Senior School or Sixth Form level, our consistently high teaching standards and varied extracurricular activities start in our Early Years Foundation Stage and continue throughout the school, enriching students' experiences and underpinning the excellent personal development of all our pupils.

The result is a vibrant community where children can flourish, learning together and achieving together, as they each follow their own path towards fulfilling their individual potential.

To experience our approach for yourself visit bridgewater-school.co.uk and take a virtual tour of our impressive grounds and facilities, or call 0161 794 1463 or email admin@bwslive.co.uk to arrange a personal visit, when we would be delighted to show you all the highly individual features which set our school apart and make it the perfect location for your child's future.

North-West

The Queen's School

(Founded 1878)
City Walls Road, Chester, Cheshire CH1 2NN

Tel: 01244 312078
Email: admissions@thequeensschool.co.uk
Website: www.thequeensschool.co.uk
Headmistress: Mrs Joanne Keville
Head of Lower School: Miss Iona Carmody
School type:
Girls' Day Preparatory, Senior & Sixth Form
Age range of girls: 4–18 years
No. of pupils enrolled as at 01/01/2025: 400

Fees as at 01/01/2025:
Lower School (Infants, Rec–Year 2):
£4,266 per term
Lower School (Juniors, Y3–Y6):
£4,776 per term
Senior School: £6,439 per term
Sixth Form: £6,439 per term
Average class size: 15
Teacher/pupil ratio: 1:8

At The Queen's School, every girl's voice is heard and celebrated. An outstanding independent school for girls aged 4–18, located in the historic city of Chester, Queen's provides the perfect setting for ambition to flourish, dreams to be realised, and a solid foundation on which to build and be happy and successful. Queen's is passionate and firmly believes in the benefits of an all-girls education and an atmosphere that fosters strong bonds and a sense of belonging, while celebrating the strengths and talents that make every girl unique.

Pupils are given self-belief and the opportunities to explore and try new things. In particular Queen's girls are encouraged to:
- Think independently
- Collaborate confidently
- Aspire globally

Providing outdoor learning opportunities is part of the fabric that makes up the curriculum at the Lower School, giving pupils the opportunity to reconnect with the outdoor world beyond the classroom, boosting environmental stewardship, academic learning and personal development. Forest and Beach School programmes help pupils develop many skills that are hard to teach in the classroom. They encourage them to be active, assess situations, take risks and make decisions, with lots of activities to develop both fine and gross motor skills. The school fosters a global perspective by immersing the girls in experiences that develop a deep understanding and appreciation of other cultures. Queen's want pupils to contribute successfully in the global community by developing the attitudes, knowledge, and skills needed to live and work in today's interconnected world, matched with global competence to participate as empathetic, engaged, and effective citizens. All of this takes place in a warm, caring environment where no one gets lost or slips through the net. Being a smaller school dedicated to the education of girls, pupils are offered a level of pastoral and academic support that is second to none. Learning is enhanced through a wide range of co-curricular opportunities and individually tailoring the approach to each child enables them to achieve outstanding academic results, while developing the skills and mindset to thrive in a changing world.

Bespoke tours and taster days are available throughout the year.

North-West

Windermere School

(Founded 1863)

Infant & Junior School
Browhead Campus, Patterdale Road,
The Lake District LA23 1NW
Tel: 01539 446164
Fax: 01539 488414
Email: admissions@windermereschool.co.uk
Website: www.windermereschool.co.uk

Head: Mrs Jenny Davies
School type: Co-educational Day & Boarding Preparatory & Nursery
Age range of pupils: 3–11 years
No. of pupils enrolled as at 01/01/2025: 72
Fees as at 01/01/2025:
Day: £7,125–£19,500

Windermere School is unique. Set amid the stunningly beautiful mountains and lakes of Cumbria, it delivers an exciting and forward-thinking curriculum, shaping the hearts and minds of the next generation. We aim to educate children to be capable and thoughtful, resourceful, courageous and caring. This is a school where young people can enjoy their schooldays and parents can be confident that their children are following the very best pathways to future success.

With adventurous learning at the heart of our provision, children learn vital skills that they take back into the classroom, as well as through life. Whether they are taking part in Forest School, adventure lessons, performing on the outdoor stage or studying wind speeds at the top of a lakeland fell, there is always challenge, fresh air and enjoyment.

As well as our innovative curriculum, which is designed to develop articulate and confident children, the one thing that makes Windermere truly special is the children themselves. The unique family atmosphere is evident the moment you walk through our blue front doors. Our children are proud of their school family and learn to look after themselves, and each other, within our caring community.

There is a warmth, vibrancy, and kindness at Windermere School that make it a very special place to learn and grow.

Why choose Windermere Junior School?
- The outdoors is as important as the indoors and both environments complement each other displaying natural resources and places in which to play, learn and discover.
- Small class sizes enable our lively, energetic teachers to quickly form close relationships with children and parents.
- A love of learning and an enthusiasm for challenges produces confident, highly motivated pupils who arrive every morning with a smile. It has been known that they even count the days off in the holidays until it is time to come back to school!
- A space where children can be children. If children are happy and feel secure in a stimulating and active environment, they are more likely to embrace the challenges and possibilities that a school like Windermere provides.
- Our innovative Adventure Programme starts from Year 3 and takes the form of adventure activities – sailing, paddle sports, climbing, caving, walking and biking. Children realise that they are capable of more than they could ever imagine. They are inspired to embrace challenges and become well-rounded, resilient, confident and independent thinkers, taking those skills with them into the classroom.

South-East

Aberdour School

(Founded 1928)

Brighton Road, Burgh Heath, Tadworth, Surrey KT20 6AJ
Tel: +44 (0)1737 354119
Email: enquiries@aberdourschool.co.uk
Website: www.aberdourschool.co.uk
Headmaster: Mr Phillip Makhouli
Appointed: April 2025

School type: Co-educational Day Preparatory & Nursery
Age range of pupils: 2–11 years
No. of pupils enrolled as at 01/01/2025: 330
Fees as at 01/01/2025:
Day: £7,785–£22,032

Finding the brilliance in every child
Enquire now for September 2025/26
Independent day school for girls and boys aged 2–11 years

Every child has the potential to shine. At Aberdour, we aim to find the brilliance in every child, by providing an individual tailored education that identifies their potential and maximises their opportunities to learn, grow and succeed.

Founded in 1928 Aberdour is a thriving and extremely successful preparatory school for girls and boys aged 2–11 years. Set in 12 acres of beautiful Surrey parkland, Aberdour is truly a hidden gem, providing a safe and happy haven for your child. With our many purpose-built facilities for learning, sport and play, your child can develop his or her talents and skills while experiencing an exceptional breadth of opportunity both inside and outside the classroom.

Our brand-new purpose built Pre-Prep opened in September 2023, allowing children and staff to learn in an innovative, creative and dynamic environment.

Aberdour developed Personalised Achievement Learning® in 2007, providing a truly personalised education with breadth and flexibility. We have supported PAL® with major investments in our staff, our systems, our buildings, our IT and our resources, and the combination of a child-focused education. Through PAL®, we believe that every child will fulfil their individual potential if we nurture the talent that is within them, whatever that talent may be. Genuinely innovative teaching has made a real difference to the children's skills, achievements and enjoyment of life. We invite you to come see for yourself.

Please visit our website for information on our admissions process and to contact our Registrar.

Barrow Hills School

(Founded 1950)

Roke Lane, Witley, Godalming, Surrey GU8 5NY
Tel: +44 (0)1428 683639
Email: info@barrowhills.org
Website: www.barrowhills.org
Headmaster: Mr John Towers
Appointed: September 2023
Chairman of Governors: Mrs Justine Voisin

School type: Co-educational Day Preparatory & Nursery
Age range of pupils: 2–13 years
No. of pupils enrolled as at 01/01/2025: 200
Fees as at 01/01/2025:
Day: from: £15,000 per annum
Average class size: 13
Teacher/pupil ratio: 1:7

Barrow Hills is a lively and aspirational independent Prep school and Nursery welcoming girls and boys aged 2–13 years.

Nestled in nature's classroom in the Surrey Hills, our beautiful woodland setting provides space and an idyllic backdrop for children's growth, exploration and wellbeing. Here, your child's early steps in their education take place in an atmosphere where every child feels happy, safe and nurtured.

Our highly qualified and dedicated teachers incorporate the very best of academic and creative practice, delivered using state-of-the-art technology and our excellent facilities. We offer academic success within a balanced and generous education and enjoy an enviable reputation for the academic performance of our children, achieving a 100% pass rate at Common Entrance and consistent graduation to preferred senior school of choice, at 11+ or 13+, including a wide range of scholarships across academics, sport, drama, music, art and all-rounder awards.

We believe that a happy educational beginning lays foundations for a life-long love for learning and a curious mind. Within small but dynamic classes we provide academic challenge for children of all abilities, where every child is encouraged to be brave and is celebrated in their individual endeavours and scholarship, aligned with our core values of compassion, curiosity, generosity, joyfulness, responsibility and truthfulness.

Expectations are high for all, and through individualised challenge and support each child is empowered to flourish academically, socially and emotionally. Through kindness, community and friendship our children discover a sense of purpose and place. They build confidence in exploring and shaping their personal identity, find their passions, develop emotional connections and empathy, learn to be ambitious for themselves and for others, and in so doing grow to know the power of a great attitude.

South-East

Ballard School

BESPOKE EDUCATION

(Founded 1895)

Fernhill Lane, New Milton, Hampshire BH25 5SU
Tel: 01425 626900
Email: registrar@ballardschool.co.uk
Website: www.ballardschool.co.uk
Headmaster: Mr Andrew McCleave

School type: Co-educational Day Preparatory, Senior & Nursery
Age range of pupils: 2–16 years
No. of pupils enrolled as at 01/01/2025: 453
Fees as at 01/01/2025:
Day: £3,455–£6,355
Average class size: 10–18

'Simply the best school every day.' – Parent

'There is only one word to describe Ballard and that is 'extraordinary!' – Pupil

'A warm, friendly school in a glorious setting, where pupils enjoy their learning, throw themselves into a plethora of activities and have fun. The performing arts are outstanding, and children seem genuinely sad to leave for pastures new at 16.' – Good Schools Guide

Ballard is a multi-award-winning, day school, set in 34 acres between the New Forest and South Coast. Ballard's dynamic leadership has turned 'excellent & outstanding' (ISI) into exceptional.

Recognised by the prestigious Independent School of the Year Awards, Ballard won Co-educational School of the Year Award (2024), having reached the finals for Sport (2023) and Performing Arts (2022). Ballard also reached the finals of the Independent School Association's Award for Fine Arts and Design and the MTI Award in Musical Theatre Provision. So, what makes an award-winning education?

Teachers at Ballard believe abilities and intelligence are not fixed – all can flourish and excel when given the tools and environment to develop self-knowledge and resilience. With over 150 co-curricular activities each week, from archaeology to Duke of Edinburgh, and many trips, pupils are encouraged to try something new. Fantastic facilities include an Olympic-sized Astroturf, swimming pool, Forest Schools, five science labs, three libraries with two librarians, 3D-printers, an iMac studio and a 200-seater performing arts centre. Ballard provides a vast array of opportunities but what sets it apart is how Ballard empowers and inspires pupils to seize them. With four alumni at the Paris Olympics (two medalling), pupils have gone onto remarkable things including successful authors, an international opera star and a pop band.

Ballard offers the perfect balance. Classes are large enough to facilitate lively, challenging lessons, yet small enough so that every pupil is known, allowing staff to help pupils successfully develop academically and pastorally. By encouraging them to be the best they can be, Ballard nurtures well-rounded, happy individuals with a healthy outlook on life.

The success of their approach is reflected in consistently superb GCSE results: with a 95% pass rate (9–4), across all pupils and all subjects, 35% attaining the top grades (9–7), and an average 0.79 added value for each pupil, across all subjects. Inspirational teachers give up weekends and holidays to provide additional revision sessions.

Staff believe in Ballard's mission – to ensure that no child gets left behind, encouraging pupils to think of others, contribute positively and make the world better. The school's values are instilled from the start: be positive, kind, curious, respectful, responsible, honest and safe. New pupils quickly feel that they belong and when they leave in Year 11, Ballard pupils do so with a powerful sense of self, equipped to build a bright future in our fast-changing world.

With key entry points in Reception, Year 3, and Year 7, find out more about Life@Ballard, contact our friendly Admissions Team; email Registrar@ballardschool.co.uk or call 01425 626900.

"It's hard to put into words what Ballard does which ignites the sparkle in the children's eyes! The way you help nurture confidence in children is incredible. I love how opportunities are given and how our children reach out and grasp them. Ballard really does nurture the whole person so a child can excel in multiple aspects. As a parent, it's joyful to see your child flourish in so many ways. We've always said our priority is to have happy and confident children and seeing them bounce into school shows that this is happening!" (Parent)

South-East

South-East

Coworth Flexlands School

Inspiring Minds, Nurturing Spirit

(Founded 1963)

Chertsey Road, Chobham, Surrey GU24 8TE
Tel: 01276 855707
Email: secretary@coworthflexlands.co.uk
Website: www.coworthflexlands.co.uk
Head of School: Miss Nicola Cowell
Appointed: September 2018

School type: Co-educational Day Preparatory & Nursery
Age range of pupils: 2.5–11 years
No. of pupils enrolled as at 01/01/2025: 150
Fees as at 01/01/2025:
Nursery: £3,907 per average term (£71 a day)
Pre-prep: £4,787 –£5,009 per term
Prep: £6,110 –£6,547 per term

Coworth Flexlands is an Independent Prep School and Nursery for boys and girls aged 2.5–11 years. The school is ideally located in acres of beautiful grounds on the Surrey/Berkshire borders with a forest school for outdoor learning and a wide range of facilities and opportunities.

'Inspiring minds' and 'Nurturing spirit' are at the heart of the school's approach. Inspiring minds is where the child's curiosity is developed through a challenging, investigative curriculum to foster a lifelong love of learning. Nurturing spirit is the aspect of childhood that brings a smile! Coworth Flexlands, has a culture of wellbeing and happiness, where happier children are healthier, learn better and display more emotional literacy.

The result of this approach sees every pupil reaching and growing their potential at a pace which is right for them. Through highly specialist teaching, led by staff who are passionate and knowledgeable about their curriculum area, pupils show high levels of understanding and attainment. Pupils are well known to staff, and as such, their individual trajectory of progress is carefully planned and monitored. Coworth Flexlands thrives on being a school community where every child's personality shines and is celebrated. Talents are nurtured and pupils are encouraged to follow their passions.

Coworth Flexlands is a school where happiness gets results! Pupils leave Coworth Flexlands as happy, confident and curious learners ready to embrace the future, having secured places at a wide range of leading senior schools, many with scholarships.

Danes Hill School

(Founded 1947)
Leatherhead Road, Oxshott,
Surrey KT22 0JG

Tel: 01372 842509
Email: registrar@daneshill.surrey.sch.uk
Website: www.daneshillschool.co.uk
Head of School: Mr Colin Baty
Appointed: April 2025
School type: Co-educational Day Preparatory & Nursery
Age range of pupils: 2–13 years
No. of pupils enrolled as at 01/01/2025: 630

Fees as at 01/01/2025:
Mini-Transition (age 2–3) minimum 5 sessions:
£470–£595 per term (excl. VAT)
Transition (age 3–4) minimum 7 sessions:
£540–£575 per term (excl. VAT)
Pre-Prep (Reception – Year 1):
£5,250 per term (excl. VAT)
Prep (Year 2 – Year 8):
£6,355–£7,420 per term (excl. VAT)

'We believe Danes Hill School develops independent, confident and caring children with strong minds and voices. We have witnessed this journey in our children and, for us, this is the school's greatest strength.'

Danes Hill School is a co-educational day Preparatory School, situated in 55 acres in the village of Oxshott, Surrey. Danes Hill provides boys and girls aged 2–13 with a dynamic and exciting curriculum. In recent years, Danes Hill has become one of the last remaining 13+ co-educational Nursery, Pre-Prep and Prep Schools in Surrey. This unique educational environment gives the children an opportunity to develop academically and socially before embarking on their Senior School journey.

Danes Hill School invests in the very best teaching staff who engage, encourage and inspire children to achieve.

'My daughter's teachers at Danes Hill School have been phenomenal. Within a few weeks they understood exactly what makes her tick and how to get the best out of her.'

From Nursery* to Year 8, children are taught by specialist teachers in languages, sport, swimming and performing arts. Regardless of a child's academic potential, the school ensures that they are supported to aim high and be the best they can be.

The Extra Curricular Activities Programme gives pupils the opportunity to participate in interests beyond the school day. There are over 100 different clubs and with everything from scuba diving to knitting, the children are sure to expand their horizons or harness an existing talent.

Danes Hill School facilities rival some of the top senior schools. A 24-acre paddock for Forest School, two swimming pools, 14 sports pitches, five science labs, three art studios, a full-sized Astro, putting green and, not to mention the *pièce de résistance*, a 10-m-high climbing wall.

A child's school days should be filled with excitement and wonder, creating memories that they will treasure for years to come. Danes Hill School is the perfect platform for children to discover their passions, days full of laughter and learning, magic moments and lifelong lessons.

*Children start in the academic year they turn 3.

South-East

Edgeborough

Part of the Charterhouse family of schools

(Founded 1906)

84 Frensham Road, Frensham, Farnham, Surrey GU10 3AH
Tel: 01252 792495
Email: office@edgeborough.co.uk
Website: www.edgeborough.co.uk
Headmaster: Mr Daniel Cox

School type: Co-educational Day & Boarding Preparatory & Nursery
Age range of pupils: 2–13 years (boarding from 7)
No. of pupils enrolled as at 01/01/2025: 360
Fees as at 01/01/2025:
£5,175–£8,404 per term

Unlocking potential, inspiring futures

Edgeborough School is a dynamic, award-winning co-educational day and boarding school for children aged two to 13. For over 80 years, Edgeborough has been at the heart of the Farnham community, shaping generations of young learners. Set within 50 acres of stunning Surrey countryside, the school is a powerhouse of academic, sporting and creative success, with pupils consistently securing places at their first-choice senior schools. At Edgeborough, learning is forward-thinking, ambitious and tailored to the individual. Teaching goes beyond the curriculum, equipping pupils with independence, critical thinking, collaboration, communication, reasoning and leadership – key skills that empower them to excel in the classroom and beyond. With expert subject specialists, an enriching curriculum and a culture of curiosity, Edgeborough pupils develop a lifelong love of learning and the confidence to thrive.

Beyond academics, Edgeborough's vibrant co-curricular life provides every child with opportunities to shine. Whether on the sports field, in a music ensemble, on stage, or exploring a vast array of clubs and activities, pupils discover their passions and build resilience, teamwork and self-belief. The Edgeborough experience ensures that every child leaves with the skills, character and ambition to make their mark.

Head, Daniel Cox, champions a school culture that nurtures individuality, adventure, responsibility, perseverance and kindness. His vision is simple: to inspire every child to be bold, curious and determined – encouraging them to be leaders, not just followers.

Edgeborough is a place where pupils develop strong personal values and build meaningful connections with those around them.

With a strong reputation both locally and further afield, Edgeborough's Open Mornings, taster days and personal tours with Mr Cox offer the perfect opportunity to experience the school's distinctive energy and ethos. These events fill quickly – don't miss out on your chance to discover the Edgeborough Advantage!

South-East

Feltonfleet School

Byfleet Road, Cobham, Surrey KT11 1DR
Tel: 01932 862264
Email: admissions@feltonfleet.co.uk
Website: www.feltonfleet.co.uk
Headmistress: Mrs Shelley Lance
School type: Co-educational Day & Boarding Preparatory & Nursery

Age range of pupils:
3–13 years (boarding from 7)
No. of pupils enrolled as at 01/01/2025: 494
Fees as at 01/01/2025:
Nursery: £2,682 (5 mornings) per term
Pre-Prep: £5,095 per term
Prep: £7,487 (day)–£8,880 (boarding) per term

Feltonfleet is a leading preparatory school for girls and boys aged 3–13, conveniently located near the A3, M25 and A245, with daily bus routes from south London and the southern Home Counties. A rural oasis among the urban hustle and bustle, Feltonfleet offers a warm and inclusive community in which **individuals really matter**.

Daily life at Feltonfleet revolves around four fundamental principles: honesty, responsibility, respect and kindness. Head, Shelley Lance, describes how children 'take time to stop, think and breathe in challenging moments', which creates a tranquil environment. The atmosphere she has cultivated fosters pupils' inquisitiveness and critical thinking – as well as immersion in their education – and is of a piece with Lance's passion for stretching childhoods and avoiding 'destination school' stress.

Each year 100% of pupils secure places at first-rate senior schools, with typically one in three pupils awarded a scholarship. The school enjoys excellent connections with a wide range of senior schools and offers families valuable guidance and support to find the right destination school for each pupil.

Every pupil benefits from specialist teaching and use of Feltonfleet's facilities, including swimming pool, MUGAs, sports hall with climbing wall, tennis courts, theatre, science labs, DT workshop, art studio and two rifle ranges, on top of scenic sports fields and woodland.

To facilitate busy family lives, co-curricular clubs and supervision are available 07:30 – 18:30. While the majority are day pupils, there is a small boarding house. Pupils may join this community of 'Feltonfleet Knights' (complete with knighting ceremony!) from Year 3. Flexi options are incredibly popular with parents, who view it as helping their children prepare for senior school by encouraging greater independence. Other parents report their children board because they 'want nothing more than to stay over at school with their friends, despite us living 10 minutes away'!

South-East

Hazelwood School

(Founded 1890)

Wolf's Hill, Limpsfield, Oxted, Surrey RH8 0QU
Tel: 01883 712194
Email: schoolsec@hazelwoodschool.com
Website: www.hazelwoodschool.co.uk
Head: Mrs Lindie Louw

School type: Co-educational Day Preparatory & Nursery
Age range of pupils: 9 months–13 years
No. of pupils enrolled as at 01/01/2025: 572
Fees as at 01/01/2025:
Day: £13,770–£22,626
Average class size: 15–18

Founded in 1890, our school motto is *'spiritu inspiratus'*, which translates as *'lungfuls of inspiration'*. It was chosen by our pupils and inspired by the 20+ acres of superb green space that we enjoy at Hazelwood.

We are a school that holds an unshakeable belief in the potential of every single child. Outside of our thriving nursery, pupils enter at age 4 into Reception or at 7+ to the Prep School. Entry at other ages is possible if space permits. Hazelwood School's Nursery and Early Year is open all year round for children from 9 months to 4 years.

A gradual transition is made towards subject specialist tuition in the middle and upper forms. Pupils are prepared for the Common Entrance examinations at 11+ and 13+ and also for Scholarships to Senior Schools.

Extracurricular activity is an important part of every pupil's education. Hazelwood offers over 45 after-school clubs across year groups, spanning sport, art, science, leisure and performing arts. We have excellent facilities including a heated indoor swimming pool, gymnasium, many games pitches, tennis courts, a food tech kitchen, graphic design suite, a design and technology studio, an innovation suite (called the BOX) and a brand new all-weather Astro pitch, completed in the summer of 2022.

Art, technology, music and drama are also strengths of the school. Our Centenary Theatre incorporates a 200-seat theatre, music school and chapel. We are also extremely proud of our musical performance space called Bawtree Hall with a 450+ seated auditorium.

For children in Years 7 and 8, our outstanding 2-year foundation programme helping prepare children for transition into Senior School education, includes an Electives programme which enables pupils to choose between a range of subjects from stockbroking, forensic science, home economics, Mandarin, fashion and more.

Our pupils develop a curiosity about the world in which they live and a real passion for learning. Most importantly of all they become confident learners, mature and articulate individuals who love coming to school each day.

South-East

Herries Preparatory School

Dean Lane, Cookham Dean, Berkshire SL6 9BD
Tel: 01628 483350
Email: admissions@herries.org.uk
Website: www.herries.org.uk

Headteacher: Mr Robert Grosse
School type: Co-educational Day Preparatory & Nursery
Age range of pupils: 2–11 years

Herries is a delightful, popular co-ed preparatory school in Berkshire for children from 2 to 11 years old. It is a small school, with a strong family ethos and excellent academic results. Herries was rated excellent in all areas by the Independent Schools Inspectorate (ISI) in 2022.

Our supportive family atmosphere enables pupils to thrive and achieve their full potential and develop life skills by following our Herries Values:

Happiness
Enthusiasm
Respect
Resilience
Independence
Excellence
Sincerity

Manners, personal responsibility, tolerance and respect are nurtured at Herries. Our pupils benefit from smaller class sizes allowing tailored teaching and more individual attention and learning time. Children leave Herries to a variety of destination schools, ranging from grammar schools to both selective and non-selective independent secondary schools.

Our ethos involves developing the whole child as a rounded individual by means of our broad educational provision. Character education and our wide-ranging curriculum provide opportunities for the children to be involved in public speaking, drama, music, art, sports and numerous extra-curricular activities and clubs.

Our distinctive setting in Cookham Dean is in the former home of Kenneth Grahame, where 'Wind in the Willows' was written. Our children use Quarry Woods next door weekly for woodland activities. We are rooted in our local area, but we also draw pupils who have lived around the world, contributing to a true community feel.

We offer a warm Herries welcome and look forward to meeting you.

Highfield and Brookham School

(Founded 1907)
Highfield Lane, Liphook,
Hampshire GU30 7LQ
Tel: 01428 728000

Email: admissions@highfieldandbrookham.co.uk
Website: www.highfieldandbrookham.co.uk
Headteacher: Mrs Suzannah Cryer BA (QTS)
School type: Co-educational Day & Boarding Preparatory & Nursery

Age range of pupils: 2–13 years
No. of pupils enrolled as at 01/01/2025: 448
Boys: 244 **Girls:** 204
Fees as at 01/01/2025: £5,400–£12,716 per term
Average class size: 16
Teacher/pupil ratio: 1:8

'We were immediately struck by the warmth of Highfield and Brookham School. It's hard to put my finger on exactly what it is, but it's like being wrapped up in a big hug! The children who showed us around were charismatic and confident without being arrogant, polite without being insincere and rosy cheeked with muddy knees as they spent so much time outside! Highfield and Brookham offered our family the whole package and it was an easy decision to make.'

Highfield and Brookham is a Nursery, Pre-prep and Prep School in Liphook for boys and girls aged 2–13. We celebrate our genuine independence and prepare children for the leading boarding and top day schools. Not being answerable to a senior school or trust results in a strong sense of togetherness and a welcoming family feel. We work together with our children and their families to ensure the children receive the very best education possible.

We have a flawless record of securing entrance to a child's chosen senior school, whether at 11+ or 13+, and our scholarship success is further evidence of our outstanding academic ambition. Our children have been awarded an impressive 111 scholarships over the past six years alone to a diverse range of top senior schools including Wellington College, Cranleigh School, Radley College, Marlborough College and Charterhouse.

Situated in 175 acres of glorious grounds on the borders of Surrey, West Sussex and Hampshire, our beautiful estate provides a stunning backdrop and a wonderful place for learning. We are committed to making the most of our amazing grounds, as well as protecting and enhancing them. Choosing Highfield and Brookham is your opportunity to make a positive impact on your child's learning journey, ensuring they grow up as happy, well-rounded individuals, full of life, keen and ready to tackle the next stage of their education.

Kent College Junior School

(Founded 1885)
Harbledown, Canterbury, Kent CT2 9AQ

Tel: 01227 762436
Email: admissions@kentcollege.co.uk
Website: kentcollege.com/junior-school
Head: Mr Simon James
Appointed: September 2020
Deputy Head: Mrs Anouska Blaza
School type: Co-educational Day & Boarding Preparatory & Nursery

Age range of pupils: 0–11 years
No. of pupils enrolled as at 01/01/2025: 220
Fees as at 01/01/2025:
Day: Reception–Year 6:
£4,810–£7,579 per term
Full Boarding: Year 6:
£12,253 per term
Teacher/pupil ratio: 1:14/18

Kent College is a happy and successful school for boys and girls aged 0–18, situated in the South-East of England in the beautiful and historic city of Canterbury – yet less than one hour away from London by train, and close to all London airports.

Our aim is for every child, every day, to be excited to come to and stay in our school, and when they leave, look forward to tomorrow. After an academic morning with accelerated learning options, pupils enjoy a creative afternoon and a wide array of co-curricular activities after school.

The Garden Cottage Nursery (0–3 years) and Prep School (3–11 years) offer an innovative British education, full of opportunities for children to grow and develop their skills and talents.

The school has a thriving music department, and our choristers regularly perform at national level. A wide range of sports are offered, from hockey to football. The school hosts regular athletic and cross-country events and takes students on sports tours during the year. The school has a new art department at the main schoolhouse and an outdoor theatre for drama.

All children in the Junior School take part in our Gifted, Really Enthusiastic, Able and Talented Programme, where specialist teachers develop individual programmes for each pupil based on their needs and interests. The areas of choice maximise each child's chances of winning a scholarship to the Senior School or gaining entry to their school of choice.

The 60 after-school clubs offer a variety of interesting, challenging and fun activities which expand pupils' skills and knowledge. The school has a working farm where students can join the Farm Club and learn to care for animals as well as take horse-riding lessons.

South-East

Ludgrove

(Founded 1892)
Wokingham, Berkshire RG40 3AB

Tel: 0118 978 9881
Email: registrar@ludgroveschool.co.uk
Website: www.ludgrove.net
Head of School: Mr Simon Barber
Appointed: 2013
School type: Boys' Fortnightly Boarding Preparatory
Religious denomination: Church of England

Age range of boys: 8–13 years
No. of pupils enrolled as at 01/01/2025: 186
Fees as at 01/01/2025:
£13,384 per term (inc. VAT)
Average class size: 14
Teacher/pupil ratio:
1:6 (based on full equivalent teacher numbers)

Ludgrove may be small in size but it has big ambitions for its 186 boys. Ludgrovians stand out from the crowd because they are full of purpose and brimming with questioning enthusiasm. This all-boys' prep school is a rare find because it continues to provide full, fortnightly boarding instead of a mixed offering. This model means the boys get a huge amount out of their day, surrounded by friends, knowing that at weekends everyone is either in school, enjoying its 130 acres of grounds in beautiful rural Berkshire, or at home for an exeat. No boy feels left out or left behind.

The school is a magical place to spend five years of childhood. Our boys enjoy a wealth of opportunities: a stimulating curriculum delivered by enthusiastic and dynamic teachers, exceptional facilities including majestic playing fields, a 350-seat theatre, the Exploration Centre (a hub for art, ceramics, CDT, coding and science) opened in 2021, Monkey House play centre, an Astroturf, 20-m indoor swimming pool, Eton Fives, tennis and squash courts, and a nine-hole golf course.

The continuity of care and education that a boarding school can offer is invaluable in providing a stable platform for a child's development. First-class academic education goes without saying but, in addition, a first-class boarding school with an outstanding pastoral care is a particularly warm and caring environment where children's confidence and character are developed, and they valued as individuals and learn to live in a community.

At Ludgrove, we are lucky to have an outstanding team of vastly experienced staff – teachers, resident matrons, school nurse and boarding house parents – who get to know the boys very well and understand what makes each individual 'tick'. Ludgrove specialises in getting to know boys as individuals, encouraging them to try new challenges and reach their potential, personally and academically.

Calling on our 133 years of experience, we ensure the 'spotlight' is on every child so that their confidence and character are nurtured at every opportunity. This close relationship enables the school to guide each to their most suitable senior school destination. Every year, approximately 70% of the Year 8 cohort go to Eton, Harrow, Radley and Winchester, with 11 boys securing awards to their senior school in 2024.

We are proud of our legacy that friendships are made for life, boys can be boys and our unique spirit allows them to thrive in an atmosphere of happiness, high achievement, good manners and kindness.

South-East

Milbourne Lodge School

(Founded 1912)
Arbrook Lane, Esher, Surrey KT10 9EG

Tel: 01372 462737
Email: registrar@milbournelodge.co.uk
Website: www.milbournelodge.co.uk
Head: Mrs Judy Waite
School type: Co-educational Day Preparatory

Age range of pupils: 4–13 years
No. of pupils enrolled as at 01/01/2025: 245
Boys: 180 **Girls:** 65
Fees as at 01/01/2025:
Day: £17,418–£23,700

Milbourne Lodge is a selective Prep School for boys and girls aged 4–13. Founded in 1912, the school has a long-standing tradition of preparing children for senior school entrance and scholarship exams to the most prestigious and well-known public schools in the country, including St Paul's, Westminster, Eton, Charterhouse, Epsom College, Wellington, Winchester and Benenden. In the past five years alone over 50 academic, art, music and sports scholarships have been won by our pupils.

We strive to set the academic bar high, to value sport and extracurricular activities, to instil a sense of responsibility and good manners and to develop children who are resilient and confident. Our academic curriculum, taught by a highly experienced and dedicated team of staff, is supported by excellent music, art, IT and sports programmes, with games played every day. A strong emphasis is also placed on pastoral care and the school provides a warm and supportive environment in which each child feels valued and can flourish.

The latest SIS Inspection awarded Milbourne Lodge 'Outstanding in all Areas' status. The inspectors stated that: *'Milbourne Lodge provides an outstanding education for its pupils. The pupils' academic attainment is very high and their achievements are exceptional.'*

Milbourne Lodge is a very energetic school which provides endless opportunities and variety. Every child is encouraged to build on their own particular talents and to discover new ones. Here at Milbourne we work hard and play hard!

'Our overriding objective is to prepare your child for his or her senior school. We will prepare each child to be ready to relish the experience of their new school, to be confident in their own skin and to be eager to take the next steps', Judy Waite, Head.

Located in Esher, Surrey, the school is situated in over 8 acres of beautiful grounds within easy access of the A3 and M25. A daily bus runs from SW London.

South-East

Spring Grove School

(Founded 1967)

Harville Road, Wye, Kent TN25 5EZ
Tel: 01233 812337
Email: office@springgroveschool.co.uk
Website: www.springgroveschool.co.uk
Head of School: Mrs Therésa Jaggard
School type: Co-educational Day Preparatory & Nursery

Age range of pupils: 2–11 years
No. of pupils enrolled as at 01/01/2025: 201
Boys: 94 **Girls:** 107
Fees as at 01/01/2025:
Day: £11,088–£17,242
Teacher/pupil ratio: 1:7

Spring Grove is a happy family school for boys and girls aged 2–11 set in 14 acres of beautiful Kent countryside. The school is located in Wye, between Ashford and Canterbury, and close to the high-speed train link into London. As a completely independent Prep school we offer support for the 11+ (Kent Test), the ISEB and scholarship applications to a wide range of senior schools, both locally and further afield.

Spring Grove achieved a double 'excellent' in its most recent (2023) inspection – both for the quality of pupils' academic and other achievements and for the quality of pupils' personal development. The school also has consistently good 11+ outcomes – in 2024, 79% of those who took the Kent Test secured grammar school placements.

The teaching and learning at Spring Grove are research-led and innovative, with a growth mindset that encourages curiosity, resilience and a love of learning. Spring Grove pupils are happy and confident, and the school is renowned for its friendly atmosphere.

Spring Grove Nursery, which caters for children from the age of 2 to 4, is on the same site as the Prep school and, while it is a safe and separate space, the preschool children benefit from sharing staff and facilities with the older children in the school. The Nursery also has its own beautiful walled garden, where the children play all year round.

Outdoor learning is integral to the Spring Grove curriculum, and all children from Nursery upwards regularly visit Forest School. The school has an active pupil-led Eco Committee and is a Green Flag school.

The importance of the creative and performing arts is recognised by an Artsmark Gold award. The school has specialist music, dance and art teachers, and all pupils have regular opportunities to perform in concerts, assemblies and shows throughout the year.

St Swithun's Prep

(Founded 1884)

Alresford Road, Winchester, Hampshire SO21 1HA
Tel: 01962 835750
Email: prepoffice@stswithuns.com
Website: www.stswithuns.com
Head of School: Mrs Liz Norris
Appointed: 2023
School type: Girls' Day Preparatory, Co-ed preschool

Age range of boys: 3–4 years
Age range of girls: 3–11 years
No. of pupils enrolled as at 01/01/2025: 208
Fees as at 01/01/2025:
Preschool: £14,037 (all day)
Reception, Years 1 and 2: £15,440 per annum
Year 3: £20,671 per annum
Years 4, 5 and 6: £20,970 per annum

St Swithun's Prep School is a magical place with children's happiness at its core. You can feel the positive energy as you walk through the door. Confidence is fundamental to success so all activities are characterised by a palpable sense of fun and enjoyable challenge to ensure that pupils flourish, while simultaneously encouraging them to be courageous in everything that they do. The children learn that not all days are perfect and are taught to persevere and develop resilience, allowing them to be ready to take all opportunities that life presents.

Children are encouraged to be compassionate – to be kind and caring – and to be respectful to everyone else. Welcoming those of all faiths and those of none and developing the children's appreciation of diversity is of the utmost importance at St Swithun's.

The weekly timetable is rich and varied, emphasising the core subjects but balancing them with a huge amount of sport, humanities, arts, languages and extracurricular opportunities, such as engineering, gardening, musical theatre workshops, music and baking. The children at St Swithun's have the chance to sample a wide range of experiences and to shine wherever their interests lie.

The teaching and learning environment is spectacular both inside and outside. Set in 45 acres of grounds overlooking the South Downs, the prep school was purpose built in 2015 and has its own specialist facilities, including a gym, theatre and teaching kitchen. It also benefits from sharing the senior school facilities, such as the swimming pool and athletics track.

To find out more about all that St Swithun's has to offer, please explore the website www.stswithuns.com or make an appointment to visit. Please contact 01962 835750 or email prepoffice@stswithuns.com. Keep up to date with the latest news by following @StSwithunsPrep on Instagram.

South-East

Wellington College Prep

(Founded 1820)
Sandhurst, Berkshire GU47 8PH

Tel: 01344 772134
Email: info@wellingtoncollegeprep.org.uk
Website: www.wellingtoncollegeprep.org.uk
Head: Mr E. Venables
Appointed: September 2023
School type: Co-educational Day & Boarding Preparatory & Nursery
Age range of pupils: 3–13 years

No. of pupils enrolled as at 01/01/2025: 385
No. of boarders: 60
Fees as at 01/01/2025:
Day: £17,280–£27,090
Full Boarding: £36,450
Average class size: 17
Teacher/pupil ratio: 1:10

Wellington College Prep is a co-educational, boarding and day Prep, Pre-Prep and Nursery located in Berkshire, but close to the borders of Surrey and Hampshire. The school was founded in 1820 and is proud of its 200-year heritage. Superb grounds and excellent facilities are the background to an experience where success, confidence and happiness are paramount. *The Good Schools Guide* describes Wellington College Prep as a 'progressive, kind and buzzy' school.

Tradition is important but putting children's learning at the heart of what we do and embracing change enables them to thrive in the 21st century.

The school is proud of its academic record, preparing children for a host of top independent schools and boasting a diverse and robust curriculum. Wellington College Prep received an 'excellent' rating in all areas from the ISI inspection team.

Younger pupils follow the International Primary Curriculum and our older children no longer sit the Common Entrance examinations, allowing pupils to embark on Curriculum 200, a new, rich, robust, assessment-led curriculum that will furnish senior schools with a valuable portfolio of academic data, removing the shackles of the traditional exam-based system.

Great teaching, new technology and a focus on the basics mean that children make good progress and love to be in the classroom. Independent learning is a focus for all children and our Extended Project programme helps drive inquisitive minds.

At Wellington College Prep we unashamedly offer lots as part of our Golden Eagle activities experience. Children benefit from a huge range of opportunities in sport, music, drama, art, outward bound and community programmes. Our focus on service means that the school regularly gets involved with the local community, particularly older people. The arts play a big part at Wellington College Prep.

Music fills every corner of the school with regular concerts both small and large consisting of choirs, ensembles and orchestras. Drama is popular and all year groups get the opportunity to join in annual year group performances with a big annual production by our oldest pupils performed at the Wellington College theatre. Art and design are part of the curriculum and children are encouraged to be creative in all sorts of ways. Technology-led projects teach pupils to experiment with software and applications.

Busy children are happy and fulfilled children and we like to think that all pupils are Learning for Life. Learning for Life means that children benefit from the best all-round education. They can feel confident in the classroom, on the games field, on stage, in the concert hall and in the community. Everyone is given the chance to stretch themselves in every area. Challenge is an important part of growing up and at Wellington College

Prep we learn that success and failure are both positive experiences. Bright learning environments including a new Pre-Prep and music complex, new science laboratories, a modern well-equipped library, design and textile workshops, outdoor learning areas and wonderful sporting facilities are important but it is the community that shapes a young person.

Through the excellent pastoral care and tutor system, coupled with a buddy structure, ensuring children have an older pupil to support them, Wellington College Prep seeks to develop wellbeing from the youngest to the oldest. Recognising how to be a positive influence within a community is also part of the Wellington College Prep journey.

Through our wonderful Learning for Life programme that teaches children about themselves and the wider community, we aim to make all our pupils responsible and independent as well as able to show empathy and understanding towards others. Time for reflection in chapel and assemblies also improves the way we look at the world and mindfulness sessions help us all take stock. Boarding is a popular option and allows children to experience a varied evening programme of activities as well as being part of a vibrant and caring community. Boarding encourages independence but it

is also great fun and whether weekly or flexi, boarders have the most wonderful time. Our new common room area allows boarders time to relax among friends on big sofas or gather around the large kitchen table for a chat while munching on a bowl of cereal!

We often say that Eagle House children have the time of their lives and we firmly believe this. Learning for Life at Wellington College Prep opens the doors to all sorts of opportunities and this results in children who are highly motivated and enthusiastic in all they do. Wellington College Prep buzzes with achievement and laughter – not a bad way to grow up!

Wellington College Prep is a registered charity (No 309093) for the furtherance of education.

South-West

Hanford School

(Founded 1947)
Child Okeford, Blandford Forum,
Dorset DT11 8HN
Tel: 01258 860219
Email: office@hanford.dorset.sch.uk
Website: www.hanfordschool.co.uk

Head of School: Hilary Phillips
School type:
Girls' Day & Boarding Preparatory
Age range of girls:
7–13 years (boarding from 7)

Hanford is a day and boarding prep school for girls, aged between 7 and 13 years old, in an idyllic countryside setting. Hanford girls enjoy a wonderful, carefree childhood and are given time and freedom to develop at their own pace. Hanford girls climb trees, ride ponies, make dens but they also learn to work hard. We are a small school where everyone knows each other, so we can build a curriculum around the needs of each child, valuing their individuality and nurturing their unique blend of talents and interests. This combination of fun, hard work and excellent teaching pays dividends when it comes to Common Entrance and scholarships, with girls achieving over 90 scholarships and awards to senior schools in the past eight years.

We are extremely proud of our 'family' atmosphere at Hanford. Older girls help look after the younger pupils, we all eat together in the beautiful Jacobean dining hall, there is no school uniform and we don't believe in lots of unnecessary rules, other than 'Be Kind'. There are no prefects but all senior girls sit on a series of committees that relate to different areas of the school. The 'Under Cover Agents' committee is made up of older girls who make it their job to know if anyone is struggling and make sure the younger girls are happy and settling in well, for example.

Boarding is central to life at Hanford and we have a very modern boarding offer to suit every family from full boarding to flexi boarding; day girls regularly stay the night at Hanford and the majority of pupils will board at some point during their time at Hanford. Dormitories are homely and cosy and always decorated by the girls with their own pictures, photos and personal treasures. Our boarding team is made up of house parents, residential matrons, school nurses and headed up by Susie, the Head of Boarding. The boarding team look after all aspects of pastoral care at school, alongside the pupils' tutors. The team know everything from the name of a beloved pet, toy animal to whose tights were left out overnight.

Parents find that their daughters quickly settle into school life with the help of the boarding team, their peer group and the older girls. There are so many fun activities and games that are part of their weekly boarding experience and each weekend the school is full of boarders who have chosen to stay at school to spend time with their friends and take part in the fun that the boarding team have in store for them. In the summer the girls spend as much time outside as possible and may end the day with a swimming pool party, a barbecue on the lawn and a game of 'Escape to Hanford'.

Hanford is well known for its riding and ponies. The stables are in the centre of the school and nearly all girls ride, either bringing their own pony back to Hanford or riding on one of the school ponies. In their free time, during the day and weekends, many girls will head over to the stables to chat to the ponies and help the Stables Team. We have three full-time members of staff who teach riding and look after the ponies. In the mornings girls take it in turns to 'catch the ponies' from the fields before breakfast and bring them into the stables. In the Summer Term, older girls take it in turns to go for 'Early Morning Rides' in the beautiful countryside before breakfast, a much-coveted tradition that younger girls eagerly look forward to doing themselves. Hanford excels in local and national riding and jumping championships and we have an outdoor and indoor arena as well as a cross-country jumping course.

Sport is incredibly strong at Hanford and recent successes have seen our teams qualify as county champions in rounders, tennis and athletics. Cross-country running is also very strong, with girls winning places on the regional teams, and we host our own Prep School Cross-Country competition. In addition, gymnastics is particularly strong and popular with the girls. Saturday and Wednesday afternoon sports fixtures throughout the year are a great opportunity for parents to come and see their daughters representing Hanford.

Creativity runs throughout Hanford across all the academic subjects, in drama, music and dance, and culminates in the wonderful new Art Barn which houses our art room, handwork (textiles) workshop and exhibition space. The Art Barn is open in the evenings and weekends and is somewhere the girls love to go and spend time with their friends. The results are impressive, last year alone eight girls were awarded art scholarships or awards to the senior schools of their choice. The girls take their creative talents outside as well; in the kitchen gardens they each have their own space to cultivate, growing vegetables and flowers. The school chefs use the vegetables, fruit and salad grown in the gardens in their homemade food, which is extremely popular. Did we even mention the daily 'Milk and Buns' which make Hanford Old Girls go misty eyed….?

South-West

Hazlegrove Prep School

(Founded 1947)

Hazlegrove House, Sparkford, Somerset BA22 7JA
Tel: 01963 442606
Email: admissions@hazlegrove.co.uk
Website: www.hazlegrove.co.uk
Headmaster: Mr Ed Benbow BA MEd PGCE
Appointed: September 2022

School type: Co-educational Day & Boarding Preparatory & Nursery
Age range of pupils: 2–13 years
No. of pupils enrolled as at 01/01/2025: 372
Fees as at 01/01/2025:
Day: £4,025–£8,161
Full Boarding: £9,468–£12,080
Average class size: 15–19
Teacher/pupil ratio: 1:9

Hazlegrove is an Independent Day and Boarding Preparatory School for 372 boys and girls. Established in 1947, the school enjoys an inspiring setting within 200 acres of parkland in Somerset and benefits from outstanding facilities. Hazlegrove believes it is important that children, from an early age, should have the breadth of opportunity to develop their abilities and potential while enjoying the benefit of a caring, nurturing and secure environment.

Hazlegrove is committed to celebrating childhood. A Hazlegrovian in the 21st century is a child who is empathetic, kind and connected to the world, one who is independent but knows that developing relationships and a sense of duty to the community are integral to a successful life. A vibrant and creative curriculum, exceptional pastoral care and stunning rural Somerset location combine to make children feel nurtured, motivated, inspired and encouraged to love learning for life.

The curriculum has a real hands-on feel where children participate and are not just spectators. Staff are passionate about developing in the children genuine awe, wonder and curiosity at the complexities of life and the world – past, present and future. The breadth and balance in the curriculum give pupils an opportunity to get excited about the lessons they have each day.

Sport is a clear strength and significant success is achieved by pupils in team and individual sports. Drama and music are part of the school's DNA with a vast array of choirs, ensemble groups and theatre productions. Every pupil performs in a drama production every year.

The children at Hazlegrove are surrounded with care. That care includes at its core, staff for whom going many extra miles is an everyday thing, and who unashamedly make time to talk about the children. It includes a dedicated Pastoral Leadership Team which meets twice a week, a tutor system, a pastoral care curriculum embedded in everything, and an ever-developing framework for social and emotional literacy and support.

Hazlegrove pupils move on to a wide variety of senior schools aged 13, having taken Common Entrance or Scholarship examinations. The destinations of leavers include Marlborough, Eton, Winchester, Sherborne, Radley and Millfield to name a few. There is excellent support and advice for parents when they are considering the 'next step' for their child. Over the last four years, 103 Scholarships and Awards have been gained to 20 different schools.

Outstanding facilities with a continual programme of investment in its buildings and facilities ensure that Hazlegrove pupils have the best start possible both now and in the future.

For further information, please contact admissions@hazlegrove.co.uk, 01963 442606.

Millfield Preparatory School

(Founded 1945)

Edgarley Hall, Glastonbury, Somerset BA6 8LD
Tel: 01458 832446
Email: prepadmissions@millfieldschool.com
Website: www.millfieldschool.com/prep
Headmaster: Dan Thornburn
Appointed: January 2022

School type: Co-educational Day & Boarding Preparatory & Nursery
Age range of pupils: 2–13 years
No. of pupils enrolled as at 01/01/2025: 472
Fees as at 01/01/2025:
£15,699–£41,796 per annum

Founded in 1945, Millfield Prep offers an exceptional, all-round educational experience that puts the individual at the centre. Nestled in 200 acres of beautiful Somerset countryside, Millfield Prep is an independent, co-educational day and boarding school for pupils aged 2–13, and provides the ideal environment in which to grow up, foster a love of learning and create lifelong childhood memories. Millfield Prep School was named the UK's Independent Prep School of the Year in 2022–23.

We pride ourselves on providing an exceptional, all-round education where every child can discover their brilliance. Our fundamental belief is that every child is unique and that they all have their own special talents which they enjoy and excel at, and the school's outstanding facilities and teaching provision help immerse pupils in limitless opportunities.

Our focus is teaching pupils a broad, balanced and individually tailored programme, and promoting confidence, health and wellbeing through involvement in sport and physical activity. Millfield Prep also runs a Wellbeing Curriculum, educating pupils about their mental health and wellbeing through a series of activities such as yoga, movement to music, mindful walk and talk, and meditation. All our pupils gain a real sense of achievement from the variety of co-curricular activities on offer. Pupils can choose from a wide range of clubs, from pottery and sailing to rock climbing and Lego modelling – there is something for everyone.

Millfield Prep's outstanding facilities allow pupils to excel. Whether it is swimming in our 25-m indoor heated swimming pool, singing in the choir in our purpose-built music department, playing golf on our nine- or 18-hole golf courses, or horse riding in our fantastic equestrian centre, which features over 120 acres of hacking trails and a British Eventing cross-country course, we provide opportunities in a wide variety of fields.

Students and staff live by the school values: Be Kind, Be You, Be Challengers, Be Curious and Be Brilliant. Millfield Prep offers full, weekly and flexi boarding from age 7, with full boarders enjoying evenings and weekends filled with trips and activities. Outstanding pastoral care is at the heart of everything the school does.

95% of Millfield Prep pupils move up to Millfield in Year 9 to continue their education.

We award a number of Academic, Art, Drama, Music and Sports Scholarships each year for entry into Years 6, 7 and 8, as well as a Millfield Prep Award, recognising Prep pupils who are talented all-rounders.

West Midlands

Moor Park

(Founded 1964)
Richards Castle, Ludlow, Shropshire SY8 4DZ

Tel: 01584 876 061
Email: registrar@moorpark.org.uk
Website: www.moorpark.org.uk
Head of School: Mr James Duffield
Appointed: January 2025
School type: Co-educational Day, Full & Flexi Boarding
Age range of pupils: 0–13 years

No. of pupils enrolled as at 01/01/2025: 202
Boys: 110 **Girls:** 92
Fees as at 01/01/2025:
Day: £3,156–£8,742
Full Boarding: £10,829–£12,936
Average class size: 15
Teacher/pupil ratio: 1:8

Muddy knees and flushed cheeks, a stick in hand and pockets bulging with natural treasures. 85 acres of Shropshire countryside in which to find adventure and joy, shared with wild deer and squirrels, with buzzards and kites on overwatch and minibeasts under the rocks.

Welcome to Moor Park, a co-educational boarding and day school for children from 3 months to 13 years of age. A school that still believes in the magic of childhood.

From their first day in our nursery, Moor Park children embrace the outdoors and learn through play and discovery, with freedom to roam and explore, create and imagine. It is in this way that children can safely, happily and wholeheartedly be themselves.

We are also ambitious. Excellent academic standards, high grades and entrance to the finest senior schools are, however, by-products of a well-rounded education. At Moor Park, we aim to develop innate curiosity, an interest in all aspects of the world, the inculcation of life-skills and mastery of a range of subjects – all while retaining the impishness of childhood. Perhaps it is because our focus is so much on the child as an inquisitive being, one who seizes opportunities and lives life with passion, that our scholarship success rate is so high and that our children are in such demand by the very best schools.

It could also be that as a non-selective school we recognise children as individuals and help them find what they love to do. Not every child can be good at everything, but every child can be good at something and finding something for every child is what we take seriously. Moor Park's space, spirit and opportunity for exploration, combined with a happy staff who love what they do, ensure that our school is well placed to get the best out of every child.

Yorkshire & Humberside

Ackworth School

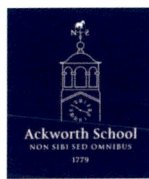

(Founded 1779)
Pontefract Road, Ackworth, Pontefract, West Yorkshire WF7 7LT

Tel: 01977 233600
Email: admissions@ackworthschool.com
Website: www.ackworthschool.com
Headteacher: Mr Martyn Beer
Appointed: April 2024
School type: Co-educational Day & Boarding Prep & Senior, Nursery & Sixth Form
Religious denomination: Quaker

Age range of pupils: 2.5–18 years (boarding from 11)
No. of pupils enrolled as at 01/01/2025: 430
Fees as at 01/01/2025:
Day: £4,440–£6,959
Full Boarding: £14,214–£15,584
Average class size: 16
Teacher/pupil ratio: 1:12

Ackworth has always been a co-educational boarding and day school. For over 245 years, we have maintained a passion for teaching and learning. We are proud of our traditions and family values, but equally proud of our innovative approach to co-education.

Ackworth is a dynamic and forward-thinking school. We strive to develop resilient individuals who not only think creatively, but also act ethically and with responsibility. We encourage our students to express themselves with confidence, to embody the Quaker value of speaking respectfully to others, but also in a way that is true to themselves and their beliefs.

First-class teaching is at the heart of any good school and Ackworth benefits greatly from the quality and experience of its teaching staff. Our aim is to provide a broad and balanced curriculum based on the National Curriculum but taking advantage of the flexibility we enjoy as an independent school. We encourage students to make curriculum choices which suit them best and much advice and guidance are on offer to help them to do this.

Located in a beautiful rural setting in Yorkshire, we offer broad educational opportunities from nursery age to sixth form, for day pupils and boarders.

Some of these opportunities are:
- proven academic performance
- a safe and supportive atmosphere
- the strength of quiet reflection
- excellent sport, music, drama, visual arts and recreational facilities.

The school embraces the Quaker ethos of looking for the good in people, encouraging the individual and providing a friendly, supportive environment. First-class teaching, a broad curriculum and superb facilities provide the foundations for a stimulating learning environment.

Yorkshire & Humberside

The Froebelian School

(Founded 1913)

Clarence Road, Horsforth, Leeds, West Yorkshire LS18 4LB
Tel: 0113 2583047
Email: office@froebelian.co.uk
Website: www.froebelian.com
Head Teacher: Mrs Anna Coulson
Appointed: 2023

School type: Co-educational Day Preparatory & Nursery
Age range of pupils: 2–11 years
No. of pupils enrolled as at 01/01/2025: 132
Fees as at 01/01/2025:
Day: £5,430–£10,095
Teacher/pupil ratio: 1:10

Love, Fairness, Respect and Honesty.

The Froebelian School, Horsforth, is one of the North's leading independent preparatory schools for all children aged 2–11 years.

Since its foundation in 1913, influenced by German educationalist, Friedrich Froebel, it has become one of the North's leading educational success stories. With 100% of our children being offered a place at their first-choice independent senior school, academic results are outstanding and the school offers so much more than an excellent academic education.

Children are loved unconditionally, enabled ambitiously, supported compassionately and are at the heart of everything we do.

We are dedicated to building strong foundations that inspire a lifelong love of learning, enabling each child to acquire knowledge, develop skills, and cultivate personal qualities essential for their future, all within a safe, nurturing, and enjoyable environment – aligning with our core values of Love, Fairness, Respect and Honesty.

The sense of community at Froebelian is second to none and we value our place in our local community, too. There is something for everyone to discover and in which to flourish and thrive. Our pupils are confident, and our talented and passionate staff guide and support each individual on their personal journeys of discovery.

A Froebelian education is a broad and varied experience and pupils are encouraged to take risks in a safe and supportive environment, discovering new talents and interests which provide happiness at school and develop their resilience, self-confidence, problem-solving abilities and interpersonal skills.

Sport, drama and music all play important roles in school life. Games receives a more generous time allocation than in many schools and our pupils represent the school in fixtures in a wide range of activities. We also have an active Outdoor Education

Curriculum which provides residential experiences across the UK and Europe.

School life is varied, exciting and fast paced. There is never a dull moment as we embody our ethos of 'Giving a Flying Start to the Citizens of Tomorrow'. Our children adore their school and are justly proud of all they do. They love learning and there is a true sense of fun. We would love you to experience the warmth of our Froebelian Family for yourselves – please do come and meet us, we'd love to see you.

'Parents are impressed by the "truly holistic ethos", having an "amazing impact" on their children. Academic challenge, traditional views with a large dose of family values, make this school stand out.' - The Good Schools Guide.

Yorkshire & Humberside

Woodhouse Grove School

(Founded 1812)
Apperley Bridge, Bradford,
West Yorkshire BD10 0NR

Tel: 0113 250 2477
Email: admissions@woodhousegrove.co.uk
Website: www.woodhousegrove.co.uk
Headmaster: Mr James Lockwood
School type: Co-educational Day & Boarding Prep & Senior, Nursery & Sixth Form
Age range of pupils: 2–18 years (boarding from 11)

No. of pupils enrolled as at 01/01/2025: 1048
Boys: 578 **Girls:** 470 **Sixth Form:** 212
Prep total: 300
Senior total: 748
No. of boarders: 58
Fees as at 01/01/2025:
Day: £11,625–£18,882
Full Boarding: £41,724–£41,958
Average class size: 18

Woodhouse Grove School – Unlock Their Potential

Woodhouse Grove School is an independent, co-educational day and boarding school in the heart of Yorkshire, offering a seamless education for children aged 2–18. Boarding begins in Year 7, and our prep school, Brontë House, provides the perfect environment for younger pupils to flourish.

Set in beautiful grounds, Brontë House offers excellent facilities for science, sport, music and technology. Nursery pupils benefit from a woodland play area, and pupils at Brontë House have access to the senior school's outstanding amenities, including a 220-seater theatre, artificial pitches and a 25m indoor competition pool.

Brontë House focuses on the holistic development of children. As quoted in our latest ISI inspection 2024: 'Children develop strong communication and language skills. They are supported by staff so that they grow intellectually and emotionally whilst also developing their creative, social and physical skills.'

Small class sizes allow teachers to tailor learning to individual needs, while co-curricular activities, wrap-around care, and swimming lessons from Reception are all included in the fees. For busy families, we offer both term-time and 51-week contracts for Nursery-age pupils.

Parents praise the nurturing environment: 'The best thing about Brontë House is how happy it makes my child. Seeing her positive, supported, and safe is invaluable.'

Sport is a vital part of life at Brontë House, fostering teamwork, leadership, and resilience. Specialist staff create an inclusive yet challenging programme that makes fitness fun. Performing arts also plays a key role, building confidence and creativity through opportunities to learn instruments and participate in performances led by our director of performing arts.

Our Grovian values – confidence, commitment, resilience and respect – are nurtured from Nursery through to Sixth Form, preparing pupils for every stage of life. Alumni, or 'Old Grovians', form a strong network across diverse fields, from the Red Arrows to the West End.

With a combination of academic excellence and co-curricular opportunities, Woodhouse Grove prepares well-rounded, entrepreneurial young people fully prepared for life in a modern world. Learn more at www.woodhousegrove.co.uk.

Prep schools in Scotland

Scotland

Merchiston Castle School

(Founded 1833)
294 Colinton Road, Edinburgh, EH13 0PU
Tel: 0131 312 2200

Email: admissions@merchiston.co.uk
Website: www.merchiston.co.uk
Headmaster: Mr Jonathan Anderson
Deputy Heads:
Mr Danny Rowlands (Wellbeing),
Dr Dale Cartwright (Learning and Teaching)
School type: Boys' Day & Boarding Senior & Sixth Form, Co-ed Prep & Nursery

Age range of boys:
3–18 years (boarding 12–18)
Age range of girls: 3–11 years
No. of pupils enrolled as at 01/01/2025: 380
No. of boarders: 245
Fees as at 01/01/2025:
Day: £18,000–£30,430
Full Boarding: £30,240–£42,255
Teacher/pupil ratio: 1:8

Building strong foundations

Many schools can boast about their exceptional academic results, university success rates, extensive sporting and co-curricular programmes, welcoming atmospheres and stunning grounds and facilities. Indeed, we can do that as well.

What makes us different, however, is a combination of things: our size, a genuine focus on the needs of the individual, and the fact that we really understand our pupils across different stages and know how to get the very best out of them.

It is a potent trio. It is what enables us to get to know our students really well and to understand what makes them tick. It is why we can support them in a way that is material and motivating to them, throughout their whole school journey. It is the reason your child will strive for personal excellence and want to be the best version of themselves. It is the secret of their, and our, success.

Our mission is to provide a caring community for every pupil, which treats them as an individual, unearths and nurtures their talents, encourages them to pursue excellence in all they do, and enables them to flourish.

Our community's wellbeing is central; without it, no one will ever achieve their best. That is why wellbeing underpins everything we do. Our students thrive because they are known, understood, valued and supported in everything they do.

Merchiston is a remarkable school where pupils make lifelong friends and community connections while gaining a world-class, global, outward-looking education.

Merchiston's pupils leave us as rounded individuals, not only having achieved the highest level of personal academic success but with a sense of who they are and with respect for others, having learnt what it means to have true integrity and character. Our success proves that what we do works.

The Forest at Merchiston – where learning happens naturally

The foundations for a Merchiston education are laid in the Forest Nursery and Forest Junior School, a co-ed provision, designed to meet the huge demand for alternative approaches and offering the very best formative early years of education.

The Forest's ground-breaking approach to education empowers children to become confident, curious and resilient learners with broad imaginations. Our outstanding curriculum nurtures cognitive and emotional growth while fostering creativity within rigorous academic learning, ensuring a well-rounded and enriching educational experience.

Scotland

Outdoor education

Outdoor education transforms the academic learning by bringing classroom lessons to life. It fosters critical thinking, enhances problem-solving skills and promotes physical wellbeing. Our cutting-edge curriculum integrates traditional learning with real-world experiences, inspiring your children to explore, discover and thrive in a natural environment, thus creating a well-rounded, engaged and resilient learner. Our innovative education encompasses enquiry-based learning, equipping your children with real skills and knowledge. This approach encourages curiosity, nurtures creativity and ensures that our children are prepared to meet the challenges of the future with confidence and competence.

Co-educational to single-sex

Following the introduction of our Forest Nursery and Junior School, Merchiston remains committed to its single-sex (all-boys) provision in the Senior School. The strength of our model is underpinned by the knowledge that boys and girls learn differently at different stages in their development; the attention to the individual being an essential pillar of our educational ethos, we strongly believe the move towards single-sex in the middle years allows us to offer a more tailored approach to education and care.

Likewise, we believe it is important for our younger pupils to have the chance to connect with and learn alongside girls during those formative early years of education, laying strong foundations for good relationships with the opposite sex.

If your daughter joins us in the Nursery or Junior School, we will then support her transition to the Senior School of your choice. At Senior School level, Merchiston continues to benefit from its strong links with girls' schools for drama performances, cultural events and social gatherings.

Admissions

A visit is the best way to get a feel of the unique ethos and junior education we offer. We would be delighted to show you around and introduce you to our staff and pupils. Contact our Admissions Department at admissions@merchiston.co.uk for more information and to arrange a visit. A warm welcome awaits!

Prep schools in Wales

Wales

St Gerard's School

(Founded 1915)

Ffriddoedd Road, Bangor, Gwynedd LL57 2EL
Tel: 01248 351656
Email: sgadmin@st-gerards.org
Website: www.st-gerards.org
Head Teacher: Mr Campbell Harrison
Appointed: September 2016

School type: Co-educational Day Preparatory, Senior & Sixth Form
Age range of pupils: 4–18 years
No. of pupils enrolled as at 01/01/2025: 100
Fees as at 01/01/2025:
Day: £11,652–£17,808
Teacher/pupil ratio: 1:10

At St Gerard's, happiness takes centre stage. We believe that a joyful atmosphere is the foundation for successful learning. As a family-orientated school, we're proud to create a safe, friendly and nurturing environment where pupils thrive.

Nestled in the picturesque surroundings of Bangor, St Gerard's is a beacon of educational excellence, shaping the futures of young minds in the heart of North Wales. Our school isn't just a place of learning; it's a vibrant community where every pupil's journey is a personalised adventure.

Our commitment to excellence shines through in our pupils remarkable achievements. What sets St Gerard's apart is its commitment to providing holistic education. The classrooms are more than spaces for lessons; they are laboratories of curiosity, fostering creativity and critical thinking. Our dedicated educators go beyond textbooks, guiding pupils to discover their passions and potentials.

The lush campus, adorned with greenery and modern facilities, provides a stimulating environment for growth. From state-of-the-art classrooms to spaces for artistic expression and athletic pursuits, St Gerard's offers a comprehensive platform for every facet of a pupil's development.

With a rich legacy spanning generations, St Gerard's is an independent Welsh and English school that has proudly welcomed learners of all backgrounds. Our all-inclusive ethos ensures that every child feels valued, supported and ready to embark on their educational adventure. We believe in nurturing not just academic excellence but also character, resilience and individuality.

Engaging in community initiatives and embracing the cultural diversity within our walls, we prepare pupils not just for exams but for life.

St Gerard's shines as a dynamic school dedicated to unlocking the full potential of each pupil. With a legacy of achievement and a future filled with promise, St Gerard's is your partner in nurturing confident, compassionate and empowered learners.

St Gerard's School Trust is nationally recognised for its outstanding academic record, regularly topping the league tables for Gwynedd schools (both state and independent), as well as featuring prominently in national league tables – this includes being ranked second in the UK for small independent schools.

Our dedication to academic excellence is the cornerstone of our educational philosophy. By combining over a century of tradition with tailored, individual support for our alumni, we consistently achieve high academic results and have all the experience to set your child on the path to fulfil their potential.

Results-based academic achievements

We take pride in our ability to not only meet, but exceed national standards, which is shown consistently in our GCSE and A-level results over the past 20 years.

Our students' performances are a testament to our rigorous curriculum and dedicated teaching staff and have resulted in St Gerard's being listed in the top 10 for independent schools in Wales by The Times Parent Power Guide 2022.

How we achieve academic success

Our consistently exceptional performance is a result of years of developing our curriculum, hours of passionate and devoted work from our teaching staff, and dedication in our belief to deliver a balanced environment for learning that provides the nurturing space students need to succeed.

Our ethos

For over a hundred years we've maintained a caring and kind ethos with high behavioural standards that have meant St Gerard's operates as more than just an educational institution. Our school community is focused on developing strong moral and ethical values to help nurture and develop analytical, critical and compassionate thinkers who can change the world around them.

Personalised education

We believe in the power of personalised education. Small class sizes in both our Senior and Junior School programmes allow us to give each student the attention they need. This approach is key to our students' remarkable achievements in both GCSE and A-level exams.

Ensuring our students develop in their own way extends to the supporting activities we provide outside of the curriculum. While academic excellence is our priority, we want to help the students become well-rounded individuals through holistic development.

To do this, we provide a range of extra-curricular activities that complements our academic rigour to help challenge and channel our students efforts into new and engaging experiences.

Discover our success for yourself

The best advertisement for our school is to see it for yourself. Arrangements can be made to visit St Gerard's throughout the whole of the year, where you can join our students and see the school in action.

We also offer access to the school via our Assessment Day. This is an opportunity for prospective students to experience our unique approach to education and witness first-hand our commitment to academic excellence and student development.

Visit our website or give us a call to embark on a journey of discovery. We're thrilled to welcome your family into the St Gerard's community.

Directory

Channels Islands D103
Central & West D105
East D109
East Midlands D115
Greater London D119
London D125
North-East D133
North-West D135
South-East D141
South-West D151
West Midlands D155
Yorkshire & Humberside D159
Northern Ireland D163
Scotland D165
Wales D169

Please note the following:
The user will find Essex and Hertfordshire in Greater London and East of England; Kent and Surrey in Greater London and South-East. When seeking schools in any of these counties, therefore, the user is advised to check both regional sections.

UK region map – Directories

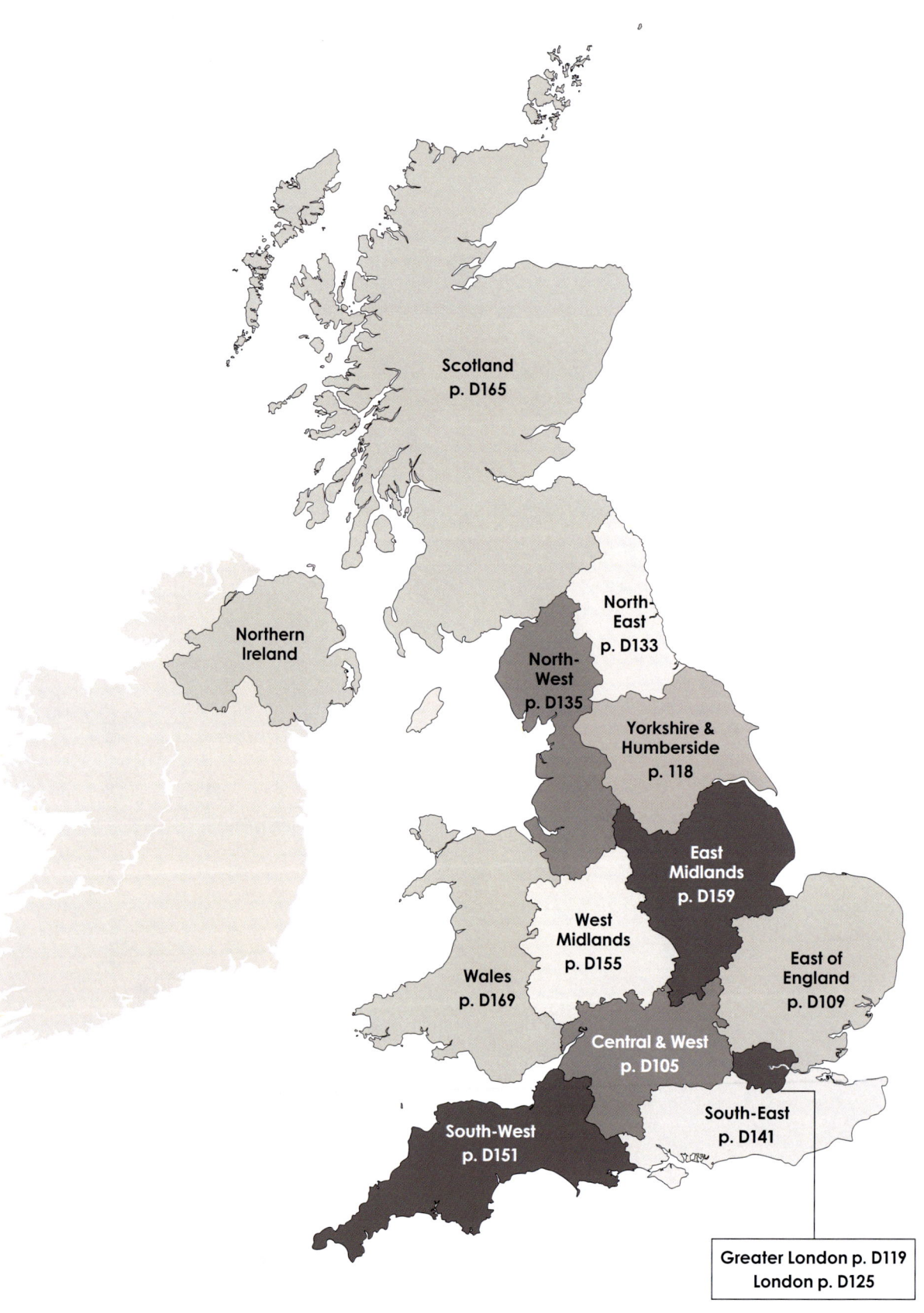

Channel Islands

KEY TO SYMBOLS
- Boys' school
- Girls' school
- International school
- Tutorial or sixth form college
- (A) A levels
- Boarding accommodation
- (£) Bursaries
- (IB) International Baccalaureate
- Learning support
- (16+) Entrance at 16+
- Vocational qualifications
- (IAPS) Independent Association of Prep Schools
- (HMC) The Headmasters' & Headmistresses' Conference
- (ISA) Independent Schools Association
- (GSA) Girls' School Association
- (BSA) Boarding Schools' Association
- (S) Society of Heads

Unless otherwise indicated, all schools are coeducational day schools. Single-sex and boarding schools will be indicated by the relevant icon.

CHANNEL ISLANDS

Guernsey

Blanchelande College
Les Vauxbelets, St Andrews,
Guernsey GY6 8XY
Tel: 01481 237200
Principal: Mr Robert O'Brien
Age range: 2.5–18 years

Elizabeth College Junior School
Beechwood, Queen's Road, St Peter Port, Guernsey GY1 1PU
Tel: 01481 722123
Headteacher: Mr Richard Fyfe
Age range: 2.5–11 years

The Ladies' College
Les Gravées, St Peter Port,
Guernsey GY1 1RW
Tel: 01481 721602
Principal: Ms Ashley Clancy
Age range: G2.5–18 years

Jersey

Beaulieu Convent School
Wellington Road, St Helier,
Jersey JE2 4RJ
Tel: 01534 731280
Executive Headmaster:
Mr Chris Beirne
Age range: B16–19 years G3–19 years

De La Salle College
Wellington Road, St Saviour,
Jersey JE2 7TH
Tel: 01534 754100
Head of College: Mr Jason Turner
Age range: B3–18 years

FCJ Primary School
Deloraine Road, St Saviour,
Jersey JE2 7XB
Tel: 01534 723063
Headteacher: Ms Donna Lenzi
Age range: 4–11 years

Helvetia House School
14 Elizabeth Place, St Helier, Jersey JE2 3PN
Tel: 01534 724928
Headmistress: Mrs Lindsey Woodward BA, DipEd
Age range: G4–11 years

St George's Preparatory School
La Hague Manor, Rue de la Hague, St Peter, Jersey JE3 7DB
Tel: 01534 481593
Headmaster: Mr Cormac Timothy
Age range: 2–11 years

St Michael's Preparatory School
La Rue de la Houguette, Five Oaks, St Saviour, Jersey JE2 7UG
Tel: 01534 856904
Headmaster: Mr Henry Marshall
Age range: 3–14 years
No. of pupils: 303
Fees: Day £13,905–£21,840

St. Christopher's School
1901 Building, Rue De La Chapelle,
St. Clement, Jersey JE2 6LN
Tel: +44 (0)1534 724758
Age range: 3–11 years

Victoria College Preparatory School
Pleasant Street, St Helier,
Jersey JE2 4RR
Tel: 01534 723468
Head Teacher: Mr Dan Pateman
Age range: B7–11 years

Central & West

Buckinghamshire D106
Gloucestershire D106
Oxfordshire D107
West Berkshire D108
Wiltshire D108

KEY TO SYMBOLS
- Boys' school
- Girls' school
- International school
- Tutorial or sixth form college
- (A) A levels
- Boarding accommodation
- (£) Bursaries
- (IB) International Baccalaureate
- Learning support
- (16+) Entrance at 16+
- Vocational qualifications
- (IAPS) Independent Association of Prep Schools
- (HMC) The Headmasters' & Headmistresses' Conference
- (ISA) Independent Schools Association
- (GSA) Girls' School Association
- (BSA) Boarding Schools' Association
- (S) Society of Heads

Unless otherwise indicated, all schools are coeducational day schools. Single-sex and boarding schools will be indicated by the relevant icon.

ENGLAND: Central & West

Buckinghamshire

Akeley Wood School
Akeley Wood House, Buckingham,
Buckinghamshire MK18 5AE
Tel: 01280 814110
Headmaster: Mr Simon Antwis
Age range: 12 months–18 years
No. of pupils: 700 VIth100
Fees: Day £10,665–£15,900

Ashfold School
Dorton House, Dorton, Aylesbury,
Buckinghamshire HP18 9NG
Tel: 01844 238237
Headmaster: Mr Colin MacIntosh
Age range: 3–13 years

Broughton Manor Preparatory School
Newport Road, Broughton, Milton
Keynes, Buckinghamshire MK10 9AA
Tel: 01908 665234
Headmistress: Mrs Katy Joiner
Age range: 2 months–11 years

Caldicott
Crown Lane, Farnham Royal,
Buckinghamshire SL2 3SL
Tel: 01753 649301
Headmaster: Mr Jeremy
Banks BA (Hons) QTS, MEd
Age range: B7–13 years
(flexi boarding from 7)
No. of pupils: 250

Chesham Preparatory School
Two Dells Lane, Chesham,
Buckinghamshire HP5 3QF
Tel: 01494 782619
Headmaster: Mr Jonathan Beale
Age range: 3–13 years

Child First Aylesbury Pre-School
35 Rickfords Hill, Aylesbury,
Buckinghamshire HP20 2RT
Tel: 01296 433224
Age range: 3–5 years

Crown House Preparatory School
Bassetsbury Manor, Bassetsbury
Lane, High Wycombe,
Buckinghamshire HP11 1QX
Tel: 01494 529927
Headteacher: Mrs Sarah Hobby
Age range: 3–11 years

DAIR HOUSE SCHOOL
For further details see p. 41
Bishops Blake, Beaconsfield
Road, Farnham Royal,
Buckinghamshire SL2 3BY
Tel: 01753 643964
Email: admissions@dairhouse.school
Website: www.dairhouseschool.co.uk
Head of School: Mrs Janine Bull
Age range: 3–11 years
No. of pupils: 125
Fees: Day £2,975–£5,555

Gateway School
1 High Street, Great Missenden,
Buckinghamshire HP16 9AA
Tel: 01494 862407
Head of School: Mrs
Cath Bufton-Green
Age range: 2–11 years

GODSTOWE PREPARATORY SCHOOL
For further details see p. 42
Shrubbery Road, High Wycombe,
Buckinghamshire HP13 6PR
Tel: 01494 529273
Email: schooloffice@godstowe.org
Website: www.godstowe.org
Headmistress: Ms Kate Bailey
Age range: B3–7 years G3–13
years (boarding from 7)

Griffin House Preparatory School
Little Kimble, Aylesbury,
Buckinghamshire HP17 0XP
Tel: 01844 346154
Headmaster: Mr Tim Walford
Age range: 3–11 years

Heatherton School
10 Copperkins Lane, Amersham,
Buckinghamshire HP6 5QB
Tel: 01494 726433
Headteacher: Mrs Nicola Nicoll
Age range: B2–4 years G2–11 years
No. of pupils: 163
Fees: Day £3,700–£5,560

High March
23 Ledborough Lane, Beaconsfield,
Buckinghamshire HP9 2PZ
Tel: 01494 675186
Head of School: Mrs Kate Gater
Age range: B3–4 years G3–11 years
No. of pupils: 297
Fees: Day £6,825–£18,705

Milton Keynes Preparatory School
Tattenhoe Lane, Milton Keynes,
Buckinghamshire MK3 7EG
Tel: 01908 642111
Headmaster: Mr Simon
Driver BA, PGCE
Age range: 2 months–11 years

Pipers Corner School
Pipers Lane, Great
Kingshill, High Wycombe,
Buckinghamshire HP15 6LP
Tel: 01494 718 255
Headmistress: Mrs H J Ness-
Gifford BA(Hons), PGCE
Age range: G4–18 years

Swanbourne House School
Swanbourne, Milton Keynes,
Buckinghamshire MK17 0HZ
Tel: 01296 720264
Head of School: Mrs Jane Thorpe
Age range: 4–13 years

The Beacon School
15 Amersham Road, Chesham Bois,
Amersham, Buckinghamshire HP6 5PF
Tel: 01494 432764
Headmaster: Mr Nick Baker
Age range: B3–13 years
No. of pupils: 510
Fees: Day £5,351–£8,604

The Webber Independent School
Soskin Drive, Stantonbury
Fields, Milton Keynes,
Buckinghamshire MK14 6DP
Tel: 01908 574740
Principal: Mrs Hilary Marsden
Age range: 6 months–16 years
No. of pupils: 285
Fees: Day £3,900–£5,450

Thornton College
College Lane, Thornton, Milton
Keynes, Buckinghamshire MK17 0HJ
Tel: 01280 812610
Headteacher: Dr Louise Shaw
Age range: G3–18 years
(boarding from 8)
No. of pupils: 367
Fees: Day £15,870–£20,220 WB
£23,940–£30,315 FB £27,780–£36,930

Walton Pre-Preparatory School & Nursery
The Old Rectory, Walton Drive, Milton
Keynes, Buckinghamshire MK7 6BB
Tel: 01908 678403
Head of School: Mrs
Chantelle McLaughlan
Age range: 2 months–5 years

Gloucestershire

Al-Ashraf Primary School
Al-Ashraf Cultural Centre,
Stratton Road, Gloucester,
Gloucestershire GL1 4HB
Tel: 01452 503533
Head Teacher: Mr Abdullah Patel
Age range: 2–11 years

Beaudesert Park School
Minchinhampton, Stroud,
Gloucestershire GL6 9AF
Tel: 01453 832072
Headmaster: Mr C D Searson
Age range: 3–13 years
(boarding from 8)

Berkhampstead School
Pittville Circus Road, Cheltenham,
Gloucestershire GL52 2QA
Tel: 01242 523263
Executive Head: Richard Cross
Age range: 3 months–11 years
No. of pupils: 252
Fees: Day £3,225–£4,635

Bredon School
Pull Court, Bushley, Tewkesbury,
Gloucestershire GL20 6AH
Tel: 01684 293156
Headmaster: Mr Nick Oldham
Age range: 7–18 years

Cheltenham College Preparatory School
Thirlestaine Road, Cheltenham,
Gloucestershire GL53 7AB
Tel: 01242 522697
Head of School: Mr Tom O'Sullivan
Age range: 3–13 years

Dean Close Airthrie
27-29 Christ Church
Road, Cheltenham,
Gloucestershire GL50 2NY
Tel: 01242 512837
Headmaster: Mr Jason Dobbie
Age range: 4–11 years
No. of pupils: 80

Dean Close Pre-Preparatory & Preparatory School
Lansdown Road, Cheltenham,
Gloucestershire GL51 6QS
Tel: +44 (0)1242 512217
Headmaster Preparatory School: Mr Paddy Moss
Age range: 2–13 years
(boarding from 7)

Dean Close St John's
Castleford Hill, Tutshill,
Gloucestershire NP16 7LE
Tel: 01291 622045
Head: Mr Nick Thrower
Age range: 3–13 years
(boarding from 7)

Edward Jenner School
The Elms, 44 London Road,
Gloucester, Gloucestershire GL1 3NZ
Tel: 01452 380808
Head Teachers: Ms. Manda
& Mr. Phil Brookes
Age range: 5–16 years

Hatherop Castle School
Hatherop, Cirencester,
Gloucestershire GL7 3NB
Tel: 01285 750206
Headmaster: Mr Nigel Reed
M.Ed, B.Sc (Hons), PGCE
Age range: 2–13 years

Hopelands Preparatory School
38/40 Regent Street, Stonehouse,
Gloucestershire GL10 2AD
Tel: 01453 822164
Heads: Mrs Sonja Jones
& Mrs Maria Boix
Age range: 3–11 years

Central & West: ENGLAND

Immanuel Christian School
Rodford Tabernacle, Westerleigh Road, Westerleigh, Gloucestershire BS37 8QG
Tel: 01454 311710
Head Teacher: Ms Joanna Gulliford
Age range: 4–16 years

Kitebrook Preparatory School
Kitebrook House, Moreton-in-Marsh, Gloucestershire GL56 0RP
Tel: 01608 674350
Headmistress: Mrs Susan McLean
Age range: 3–13 years

OneSchool Global UK Bristol Campus
Station Road, Wanswell, Berkeley, Gloucestershire GL13 9RS
Tel: 01453 511282
Age range: 7–18 years

OneSchool Global UK Gloucester Campus
Eastbrook Road, Gloucester, Gloucestershire GL4 3DB
Tel: 01452 417722
Age range: 7–18 years

Rendcomb College
Rendcomb, Cirencester, Gloucestershire GL7 7HA
Tel: 01285 831213
Head of School: Mr Rob Jones
Age range: 3–18 years

St Edward's Preparatory School
London Road, Charlton Kings, Cheltenham, Gloucestershire GL52 6NR
Tel: +44 (0)1242 388550
Head of Prep School: Mr Paul Fathers BA (Hons) PGCE
Age range: 1–11 years

The Acorn School
Church Street, Nailsworth, Stroud, Gloucestershire GL6 0BP
Tel: 01453 836508
Head of School: Mr Mario Peters
Age range: 6–18 years

The King's School
Gloucester, Gloucestershire GL1 2BG
Tel: 01452 337337
Headmaster: Mr David Morton
Age range: 3–18 years

The Richard Pate School
Southern Road, Leckhampton, Cheltenham, Gloucestershire GL53 9RP
Tel: 01242 522086
Headmaster: Mr Robert MacDonald
Age range: 3–11 years

Westonbirt Prep School
Westonbirt, Tetbury, Gloucestershire GL8 8QG
Tel: 01666 881400
Headmaster: Mr Sean Price
Age range: 2–11 years

Wycliffe College
Bristol Road, Stonehouse, Gloucestershire GL10 2AF
Tel: 01453 822432
Senior School Head: Mr Nick Gregory BA, MEd
Age range: 3–19 years (boarding from 7)
No. of pupils: 696
Fees: Day £9,675–£20,985 FB £20,625–£38,115

Oxfordshire

Abingdon Preparatory School
Josca's House, Kingston Road, Frilford, Oxfordshire OX13 5NX
Tel: +44 (0)1865 391570
Headmaster: Mr Craig Williams
Age range: B4–13 years

Carrdus School
Overthorpe Hall, Banbury, Oxfordshire OX17 2BS
Tel: 01295 263733
Head: Mr Edward Way
Age range: 3–11 years

Chandlings
Bagley Wood, Kennington, Oxford, Oxfordshire OX1 5ND
Tel: 01865 730771
Head: Christine Cook
Age range: 2–11 years

Christ Church Cathedral School
3 Brewer Street, Oxford, Oxfordshire OX1 1QW
Tel: 01865 242561
Headmaster: Mr Richard Murray
Age range: B2–13 years (boarding from 7) G2–4 years

Cokethorpe School
Witney, Oxfordshire OX29 7PU
Tel: 01993 703921
Headmaster: Mr D Ettinger BA, MA, PGCE
Age range: 4–18 years

Cothill House
Cothill, Oxfordshire OX13 6JL
Tel: 01865 390800
Headmaster: Mr D M Bailey
Age range: B8–13 years

CRANFORD SCHOOL
For further details see p. 40
Moulsford, Wallingford, Oxfordshire OX10 9HT
Tel: 01491 651218
Email: admissions@cranfordschool.co.uk
Website: www.cranfordschool.co.uk
Headmaster: Dr James Raymond
Age range: 3–18 years
No. of pupils: 575
Fees: Day £4,000–£7,125

Dragon School
Bardwell Road, Oxford, Oxfordshire OX2 6SS
Tel: 01865 315405
Head: Emma Goldsmith
Age range: 4–13 years
No. of pupils: 798
Fees: Day £7,473 FB £10,931

Emmanuel Christian School
Sandford Road, Littlemore, Oxford, Oxfordshire OX4 4PU
Tel: 01865 395236
Principal: Mrs Elizabeth Nesbitt
Age range: 3–11 years

Headington Preparatory School
26 London Road, Oxford, Oxfordshire OX3 7PB
Tel: +44 (0)1865 759400
Head: Mrs Jane Crouch BA (Hons), MA
Age range: G3–11 years

Magdalen College School
Cowley Place, Oxford, Oxfordshire OX4 1DZ
Tel: 01865 242191
Master: Miss Helen Pike
Age range: B7–18 years G16–18 years

MOULSFORD PREPARATORY SCHOOL
For further details see p. 43
Moulsford-on-Thames, Oxfordshire OX10 9HR
Tel: 01491 651438
Email: admissions@moulsford.com
Website: www.moulsford.com
Headmaster: Mr B. Beardmore-Gray
Age range: B3–13 years G3–7 years
No. of pupils: 360
Fees: FB £10,298

New College School
2 Savile Road, Oxford, Oxfordshire OX1 3UA
Tel: 01865 285 560
Head of School: Dr Matthew Jenkinson
Age range: B4–13 years
No. of pupils: 156
Fees: Day £11,100–£17,700

Our Lady's Abingdon School
Radley Road, Abingdon-on-Thames, Oxfordshire OX14 3PS
Tel: 01235 524658
Principal: Mr Daniel Gibbons
Age range: 7–18 years
No. of pupils: 374 VIth61
Fees: Day £11,280–£16,815

Oxford High School GDST
Belbroughton Road, Oxford, Oxfordshire OX2 6XA
Tel: 01865 559888
Headmistress: Ms Marina Gardiner Legge
Age range: G4–18 years

Oxford Montessori School
Forest Farm School, Elsfield, Oxford, Oxfordshire OX3 9UW
Tel: 01865 352062
Age range: 2–16 years

Rupert House School
90-92 Bell Street, Henley-on-Thames, Oxfordshire RG9 2BN
Tel: 01491 574263
Head: Mr Nick Armitage
Age range: 3–11 years

Sibford School
Sibford Ferris, Banbury, Oxfordshire OX15 5QL
Tel: 01295 781200
Head: Mr Toby Spence
Age range: 3–18 years

St Helen and St Katharine
Faringdon Road, Abingdon, Oxfordshire OX14 1BE
Tel: 01235 520173
Headmistress: Mrs Rebecca Dougall BA MA
Age range: G9–18 years

St Hugh's School
Carswell Manor, Faringdon, Oxfordshire SN7 8PT
Tel: 01367 870700
Headmaster: Mr James Thompson
Age range: 3–13 years
Fees: Day £12,285–£21,195 WB £23,655–£25,350

St John's Priory School
St John's Road, Banbury, Oxfordshire OX16 5HX
Tel: 01295 259607
Headmistress: Mrs Tracey Wilson
Age range: 3–11 years

St Mary's Preparatory School
11-13 St Andrew's Road, Henley-on-Thames, Oxfordshire RG9 1HS
Tel: 01491 573118
Headteacher: Mr Stephen Blundell
Age range: 2.5–11 years
No. of pupils: 130

ENGLAND: Central & West

Summer Fields
Mayfield Road, Oxford,
Oxfordshire OX2 7EN
Tel: 01865 454433
Headmaster: Mr David
Faber MA(Oxon)
Age range: B4–13 years
(boarding from 8)

The King's School, Witney
New Yatt Road, Witney,
Oxfordshire OX29 6TA
Tel: 01993 778463
Principal: Mr Matthew Cripps
Age range: 3–16 years

The Manor Preparatory School
Faringdon Road, Abingdon,
Oxfordshire OX13 6LN
Tel: 01235 858458
Head of School: Mrs Rachel Hamlyn
Age range: 2–11 years
No. of pupils: 372

Windrush Valley School
The Green, London Lane,
Ascott-under-Wychwood,
Oxfordshire OX7 6AN
Tel: 01993 831793
Headteacher: Mrs Amanda Douglas
Age range: 3–11 years
No. of pupils: 120
Fees: Day £7,005–£7,341

West Berkshire

Brockhurst & Marlston House Schools
Hermitage, Newbury, West
Berkshire RG18 9UL
Tel: 01635 200293
Headmaster: Mr David
Fleming MA (Oxon), MSc
Age range: 2–13 years
(boarding from 7)

Cheam School
Headley, Newbury, West
Berkshire RG19 8LD
Tel: +44 (0)1635 268242
Headteacher: Mr Nick Milbank
Age range: 3–13 years
(boarding from 8)
No. of pupils: 400
Fees: Day £4,315–£8,475
WB £10,495–£10,865

Horris Hill
Newtown, Newbury, West
Berkshire RG20 9DJ
Tel: 01635 40594
Headmaster: Mr Rob Stewart
Age range: 2–13 years
(boarding from 8)

St Gabriel's
Sandleford Priory, Newbury,
West Berkshire RG20 9BD
Tel: 01635 555680
Principal: Mr Ricki Smith
Age range: 6 months–18 years

St. Michael's School
Harts Lane, Burghclere, Newbury,
West Berkshire RG20 9JW
Tel: 01635 278137
Headmaster: Rev. Fr. John Brucciani
Age range: B4–18 years (boarding from 11) G4–11 years

Wiltshire

Avondale Preparatory School
27-29 High Street, Bulford,
Salisbury, Wiltshire SP4 9DR
Tel: 01980 632387
Co-Heads: Celina Rae &
Georgina Barrington-Tolan
Age range: 2–11 years

Chafyn Grove School
33 Bourne Avenue, Salisbury,
Wiltshire SP1 1LR
Tel: 01722 333423
Headmaster: Mr Simon Head
Age range: 3–13 years
(boarding from 7)

Cricklade Manor Prep
The Manor House, Calcutt Street,
Cricklade, Wiltshire SN6 6BB
Tel: 01793 750275
Headmaster: Mr Guy Barrett
Age range: 2–11 years

Emmaus School
School Lane, Staverton,
Trowbridge, Wiltshire BA14 6NZ
Tel: 01225 782684
Headteacher: Ms Miriam Wiltshire
Age range: 5–16 years

Godolphin Preparatory School
Laverstock Road, Salisbury,
Wiltshire SP1 2RB
Tel: +44 (0)1722 430545
Head: Ms Julia Miller
Age range: G3–11 years
(boarding from 7)

Heywood Prep
The Priory, Priory Street,
Corsham, Wiltshire SN13 0AP
Tel: 01249 713379
Headmistress: Ms Rebecca Mitchell
Age range: 2–11 years
No. of pupils: 200
Fees: Day £9,525–£10,755

Leehurst Swan School
19 Campbell Road, Salisbury,
Wiltshire SP1 3BQ
Tel: 01722 333094
Headteacher: Mrs Mandy Bateman
Age range: 4–16 years

Maranatha Christian School
Queenlaines Farm, Sevenhampton,
Swindon, Wiltshire SN6 7SQ
Tel: 01793 762075
Headteacher: Mr Tom Price
Age range: 3–18 years

OneSchool Global UK Salisbury Campus
The Hollows, Wilton, Salisbury,
Wiltshire SP2 0JE
Tel: 01722 741910
Age range: 7–18 years

Pinewood School
Bourton, Shrivenham,
Swindon, Wiltshire SN6 8HZ
Tel: 01793 782205
Headmaster: Mr Neal Bailey
Age range: 3–13 years
(boarding from 9)

Salisbury Cathedral School
The Old Palace, 1 The Close,
Salisbury, Wiltshire SP1 2EQ
Tel: 01722 555300
Head Master: Mr Clive
Marriott BEd MA
Age range: 3–13 years
(boarding from 7)

Sandroyd School
Rushmore, Tollard Royal,
Salisbury, Wiltshire SP5 5QD
Tel: 01725 516264
Headmaster: Mr Alastair Speers
Age range: 2–13 years

St Francis School
Marlborough Road, Pewsey,
Wiltshire SN9 5NT
Tel: 01672 563228
Headmaster: Mr David Lee
Age range: 0–13 years

St Margaret's Preparatory School
Curzon Street, Calne,
Wiltshire SN11 0DF
Tel: 01249 857220
Headmaster: Mr Luke Bromwich
Age range: 2–11 years

Stonar School
Cottles Park, Atworth,
Melksham, Wiltshire SN12 8NT
Tel: 01225 701740
Head of School: Mr Matthew Way
Age range: 2–18 years
(boarding from 10)

Warminster School
Church Street, Warminster,
Wiltshire BA12 8PJ
Tel: +44 (0)1985 210100
Headmaster: Mr Matt Williams BA MA
Age range: 2–18 years
(boarding from 7)
No. of pupils: 551
Fees: Day £5,970 FB £12,241

East

Bedfordshire D110
Cambridgeshire D110
Essex D111
Hertfordshire D112
Norfolk D113
Suffolk D114

*See also Greater London (D119)
for schools in Essex and Hertfordshire

KEY TO SYMBOLS
- Boys' school
- Girls' school
- International school
- Tutorial or sixth form college
- A levels
- Boarding accommodation
- Bursaries
- International Baccalaureate
- Learning support
- Entrance at 16+
- Vocational qualifications
- Independent Association of Prep Schools
- The Headmasters' & Headmistresses' Conference
- Independent Schools Association
- Girls' School Association
- Boarding Schools' Association
- Society of Heads

Unless otherwise indicated, all schools are coeducational day schools. Single-sex and boarding schools will be indicated by the relevant icon.

ENGLAND: East

Bedfordshire

Bedford Girls' School
Cardington Road, Bedford,
Bedfordshire MK42 0BX
Tel: 01234 361900
Headmistress: Ms Gemma Gibson
Age range: G7–18 years

Bedford Greenacre Independent School
58-60 Shakespeare Road,
Bedford, Bedfordshire MK40 2DL
Tel: 01234 352031
Principal: Mr Ian Daniel
Age range: 3–18 years

Bedford Modern School
Manton Lane, Bedford,
Bedfordshire MK41 7NT
Tel: 01234 332500
Headmaster: Mr Alex Tate
Age range: 7–18 years
No. of pupils: 1289
Fees: Day £10,528–£14,443

Bedford Preparatory School
De Parys Avenue, Bedford,
Bedfordshire MK40 2TU
Tel: 01234 362274
Headmaster: Mr Ian Silk
Age range: B7–13 years

King's House School
33-43 High Street, Leagrave,
Luton, Bedfordshire LU4 9JY
Tel: 01582 491430
Head of School: Ms Jade Pawaar
Age range: 2–11 years

Mehria Primary School
23 Westbourne Road, Luton,
Bedfordshire LU4 8JD
Tel: 01582 484617
Headteacher: Mr Zia Qazi
Age range: 4–11 years

Oakwood Primary School
117 Tennyson Road, Luton,
Bedfordshire LU1 3RR
Tel: 01582 518800
Headteacher: Mrs F Salihi
Age range: 3–11 years

OneSchool Global UK Biggleswade Campus
The Oaks, Potton Road, Biggleswade,
Bedfordshire SG18 0EP
Tel: 01767 602800
Age range: 7–18 years

OneSchool Global UK Dunstable Campus
Ridgeway Avenue, Dunstable,
Bedfordshire LU5 4QL
Tel: 01582 665676
Age range: 7–18 years

Orchard School & Nursery
Higham Gobion Road, Barton le Clay, Bedford, Bedfordshire MK45 4RB
Tel: 01582 882054
Headmistress: Mrs Anne Burton
Age range: 0–9 years

Pilgrims Pre-Preparatory School
Brickhill Drive, Bedford,
Bedfordshire MK41 7QZ
Tel: 01234 369555
Head: Mrs J Webster BEd(Hons), EYPS
Age range: 3 months–7 years

Polam School
45 Lansdowne Road, Bedford,
Bedfordshire MK40 2BU
Tel: 01234 261864
Head: Darren O'Neil
Age range: 1–7 years
No. of pupils: 95

Cambridgeshire

Cambridge International School
Cherry Hinton Road, Cambridge,
Cambridgeshire CB1 8DW
Tel: +44 (0) 1223 416938
Headteacher: Ms Amanda Gibbard
Age range: 2–11 years

Cambridge Steiner School
Hinton Road, Fulbourn, Cambridge,
Cambridgeshire CB21 5DZ
Tel: 01223 882727
Education Manager: Ms Sarah Fox
Age range: 2.5–16 years

Heritage School
17-19 Brookside, Cambridge,
Cambridgeshire CB2 1JE
Tel: 01223 350615
Headmaster: Mr Jason Fletcher
Age range: 4–16 years

Kimbolton School
Kimbolton, Huntingdon,
Cambridgeshire PE28 0EA
Tel: 01480 860505
Head of School: Mr Will Chuter
Age range: 4–18 years

King's College School
West Road, Cambridge,
Cambridgeshire CB3 9DN
Tel: 01223 365814
Head: Mrs Yvette Day BMus, MMus, GDL
Age range: 4–13 years

King's Ely Acremont & Nursery
30 Egremont Street, Ely,
Cambridgeshire CB6 1AE
Tel: 01353 660700
Head of School: Ms Faye Fenton-Stone
Age range: 2–7 years

KING'S ELY PREP
For further details see p. 48
Ely, Cambridgeshire CB7 4DB
Tel: 01353 660707
Email: admissions@kingsely.org
Website: www.kingsely.org
Head: Mr Simon Kibler
Age range: 7–13 years
No. of pupils: 412
Fees: Day £20,721–£23,103
FB £32,976–£35,313

Magdalene House Preparatory School
Chapel Road, Wisbech,
Cambridgeshire PE13 1RH
Tel: 01945 583631
Senior Deputy Head, Prep School: Mrs Keryn Neaves
Age range: 3–11 years

Sancton Wood School
2 St Paul's Road, Cambridge,
Cambridgeshire CB1 2EZ
Tel: +44 (0)1223 471703
Head of School: Mr Richard Settle
Age range: 1–16 years

St Faith's
Trumpington Road, Cambridge,
Cambridgeshire CB2 8AG
Tel: 01223 229421
Headmaster: Dr C Hyde-Dunn
Age range: 4–13 years
No. of pupils: 555
Fees: Day £16,515–£20,805

ST JOHN'S COLLEGE SCHOOL
For further details see p. 50
73 Grange Road, Cambridge,
Cambridgeshire CB3 9AB
Tel: 01223 353652
Email: admissions@sjcs.co.uk
Website: www.sjcs.co.uk
Headmaster: Mr N. Chippington MA(Cantab), FRCO
Age range: 4–13 years
No. of pupils: 409

St Mary's School, Cambridge
Bateman Street, Cambridge,
Cambridgeshire CB2 1LY
Tel: +44 (0)1223 224167
Headmistress: Ms Charlotte Avery
Age range: G3–18 years (boarding from 9)
No. of pupils: 630
Fees: Day £12,663–£19,740
FB £39,444–£41,676

Stephen Perse Junior School, Fitzwilliam Building
Shaftesbury Road, Cambridge,
Cambridgeshire CB2 8AA
Tel: 01223 454700 (Ext:2000)
Age range: 5–11 years

Stephen Perse Nurseries & Early Years
Cambridge Road,
Madingley, Cambridge,
Cambridgeshire CB23 8AH
Tel: 01223 454700 (Ext:5000)
Age range: 1–5 years

The Perse Pelican Pre-Prep & Nursery
92 Glebe Road, Cambridge,
Cambridgeshire CB1 7TD
Tel: 01223 403940
Head: Ms Francesca Heftman
Age range: 3–7 years

The Perse Prep School
Trumpington Road, Cambridge,
Cambridgeshire CB2 8EX
Tel: 01223 403920
Head: Mr James Piper
Age range: 7–11 years

The Peterborough School
Thorpe Road, Peterborough,
Cambridgeshire PE3 6AP
Tel: 01733 343357
Headmaster: Mr A D Meadows BSc(Hons), NPQH
Age range: 6 weeks–18 years
No. of pupils: 500
Fees: Day £12,900–£20,800

Whitehall School
117 High Street, Somersham,
Cambridgeshire PE28 3EH
Tel: 01487 840966
Head of School: Chris Holmes
Age range: 6 months–11 years

East: ENGLAND

Essex

Alleyn Court School
Wakering Road, Southend-on-Sea, Essex SS3 0PW
Tel: 01702 582553
Headmaster: Mr Rupert W.J. Snow B.Ed, NPQH
Age range: 2.5–11 years

BRENTWOOD PREPARATORY SCHOOL
For further details see p. 44
Shenfield Road, Brentwood, Essex CM15 8BD
Tel: +44 (0)1277 243300
Email: prepadmissions@brentwood.essex.sch.uk
Website: www.brentwoodschool.co.uk
Head of School: Mrs Alice Goodfellow
Age range: 3–11 years
No. of pupils: 564
Fees: Day £7,077

Colchester High School
Wellesley Road, Colchester, Essex CO3 3HD
Tel: 01206 573389
Headteacher: Ms Karen Gracie-Langrick
Age range: 2.5–16 years
No. of pupils: 320
Fees: Day £9,465–£13,620

Coopersale Hall School
Flux's Lane, off Stewards Green Road, Epping, Essex CM16 7PE
Tel: 01992 577133
Headmistress: Ms Moreen Barnard
Age range: 2.5–11 years

Elm Green Preparatory School
Parsonage Lane, Little Baddow, Chelmsford, Essex CM3 4SU
Tel: 01245 225230
Principal: Ms Ann Milner
Age range: 4–11 years

Felsted Preparatory School
Felsted, Great Dunmow, Essex CM6 3JL
Tel: 01371 822610
Headmaster: Mr Simon James
Age range: 4–13 years

Gosfield School
Cut Hedge Park, Halstead Road, Gosfield, Halstead, Essex CO9 1PF
Tel: 01787 474040
Head of School: Mr Rod Jackson
Age range: 2–18 years
Fees: Day £7,680–£17,250

Heathcote School
Eves Corner, Danbury, Chelmsford, Essex CM3 4QB
Tel: 01245 223131
Head of School: Mrs Samantha Scott
Age range: 2–11 years
No. of pupils: 105
Fees: Day £9,450

Holmwood House School
Chitts Hill, Lexden, Colchester, Essex CO3 9ST
Tel: 01206 574305
Headmaster: Mr Edward Bond
Age range: 6 months–16 years

Littlegarth School
Horkesley Park, Nayland, Colchester, Essex CO6 4JR
Tel: 01206 262332
Head of School: Ms Kathy Uttley
Age range: 2–11 years
No. of pupils: 330
Fees: Day £4,259–£5,197

Maldon Court Preparatory School
Silver Street, Maldon, Essex CM9 4QE
Tel: 01621 853529
Headteacher: Elaine Mason
Age range: 1–11 years

New Hall School
The Avenue, Boreham, Chelmsford, Essex CM3 3HS
Tel: 01245 467588
Principal: Mrs Katherine Jeffrey MA, BA, PGCE, MA(Ed Mg), NPQH
Age range: 1–19 years (boarding from 7)
No. of pupils: 1339
Fees: Day £13,068–£27,864 WB £24,849–£38,205 FB £28,899–£44,316

Octavia House School, Great Baddow
High Street, Great Baddow, Essex CM2 7HH
Tel: 020 3651 4396 (option 4)
Assistant Principal: Ms Aboukhshem
Age range: 5–11 years

OneSchool Global UK Colchester Campus
Sudbury Road, Stoke By Nayland, Colchester, Essex CO6 4RW
Tel: 01206 264230
Age range: 7–18 years

Oxford House School
2-4 Lexden Road, Colchester, Essex CO3 3NE
Tel: 01206 576686
Head Teacher: Mrs Sarah Leyshon
Age range: 2.5–11 years

Saint Nicholas School
Hillingdon House, Hobbs Cross Road, Harlow, Essex CM17 0NJ
Tel: 01279 429910
Headmaster: Mr Terence Ayres
Age range: 2.5–16 years

Saint Pierre School
16 Leigh Road, Leigh-on-Sea, Southend-on-Sea, Essex SS9 1LE
Tel: 01702 474164
Headmaster: Mr Peter Spencer-Lane
Age range: 2.5–11 years

ST CEDD'S SCHOOL
For further details see p. 52
178a New London Road, Chelmsford, Essex CM2 0AR
Tel: 01245 392810
Email: info@stcedds.org.uk
Website: www.stcedds.org.uk
Head: Mr Matthew Clarke
Age range: 3–11 years
No. of pupils: 400
Fees: Day £3,700–£5,432

St John's School
Stock Road, Billericay, Essex CM12 0AR
Tel: 01277 623070
Headteacher: Mr A. Angeli BA (Hons)
Age range: 2–16 years

St Margaret's Preparatory School
Gosfield Hall Park, Gosfield, Halstead, Essex CO9 1SE
Tel: 01787 472134
Headteacher: Mrs Carolyn Moss
Age range: 2–11 years

St Mary's School
91 Lexden Road, Colchester, Essex CO3 3RB
Tel: 01206 572544
Principal: Mrs Nicola Griffiths
Age range: B3–4 years G3–16 years

St Michael's Church Of England Preparatory School
198 Hadleigh Road, Leigh-on-Sea, Southend-on-Sea, Essex SS9 2LP
Tel: 01702 478719
Headmaster: Mr James Mobbs
Age range: 3–11 years

St Philomena's Catholic School
Hadleigh Road, Frinton-on-Sea, Essex CO13 9HQ
Tel: 01255 674492
Head of School: Mrs P Mathews ACIS, BA Hons, PGCE, MA, NPQH
Age range: 4–11 years

St. Anne's Preparatory School
154 New London Road, Chelmsford, Essex CM2 0AW
Tel: 01245 353488
Head of School: Valerie Eveleigh
Age range: 3–11 years

Stephen Perse Junior School, Dame Bradbury's School
Ashdon Road, Saffron Walden, Essex CB10 2AL
Tel: 01223 454700 (Ext: 4000)
Age range: 1–11 years

Thorpe Hall School
Wakering Road, Southend-on-Sea, Essex SS1 3RD
Tel: 01702 582340
Headmaster: Mr Stephen Duckitt
Age range: 2–16 years

Ursuline Preparatory School
Old Great Ropers, Great Ropers Lane, Warley, Brentwood, Essex CM13 3HR
Tel: 01277 227152
Headmistress: Mrs Pauline Wilson MSc
Age range: 3–11 years

Widford Lodge Preparatory School
Widford Road, Chelmsford, Essex CM2 9AN
Tel: 01245 352581
Headteacher: Miss Michelle Cole A.C.I.B. – P.G.C.E.
Age range: 2.5–11 years

Woodlands School, Great Warley
Warley Street, Great Warley, Brentwood, Essex CM13 3LA
Tel: 01277 233288
Head: Mr David Bell
Age range: 2–11 years

Woodlands School, Hutton Manor
428 Rayleigh Road, Hutton, Brentwood, Essex CM13 1SD
Tel: 01277 245585
Head: Ms Paula Hobbs
Age range: 3–11 years

ENGLAND: East

Hertfordshire

Abbot's Hill School
Bunkers Lane, Hemel Hempstead, Hertfordshire HP3 8RP
Tel: 01442 240333
Headmistress: Mrs K Gorman BA, MEd (Cantab)
Age range: G4–16 years
No. of pupils: 482

Aldenham School
Elstree, Hertfordshire WD6 3AJ
Tel: 01923 858122
Headmaster: Mr James Fowler
Age range: 3–18 years

Aldwickbury School
Wheathampstead Road, Harpenden, Hertfordshire AL5 1AD
Tel: 01582 713022
Headmaster: Mr Paul Symes
Age range: B4–13 years

Beechwood Park School
Beechwood Park, Pickford Road, Markyate, Nr St Albans, Hertfordshire AL3 8AW
Tel: 01582 840333
Head of School: Mr Christian Pritchard
Age range: 3–13 years
No. of pupils: 520

Berkhamsted School
Overton House, 131 High Street, Berkhamsted, Hertfordshire HP4 2DJ
Tel: 01442 358001
Principal: Mr Richard Backhouse MA(Cantab)
Age range: 3–18 years
No. of pupils: 1994 VIth462
Fees: Day £11,565–£26,520 WB £36,600 FB £43,740

Bishop's Stortford College Prep School
School House, Maze Green Road, Bishop's Stortford, Hertfordshire CM23 2PQ
Tel: +44 (0)1279 838583
Head of the Prep School: Mr Bill Toleman
Age range: 4–13 years

Charlotte House Preparatory School
88 The Drive, Rickmansworth, Hertfordshire WD3 4DU
Tel: 01923 772101
Head: Miss P Woodcock
Age range: G3–11 years

Duncombe School
4 Warren Park Road, Bengeo, Hertford, Hertfordshire SG14 3JA
Tel: 01992 414100
Headmaster: Mr Jeremy Phelan M.A. (Ed)
Age range: 2–11 years

EDGE GROVE SCHOOL
For further details see p. 45
High Cross, Aldenham Village, Hertfordshire WD25 8NL
Tel: 01923 855724
Email: admissions@edgegrove.com
Website: www.edgegrove.com
Headmaster: Mr Richard Stanley
Age range: 2–13 years
No. of pupils: 397

Egerton Rothesay School
Durrants Lane, Berkhamsted, Hertfordshire HP4 3UJ
Tel: 01442 865275
Headteacher: Mr Colin Parker BSc(Hons), Dip.Ed (Oxon), PGCE, C.Math MIMA
Age range: 6–19 years

Gurukula - The Hare Krishna Primary School
Hartspring Cottage, Elton Way, Watford, Hertfordshire WD25 8HB
Tel: 01923 851 005
Head of School: Ms Gunacuda Dasi (Gwyneth Milan)
Age range: 4–12 years

Haberdashers' Boys' School
Butterfly Lane, Elstree, Borehamwood, Hertfordshire WD6 3AF
Tel: 020 8266 1700
Headmaster: Mr Robert Sykes
Age range: B4–18 years
No. of pupils: 1481

Haberdashers' Girls' School
Aldenham Road, Elstree, Borehamwood, Hertfordshire WD6 3BT
Tel: 020 8266 2300
Headmistress: Dr Hazel Bagworth-Mann
Age range: G4–18 years
No. of pupils: 1162

Heath Mount School
Woodhall Park, Watton-at-Stone, Hertford, Hertfordshire SG14 3NG
Tel: 01920 830230
Headmaster: Mr Chris Gillam BEd(Hons)
Age range: 2–13 years
No. of pupils: 520
Fees: Day £12,435–£19,185

Howe Green House School
Great Hallingbury, Bishop's Stortford, Hertfordshire CM22 7UF
Tel: 01279 657706
Co-Heads: Mrs Anna Lipani & Mr Paul Bailey
Age range: 2–11 years
No. of pupils: 177
Fees: Day £499–£5,088

Kingshott
Stevenage Road, St Ippolyts, Hitchin, Hertfordshire SG4 7JX
Tel: 01462 432009
Headmaster: Mr David Weston
Age range: 3–13 years
No. of pupils: 400
Fees: Day £6,555–£14,115

Little Acorns Montessori School
Building 19 & 21, The Lincolnsfield Centre, Bushey Hall Drive, Bushey, Hertfordshire WD23 2ES
Tel: 01923 230705
Age range: 3 months–5 years

Lochinver House School
Heath Road, Little Heath, Potters Bar, Hertfordshire EN6 1LW
Tel: 01707 653064
Head of School: Mr Jonathan Wadge
Age range: B3–13 years
No. of pupils: 345
Fees: Day £14,250–£18,225

Lockers Park
Lockers Park Lane, Hemel Hempstead, Hertfordshire HP1 1TL
Tel: 01442 251712
Headmaster: Mr Gavin Taylor
Age range: B4–13 years
No. of pupils: 171
Fees: Day £13,785–£21,885 FB £32,340

Longwood School
Bushey Hall Drive, Bushey, Hertfordshire WD23 2QG
Tel: 01923 253715
Headteacher: Ms Claire May
Age range: 3 months–11 years

Manor Lodge School
Rectory Lane, Ridge Hill, Shenley, Hertfordshire WD7 9BG
Tel: 01707 642424
Head Teacher: Mrs A Lobo BEd(Hons)
Age range: 3–11 years
No. of pupils: 456
Fees: Day £3,820–£4,500

Merchant Taylors' Prep
Moor Farm, Sandy Lodge Road, Rickmansworth, Hertfordshire WD3 1LW
Tel: 01923 825648
Head of School: Dr Karen McNerney
Age range: B3–13 years

Radlett Preparatory School
Kendal Hall, Watling Street, Radlett, Hertfordshire WD7 7LY
Tel: 01923 856812
Principal: Mr M Pipe BA Hons, QTS
Age range: 4–11 years

Sherrardswood School
Lockleys, Welwyn, Hertfordshire AL6 0BJ
Tel: 01438 714282
Headmistress: Mrs Anna Wright
Age range: 2–18 years

St Albans High School for Girls
Townsend Avenue, St Albans, Hertfordshire AL1 3SJ
Tel: 01727 853800
Head: Ms Amber Waite
Age range: G4–18 years

St Christopher School
Barrington Road, Letchworth Garden City, Hertfordshire SG6 3JZ
Tel: 01462 650 850
Head of School: Ms Emma-Kate Henry
Age range: 3–18 years

St Columba's College Prep School
King Harry Lane, St Albans, Hertfordshire AL3 4AW
Tel: 01727 862616
Head of Prep: Mr Richard McCann
Age range: 4–11 years

St Edmund's College & Prep School
Old Hall Green, Nr Ware, Hertfordshire SG11 1DS
Tel: 01920 824247
Headmaster: Mr Matthew Mostyn BA (Hons) MA (Ed)
Age range: 3–18 years (boarding from 11)

St Francis' College
Broadway, Letchworth Garden City, Hertfordshire SG6 3PJ
Tel: 01462 670511
Headmistress: Mrs B Goulding
Age range: B3–11 years G3–18 years (boarding from 10)

St Hilda's School
28 Douglas Road, Harpenden, Hertfordshire AL5 2ES
Tel: 01582 712307
Headmaster: Mr Dan Sayers
Age range: B2.5–4 years G2.5–11 years
No. of pupils: 150
Fees: Day £3,285–£4,260

St Hilda's School, Bushey
High Street, Bushey, Hertfordshire WD23 3DA
Tel: 020 8950 1751
Headmistress: Miss Sarah-Jane Styles MA
Age range: B2–4 years G2–11 years

East: ENGLAND

St Joseph's In The Park
St Mary's Lane, Hertingfordbury,
Hertford, Hertfordshire SG14 2LX
Tel: 01992 513810
Head of School: Mr Douglas Brown
Age range: 2–11 years

St Margaret's School, Bushey
Merry Hill Road, Bushey,
Hertfordshire WD23 1DT
Tel: +44 (0)20 8416 4400
Headteacher: Lara Péchard
Age range: 2–18 years
No. of pupils: 830

St. John's Prep School
The Ridgeway, Potters Bar,
Hertfordshire EN6 5QT
Tel: +44 (0)1707 657294
Head Teacher: Mrs C Tardios
Age range: 3–11 years

Stanborough Primary School
Appletree Walk, Watford,
Hertfordshire WD25 0DQ
Tel: 01923 673291
Head of School: Mrs T Madden
Age range: 3–11 years

Stormont
The Causeway, Potters Bar,
Hertfordshire EN6 5HA
Tel: 01707 654037
Head Teacher: Miss Louise Martin
Age range: G4–11 years

The King's School
Elmfield, Ambrose Lane, Harpenden,
Hertfordshire AL5 4DU
Tel: 01582 767566
Headteacher: Mr Andy Reeves
Age range: 2–16 years

The Purcell School, London
Aldenham Road, Bushey,
Hertfordshire WD23 2TS
Tel: 01923 331100
Principal: Mr Paul Bambrough
Age range: 10–18 years

Tring Park School for the Performing Arts
Mansion Drive, Tring,
Hertfordshire HP23 5LX
Tel: 01442 824255
Principal: Mr Stefan Anderson MA, ARCM, ARCT
Age range: 8–19 years
No. of pupils: 370 VIth171
Fees: Day £15,405–£24,885
FB £26,190–£37,605

Westbrook Hay Prep School
London Road, Hemel Hempstead,
Hertfordshire HP1 2RF
Tel: 01442 256143
Headmaster: Mark Brain
Age range: 3–16 years
No. of pupils: 340
Fees: Day £10,905–£15,690

York House School
Sarratt Road, Croxley Green, Rickmansworth,
Hertfordshire WD3 4LW
Tel: 01923 772395
Headmaster: Mr Jon Gray BA(Ed)
Age range: 3–13 years
No. of pupils: 401
Fees: Day £3,923–£5,773

Norfolk

All Saints School
School Road, Lessingham,
Norwich, Norfolk NR12 0DJ
Tel: 01692 582083
Head of School: Samantha Dangerfield
Age range: 7–16 years

Beeston Hall School
Beeston Regis, West Runton,
Cromer, Norfolk NR27 9NQ
Tel: 01263 837324
Headmaster: Mr Fred de Falbe BA(Hons) PGCE
Age range: 4–13 years

Gresham's Nursery and Pre-Prep School
Market Place, Holt, Norfolk NR25 6BB
Tel: 01263 714575
Head: Ms Sarah Hollingsworth
Age range: 2–7 years

Gresham's Prep School
Holt, Norfolk NR25 6EY
Tel: 01263 714600
Head: Mrs Cathy Braithwaite
Age range: 7–13 years

Langley Pre-Prep & Prep School
Taverham, Norwich, Norfolk NR8 6HU
Tel: 01603 868206
Head of Prep: Mr Mike A Crossley NPQH, BEd(Hons)
Age range: 6 months–13 years

Norwich High School for Girls GDST
95 Newmarket Road,
Norwich, Norfolk NR2 2HU
Tel: 01603 453265
Head: Ms Alison Sefton
Age range: G3–18 years

Norwich School
71a The Close, Norwich,
Norfolk NR1 4DD
Tel: 01603 728430
Head: Mr Steffan D A Griffiths
Age range: 4–18 years
No. of pupils: 1198 VIth341

Norwich Steiner School
Hospital Lane, Norwich,
Norfolk NR1 2HW
Tel: 01603 611175
Age range: 3–19 years

NOTRE DAME PREPARATORY SCHOOL
For further details see p. 49
147 Dereham Road,
Norwich, Norfolk NR2 3TA
Tel: 01603 625593
Email: admissions@notredameprepschool.co.uk
Website: www.notredameprepschool.co.uk
Headteachers: Mrs K. Laudan & Dr L. Campbell
Age range: 2–11 years

OneSchool Global UK Swaffham Campus
Turbine Way, Swaffham,
Norfolk PE37 7XD
Tel: 01760 336939
Age range: 7–18 years

Thetford Grammar School
Bridge Street, Thetford,
Norfolk IP24 3AF
Tel: 01842 752840
Head of School: Ms Amanda Faye
Age range: 3–19 years

Town Close School
14 Ipswich Road, Norwich,
Norfolk NR2 2LR
Tel: 01603 620180
Head of School: Mr Nick Tiley-Nunn
Age range: 3–13 years
No. of pupils: 450
Fees: Day £3,737–£5,668

Wymondham College Prep School
Golf Links Road, Wymondham,
Norfolk NR18 9SZ
Tel: 01953 609000 (option 3)
Headteacher: Mr Simon Underhill
Age range: 4–11 years
No. of pupils: 150
Fees: FB £12,165

ENGLAND: East

Suffolk

Barnardiston Hall Preparatory School
Hall Road, Barnardiston, Nr Haverhill, Suffolk CB9 7TG
Tel: 01440 786316
Headmaster: Lt Col K A Boulter MA(Cantab)
Age range: 6 months–13 years

Brookes UK
Flempton Road, Risby, Bury St Edmunds, Suffolk IP28 6QJ
Tel: 01284 760531
Principal: Ms Natalie Taylor
Age range: 2–16 years

Culford Preparatory School
Bury St Edmunds, Suffolk IP28 6TX
Tel: +44 (0)1284 728615
Head of School: Mrs Claire Bentley
Age range: 7–13 years

Culford Pre-Preparatory School
Bury St Edmunds, Suffolk IP28 6TX
Tel: +44 (0)1284 728615
Head of School: Mrs Claire Bentley
Age range: 1–7 years

FAIRSTEAD HOUSE SCHOOL
For further details see p. 46
Fairstead House, Fordham Road, Newmarket, Suffolk CB8 7AA
Tel: 01638 662318
Email: secretary@fairsteadhouse.org
Website: www.fairsteadhouse.org
Head of School: Mr Michael Radford
Age range: 1–11 years
No. of pupils: 216
Fees: Day £14,508–£16,170

Finborough School
The Hall, Great Finborough, Stowmarket, Suffolk IP14 3EF
Tel: +44 (0)1449 773600
Headmaster: Mr Steven T. Clark
Age range: 2–18 years
No. of pupils: 663
Fees: Day £10,800–£16,650 WB £20,250–£27,150 FB £25,260–£33,840

Framlingham College Prep School
Brandeston, Suffolk IP13 7AH
Tel: +44 (0)1728 685331
Head of School: Mr Simon Roche
Age range: 3–13 years

Ipswich High School
Woolverstone, Ipswich, Suffolk IP9 1AZ
Tel: 01473 780201
Head of School: Mr Dan Browning
Age range: 3–18 years
No. of pupils: 530
Fees: Day £12,105–£19,305 WB £32,120 FB £42,120

IPSWICH PREP SCHOOL
For further details see p. 47
3 Ivry Street, Ipswich, Suffolk IP1 3QW
Tel: 01473 282800
Email: prepenquiries@ipswich.school
Website: www.ipswich.school
Headmistress: Ms Claire Jackson
Age range: 4–11 years
No. of pupils: 234
Fees: Day £12,705–£15,612

Old Buckenham Hall School
Old Buckenham Hall, Brettenham Park, Ipswich, Suffolk IP7 7PH
Tel: 01449 740252
Headmaster: Mr David Griffiths
Age range: 3–13 years
No. of pupils: 221
Fees: Day £7,295 FB £9,505

Orwell Park School
Nacton, Ipswich, Suffolk IP10 0ER
Tel: 01473 659225
Headmaster: Mr Guy Musson
Age range: 2–13 years
No. of pupils: 240

Saint Felix School
Halesworth Road, Southwold, Suffolk IP18 6SD
Tel: +44 (0)15027 22175
Headmaster: Mr. James Harrison
Age range: 2–18 years (boarding from 7)

South Lee Preparatory School
Nowton Road, Bury St Edmunds, Suffolk IP33 2BT
Tel: 01284 754654
Acting Head: Mrs Sarah Catchpole
Age range: 4 months–13 years

St Joseph's College
Belstead Road, Ipswich, Suffolk IP2 9DR
Tel: +44 (0)1473 690281
Principal: Mrs Danielle Clarke
Age range: 2–18 years

Stoke College
Ashen Lane, Stoke by Clare, Sudbury, Suffolk CO10 8JE
Tel: +44 (0)1787 278141
Principal: Dr. Gareth P. Lloyd
Age range: 11–18 years

Summerhill School
Westward Ho, Leiston, Suffolk IP16 4HY
Tel: 01728 830540
Principal: Mrs Zoe Readhead
Age range: 5–18 years

The Meadows Montessori School
32 Larchcroft Road, Ipswich, Suffolk IP1 6AR
Tel: 01473 233782
Headteacher: Ms Samantha Sims
Age range: 3–16 years

The Old School Henstead
Toad Row, Henstead, Beccles, Suffolk NR34 7LG
Tel: 01502 741150
Head of School: Miss Melissa Clifton
Age range: 2.5–11 years

Woodbridge School Prep
Church Street, Woodbridge, Suffolk IP12 1DS
Tel: +44 (0)1394 382673
Head of School: Mrs Nicola Mitchell
Age range: 4–11 years

East Midlands

Derbyshire D116
Leicestershire D116
Lincolnshire D117
Northamptonshire D117
Nottinghamshire D118
Rutland D118

KEY TO SYMBOLS
- Boys' school
- Girls' school
- International school
- Tutorial or sixth form college
- (A) A levels
- Boarding accommodation
- (£) Bursaries
- (IB) International Baccalaureate
- Learning support
- (16+) Entrance at 16+
- Vocational qualifications
- (IAPS) Independent Association of Prep Schools
- (HMC) The Headmasters' & Headmistresses' Conference
- (ISA) Independent Schools Association
- (GSA) Girls' School Association
- (BSA) Boarding Schools' Association
- (S) Society of Heads

Unless otherwise indicated, all schools are coeducational day schools. Single-sex and boarding schools will be indicated by the relevant icon.

ENGLAND: East Midlands

Derbyshire

Barlborough Hall School
Park Street, Barlborough,
Chesterfield, Derbyshire S43 4ES
Tel: 01246 810511
Headteacher: Mrs Karen Keeton
Age range: 3–11 years

Dame Catherine Harpur's School
Rose Lane, Ticknall, Derby,
Derbyshire DE73 7JW
Tel: 01332 862792
Headteacher: Lorna Harvey
Age range: 3–11 years

Derby Grammar School
Rykneld Hall, Rykneld Road,
Littleover, Derby, Derbyshire DE23 4BX
Tel: 01332 523027
Acting Head: Mr Paul Hilliam
Age range: 4–18 years

Derby High School
Hillsway, Littleover, Derby,
Derbyshire DE23 3DT
Tel: 01332 514267
Headteacher: Mrs Amy Chapman
Age range: 3–18 years

Emmanuel School
Juniper Lodge, 43 Kedleston Road,
Derby, Derbyshire DE22 1FP
Tel: 01332 340505
Headteacher: Mr Ben Snowdon
Age range: 3–11 years

Normanton House School
Normanton House, Village Street,
Derby, Derbyshire DE23 8DF
Tel: 01332 769333
Head of School: Ms A Ahmed
Age range: 5–16 years

Old Vicarage School
11 Church Lane, Darley Abbey,
Derby, Derbyshire DE22 1EW
Tel: 01332 557130
Head of School: Mrs Kerry Wise
Age range: 3–13 years

Repton Prep
Milton, Derby, Derbyshire DE65 6EJ
Tel: 01283 707100
Head of School: Mrs Vicky Harding
Age range: 3–13 years

S. Anselm's School
Stanedge Road, Bakewell,
Derbyshire DE45 1DP
Tel: 01629 812734
Headmaster: Mr Frank Thompson
Age range: 2–13 years

St Peter & St Paul School
Brambling House, Hady Hill,
Chesterfield, Derbyshire S41 0EF
Tel: 01246 278522
Headteacher: Mrs Jill Phinn
Age range: 3 months–11 years

St Wystan's School
High Street, Repton,
Derbyshire DE65 6GE
Tel: 01283 703258
Head Teacher: Ms Kara Lebihan
Age range: 2.5–11 years

Watchorn Christian School
Watchorn Church, Derby Road,
Alfreton, Derbyshire DE55 7AQ
Tel: 07387 721877
Age range: 3–11 years

Leicestershire

Al-Aqsa Schools Trust
The Wayne Way, Leicester,
Leicestershire LE5 4PP
Tel: 01162 760953
Headteacher: Arafat Q Hingora
Age range: 4–16 years

Brooke House School
Croft Road, Cosby, Leicester,
Leicestershire LE9 1SE
Tel: 0116 286 7770
Principal: Mrs Joy Parker
Age range: 3–18 years

Emmanuel Christian School, Leicester
Didsbury Street, Braunstone,
Leicester, Leicestershire LE3 1QP
Tel: 0116 222 0792
Age range: 4–16 years

Fairfield Prep School
Leicester Road, Loughborough,
Leicestershire LE11 2AE
Tel: 01509 215172
Headmaster: Mr Andrew Earnshaw
Age range: 3–11 years
No. of pupils: 500

Jameah Boys Academy
33 Wood Hill, Leicester,
Leicestershire LE5 3SQ
Tel: 01162 927746
Age range: B5–16 years

Jameah Girls Academy
49 Rolleston Street, Leicester,
Leicestershire LE5 3SD
Tel: 0116 262 7745
Age range: G5–16 years

Leicester Grammar Junior School
London Road, Great Glen,
Leicester, Leicestershire LE8 9FL
Tel: 0116 259 1950
Head of School: Mrs S Ashworth Jones
Age range: 3–11 years
No. of pupils: 391
Fees: Day £11,493–£12,212

Leicester High School for Girls
454 London Road, Leicester,
Leicestershire LE2 2PP
Tel: 0116 2705338
Headmaster: Mr Alan Whelpdale
Age range: G3–18 years

Leicester Islamic Academy
320 London Road, Leicester,
Leicestershire LE2 2PJ
Tel: 01162 705343
Headteacher: Mrs T. Jakhura
Age range: 3–11 years

Leicester Preparatory School
2 Albert Road, Leicester,
Leicestershire LE2 2AA
Tel: 01162 707414
Headmistress: Ms Claudette Salmon
Age range: 2–11 years

LGS Stoneygate
London Road, Great Glen,
Leicester, Leicestershire LE8 9DJ
Tel: 01162 592282
Headmaster: Mr J F Dobson
Age range: 4–16 years

Loughborough Amherst School
Gray Street, Loughborough,
Leicestershire LE11 2DZ
Tel: 01509 263901
Interim Head: Miss Grace Davies
Age range: 4–18 years
No. of pupils: 300

Ratcliffe College
Fosse Way, Ratcliffe on the Wreake,
Leicester, Leicestershire LE7 4SG
Tel: +44 (0)1509 817000
Headmaster: Mr Jon Reddin
BSc, MSc, NPQH
Age range: 3–18 years
(boarding from 11)

St Crispin's School
6 St Mary's Road, Stoneygate,
Leicester, Leicestershire LE2 1XA
Tel: 01162 707648
Headmaster: Mr Andrew Atkin
Age range: 2–16 years

The Dixie Grammar School
Market Place, Market Bosworth,
Leicestershire CV13 0LE
Tel: 01455 292244
Headmaster: Mr Richard Lynn MA
Age range: 3–18 years

East Midlands: ENGLAND

Lincolnshire

Ayscoughfee Hall School
Welland Hall, London Road, Spalding, Lincolnshire PE11 2TE
Tel: 01775 724733
Headteacher: Ms Theresa Wright
Age range: 3–11 years

Burton Hathow Preparatory School
Odder Farm, Saxilby Road, Burton, Lincoln, Lincolnshire LN1 2BB
Tel: 01522 274616
Head Teacher: Ms Penny Ford
Age range: 2–11 years

Copthill School
Barnack Road, Uffington, Stamford, Lincolnshire PE9 3AD
Tel: 01780 757506
Headmaster: Mr J A Teesdale BA(Hons), PGCE
Age range: 2–11 years

Dudley House School
1 Dudley Road, Grantham, Lincolnshire NG31 9AA
Tel: 01476 400184
Headteacher: Ms Jenny Johnson
Age range: 3–11 years

Grantham Preparatory International School
Gorse Lane, Grantham, Lincolnshire NG31 7UF
Tel: +44 (0)1476 593293
Headmistress: Mrs K A Korcz
Age range: 3–11 years

Greenwich House Independent School
106 High Holme Road, Louth, Lincolnshire LN11 0HE
Tel: 01507 609252
Headmistress: Mrs J Brindle
Age range: 9 months–11 years

Handel House Preparatory School
The Northolme, Gainsborough, Lincolnshire DN21 2JB
Tel: 01427 612426
Headteacher: Mr Mark Raisborough
Age range: 3–11 years

Kirkstone House School
Main Street, Baston, Peterborough, Lincolnshire PE6 9PA
Tel: 01778 560350
Headteacher: Mr Stuart Judge
Age range: 5–18 years

Lincoln Minster School
The Prior Building, Upper Lindum Street, Lincoln, Lincolnshire LN2 5RW
Tel: 01522 551300
Headmistress: Mrs Maria Young
Age range: 4–18 years
No. of pupils: 500

St George's Preparatory School & Little Dragons Nursery
126 London Road, Boston, Lincolnshire PE21 7HB
Tel: 01205 317600
Directors: Mark & Sarah Whelan
Age range: 3–11 years

St Hugh's School
Cromwell Avenue, Woodhall Spa, Lincolnshire LN10 6TQ
Tel: 01526 352169
Headmaster: Mr Jeremy Wyld
Age range: 2–13 years

Stamford Junior School
Kettering Road, Stamford, Lincolnshire PE9 2LR
Tel: 01780 484400
Headteacher: Mr Matthew O'Reilly
Age range: 2–11 years (boarding from 7)

Witham Hall Preparatory School
Witham-on-the-Hill, Stamford, Lincolnshire PE10 0JJ
Tel: +44(0)1778 590222
Headmaster: Mr William Austen
Age range: 4–13 years

Northamptonshire

Beachborough School
Westbury, Nr. Brackley, Northamptonshire NN13 5LB
Tel: 01280 700071
Headteacher: Mrs Simone Mitchell
Age range: 2–13 years
No. of pupils: 400
Fees: Day £12,885–£20,235

Laxton Junior School
East Road, Oundle, Northamptonshire PE8 4BX
Tel: 01832 277275
Head: Mr Sam Robertson
Age range: 4–11 years

Northampton High School GDST
Newport Pagnell Road, Hardingstone, Northampton, Northamptonshire NN4 6UU
Tel: 01604 765765
Head: Dr May Lee
Age range: G2–18 years
No. of pupils: 600
Fees: Day £3,576–£5,254

OneSchool Global UK Northampton Campus
Billing Road East, Northampton, Northamptonshire NN3 3LF
Tel: 01604 633819
Age range: 7–18 years

Overstone Park School
Overstone Park, Overstone, Northampton, Northamptonshire NN6 0DT
Tel: 01604 643787
Principal: Mrs M F Brown BA(Hons), PGCE
Age range: 2–18 years

Pitsford School
Pitsford Hall, Pitsford, Northampton, Northamptonshire NN6 9AX
Tel: 01604 880306
Headteacher: Dr Craig Walker
Age range: 3–18 years
Fees: Day £9,600–£16,656

Quinton House School
Upton Hall, Upton, Northampton, Northamptonshire NN5 4UX
Tel: 01604 752050
Headteacher: Mr Tim Hoyle
Age range: 2–18 years
No. of pupils: 390
Fees: Day £8,040–£11,985

SPRATTON HALL
For further details see p. 53
Smith Street, Spratton, Northamptonshire NN6 8HP
Tel: 01604 847292
Email: registrar@sprattonhall.com
Website: www.sprattonhall.com
Head Master: Mr Simon Clarke
Age range: 4–13 years
No. of pupils: 390

St Peter's School
52 Headlands, Kettering, Northamptonshire NN15 6DJ
Tel: 01536 512066
Headteacher: Mr Mark Thomas
Age range: 3–11 years

Wellingborough School
London Road, Wellingborough, Northamptonshire NN8 2BX
Tel: 01933 222427
Headmaster: Mr A N Holman
Age range: 3–18 years

Winchester House School
High Street, Brackley, Northamptonshire NN13 7AZ
Tel: 01280 702483
Head: Ms Antonia Lee
Age range: 3–13 years (boarding from 7)

ENGLAND: East Midlands

Nottinghamshire

Colston Bassett Preparatory School
School Lane, Colston bassett, Nottingham, Nottinghamshire NG12 3FD
Tel: 01949 81118
Headteacher: Mrs C Newcombe
Age range: 4–11 years

Coteswood House Pre-school & Day Nursery
19 Thackeray's Lane, Woodthorpe, Nottingham, Nottinghamshire NG5 4HT
Tel: 01159 676551
Age range: 9 months–5 years

Fig Tree Primary School
30 Bentinck Road, Nottingham, Nottinghamshire NG7 4AF
Tel: 01159 788152
Headteacher: Mrs Nabeela Hussain
Age range: 5–11 years

Highfields School
London Road, Newark, Nottinghamshire NG24 3AL
Tel: 01636 704103
Headteacher: Mrs Sarah H Lyons
Age range: 2–11 years

Hollygirt School
Elm Avenue, Nottingham, Nottinghamshire NG3 4GF
Tel: 0115 958 0596
Head of School: Dr. Helen Barsham
Age range: 3–19 years

Jamia Al-Hudaa Residential College
Forest House, Berkeley Avenue, Mapperley Park, Nottingham, Nottinghamshire NG3 5TT
Tel: 01159 690800
Principal: Raza ul-Haq Siakhvy
Age range: 11–19 years

Nottingham Girls' High School GDST
9 Arboretum Street, Nottingham, Nottinghamshire NG1 4JB
Tel: 01159 417663
Head: Julie Keller
Age range: G3–18 years
No. of pupils: 690

Nottingham High Infant and Junior School
Waverley Mount, Nottingham, Nottinghamshire NG7 4ED
Tel: 01158 452214
Age range: 4–11 years
No. of pupils: 1158
Fees: Day 10,986–16,047

OneSchool Global UK Nottingham Campus
Wellington Street, Long Eaton, Nottingham, Nottinghamshire NG10 4HR
Tel: 0115 973 3568
Age range: 7–18 years

Plumtree School
Church Hill, Plumtree, Nottingham, Nottinghamshire NG12 5ND
Tel: 0115 937 5859
Head Teacher: Phil Simpson
Age range: 3–11 years

Salterford House School
Salterford Lane, Calverton, Nottingham, Nottinghamshire NG14 6NZ
Tel: 01159 652127
Head: Ms Kimberley Venables
Age range: 3–11 years

Saville House School
11 Church Street, Mansfield Woodhouse, Mansfield, Nottinghamshire NG19 8AH
Tel: 01623 904418
Headteacher: Ms Claire King
Age range: 3–11 years

St Joseph's School
33 Derby Road, Nottingham, Nottinghamshire NG1 5AW
Tel: 01159 418356
Head Teacher: Mr Ashley Crawshaw
Age range: 1–11 years

The Orchard School
South Leverton, Retford, Nottinghamshire DN22 0DJ
Tel: 01427 880395
Head Teacher: Mrs Sandra Fox BA, PGCE
Age range: 5–16 years

Trent College and The Elms
Derby Road, Long Eaton, Nottingham, Nottinghamshire NG10 4AD
Tel: 0115 8494949
Head: Mr Bill Penty
Age range: 0–18 years
No. of pupils: 1121
Fees: Day £14,994–£18,789

Wellow House School
Wellow, Newark, Nottinghamshire NG22 0EA
Tel: 01623 861054
Head of School: Mr Stephen Thompson
Age range: 3–13 years

Worksop College, Ranby House
Retford, Nottinghamshire DN22 8HX
Tel: 01777 703138
Headmaster: Mr David Thorpe
Age range: 3–11 years

Rutland

Brooke Priory School
Station Approach, Oakham, Rutland LE15 6QW
Tel: 01572 724778
Headmaster: Mr Duncan Flint
Age range: 2–11 years

Greater London

Essex D120
Hertfordshire D120
Kent D121
Middlesex D121
Surrey D122

*See also East (D109) for schools in Essex and Hertfordshire; South-East (D141) for schools in Kent and Surrey

KEY TO SYMBOLS

- Boys' school
- Girls' school
- International school
- Tutorial or sixth form college
- A levels
- Boarding accommodation
- Bursaries
- International Baccalaureate
- Learning support
- Entrance at 16+
- Vocational qualifications
- Independent Association of Prep Schools
- The Headmasters' & Headmistresses' Conference
- Independent Schools Association
- Girls' School Association
- Boarding Schools' Association
- Society of Heads

Unless otherwise indicated, all schools are coeducational day schools. Single-sex and boarding schools will be indicated by the relevant icon.

ENGLAND: Greater London

Essex

Apex Primary School
60-62 Argyle Road, Ilford,
Essex IG1 3BG
Tel: 020 8554 1208
Head Teacher: Ms Meherun Hamid
Age range: 3–11 years

Avon House Preparatory School
490 High Road, Woodford Green, Essex IG8 0PN
Tel: 020 8504 1749
Headteacher: Mrs Amanda Campbell
Age range: 3–11 years
No. of pupils: 268
Fees: Day £3,530–£3,950

Bancroft's School
High Road, Woodford Green, Essex IG8 0RF
Tel: 020 8505 4821
Head: Mr Simon Marshall MA, PGCE (Cantab), MA, MPhil (Oxon)
Age range: 7–18 years

Beehive Preparatory School
233 Beehive Lane, Redbridge, Ilford, Essex IG4 5ED
Tel: 020 8550 3224
Head Teacher: Mr Jamie Gurr
Age range: 2.5–11 years

Braeside School
130 High Road, Buckhurst Hill, Essex IG9 5SD
Tel: 020 8504 1133
Headmistress: Ms Chloe Moon
Age range: 2.5–16 years

CHIGWELL SCHOOL
For further details see p. 54
High Road, Chigwell, Essex IG7 6QF
Tel: 020 8501 5700
Email: admissions@chigwell-school.org
Website: www.chigwell-school.org
Head Teacher: Mr Damian King
Age range: 4–18 years
No. of pupils: 1111

Daiglen School
68 Palmerston Road, Buckhurst Hill, Essex IG9 5LG
Tel: 020 8504 7108
Headteacher: Mrs P Dear
Age range: 3–11 years

Eastcourt Independent School
1-5 Eastwood Road, Goodmayes, Ilford, Essex IG3 8UW
Tel: 020 8590 5472
Headmistress: Mrs Christine Redgrave BSc(Hons), DipEd, MEd
Age range: 3–11 years
No. of pupils: 220
Fees: Day £2,600

Gidea Park Preparatory School & Nursery
2 Balgores Lane, Gidea Park, Romford, Essex RM2 5JR
Tel: 01708 740381
Head of School: Mr Callum Douglas
Age range: 2–11 years
No. of pupils: 100
Fees: Day £10,775

Guru Gobind Singh Khalsa College
Roding Lane, Chigwell, Essex IG7 6BQ
Tel: 020 8559 9160
Principal: Mr Amarjit Singh Toor BSc(Hons), BSc, BT
Age range: 3–19 years

Immanuel School
Havering Grange, Havering Road, Romford, Essex RM1 4HR
Tel: 01708 764449
Principal: Ms Sarah Williams
Age range: 3–16 years

Loyola Preparatory School
103 Palmerston Road, Buckhurst Hill, Essex IG9 5NH
Tel: 020 8504 7372
Headmistress: Mrs K R Anthony
Age range: B3–11 years
No. of pupils: 200
Fees: Day £11,610

Oakfields Preparatory School
Harwood Hall, Harwood Hall Lane, Upminster, Essex RM14 2YG
Tel: 01708 220117
Head of School: Matthew Booth
Age range: 3–11 years
No. of pupils: 215
Fees: Day £12,597–£13,497

Oaklands School
6-8 Albion Hill, Loughton, Essex IG10 4RA
Tel: 020 8508 3517
Headmistress: Ms Sue Belej
Age range: 2.5–11 years

St Aubyn's School
Bunces Lane, Woodford Green, Essex IG8 9DU
Tel: 020 8504 1577
Headmaster: Mr Leonard Blom BEd(Hons) BA NPQH
Age range: 3–13 years

St Mary's Hare Park School & Nursery
South Drive, Gidea Park, Romford, Essex RM2 6HH
Tel: 01708 761220
Headteacher: Mr Ludovic Bernard
Age range: 2.5–11 years

The Ursuline Preparatory School Ilford
2-4 Coventry Road, Ilford, Essex IG1 4QR
Tel: 020 8518 4050
Acting Headteacher: Mrs Lorraine Pereira
Age range: 3–11 years

WOODFORD GREEN PREPARATORY SCHOOL
For further details see p. 60
Glengall Road, Woodford Green, Essex IG8 0BZ
Tel: 020 8504 5045
Email: admissions@wgprep.co.uk
Website: www.wgprep.co.uk
Head of School: Miss Jenny Maslen
Age range: 3–11 years
No. of pupils: 381

Hertfordshire

Lyonsdown School
3 Richmond Road, New Barnet, Barnet, Hertfordshire EN5 1SA
Tel: 020 8449 0225
Head: Mrs Rittu Hall
Age range: G3–11 years
No. of pupils: 180
Fees: Day £11,985–£12,975

The Royal Masonic School for Girls
Rickmansworth Park, Rickmansworth, Hertfordshire WD3 4HF
Tel: 01923 725354
Headmaster: Mr Kevin Carson M.Phil (Cambridge)
Age range: B2–3 years G2–18 years (boarding from 8)
No. of pupils: 985
Fees: Day £4,710–£8,015
FB £10,585–£14,585

Greater London: ENGLAND

Kent

Babington House School
Grange Drive, Chislehurst,
Kent BR7 5ES
Tel: 020 8467 5537
Headmaster: Mr Tim Lello
MA, FRSA, NPQH
Age range: 3–18 years
No. of pupils: 500

Benedict House Preparatory School
1-5 Victoria Road, Sidcup,
Kent DA15 7HD
Tel: 020 8300 7206
Headteacher: Mr Craig Wardle
Age range: 3–11 years

Bickley Park School
14 & 24 Page Heath Lane,
Bickley, Bromley, Kent BR1 2DS
Tel: 020 8467 2195
Head of School: Ms Tammy Howard
Age range: B2.5–13 years G2.5–4 years

Bishop Challoner School
228 Bromley Road, Shortlands,
Bromley, Kent BR2 0BS
Tel: 020 8460 3546
Headteacher: Mr Mark Wallace BA (Hons), MBA
Age range: 3–18 years
No. of pupils: 319

Breaside Preparatory School
41-43 Orchard Road,
Bromley, Kent BR1 2PR
Tel: 020 8460 0916
Executive Principal: Mrs Karen A Nicholson B.Ed, NPQH, Dip EYs
Age range: 2.5–11 years
No. of pupils: 415
Fees: Day £14,475–£16,620

Bromley High School GDST
Blackbrook Lane, Bickley,
Bromley, Kent BR1 2TW
Tel: 020 8781 7000/1
Head: Mrs A M Drew BA(Hons), MBA (Dunelm)
Age range: G4–18 years

Farringtons Junior School
Perry Street, Chislehurst, Kent BR7 6LR
Tel: 020 8467 0395
Head of Junior School: Mr Rishi Boyjoonauth
Age range: 3–11 years

> **MERTON COURT PREPARATORY SCHOOL**
> *For further details see p. 57*
> 38 Knoll Road, Sidcup,
> Kent DA14 4QU
> Tel: 020 8300 2112
> Email: office@mertoncourtprep.co.uk
> Website: mertoncourtprep.co.uk
> Headmaster: Mr Dominic Price BEd, MBA
> Age range: 3–11 years
> No. of pupils: 315
> Fees: Day £3,700–£5,625

St Christopher's The Hall School
49 Bromley Road, Beckenham,
Kent BR3 5PA
Tel: 020 8650 2200
Headteacher: Mr Tom Carter
Age range: 3–11 years

St David's Prep
Justin Hall, Beckenham Road,
West Wickham, Kent BR4 0QS
Tel: 020 8777 5852
Head Teacher: Ms Julia Foulger
Age range: 3–11 years

West Lodge School
36 Station Road, Sidcup,
Kent DA15 7DU
Tel: 020 8300 2489
Head Teacher: Mr Robert Francis
Age range: 3–11 years

Middlesex

ACS Hillingdon International School
108 Vine Lane, Hillingdon,
Uxbridge, Middlesex UB10 0BE
Tel: +44 (0) 1895 259771
Head of School: Mr Martin Hall
Age range: 4–18 years

Alpha Preparatory School
21 Hindes Road, Harrow,
Middlesex HA1 1SH
Tel: 020 8427 1471
Headmaster: Mr Pádraic Fahy
Age range: 3–11 years

Ashton House School
50-52 Eversley Crescent,
Isleworth, Middlesex TW7 4LW
Tel: 020 8560 3902
Head of School: Mr Graeme Smith
Age range: 3–11 years

Buckingham Preparatory School
458 Rayners Lane, Pinner,
Harrow, Middlesex HA5 5DJ
Tel: 020 8866 2737
Head of School: Mrs Sarah Hollis
Age range: B3–11 years

Buxlow Preparatory School
5/6 Castleton Gardens,
Wembley, Middlesex HA9 7QJ
Tel: 020 8904 3615
Headteacher: Mr D May
Age range: 2–11 years

Edgware Jewish Girls - Beis Chinuch
296 Hale Lane, Edgware,
Middlesex HA8 8NP
Tel: 020 8905 4376
Headteacher: Mr M Cohen
Age range: G3–11 years

Hampton Prep and Pre-Prep School
Gloucester Road, Hampton,
Middlesex TW12 2UQ
Tel: 020 8979 1844
Headmaster: Mr Tim Smith
Age range: B3–11 years G3–7 years

Holland House School
1 Broadhurst Avenue, Edgware,
Middlesex HA8 8TP
Tel: 020 8958 6979
Headteacher: Mrs Emily Brown
Age range: 4–11 years
No. of pupils: 147

Jack & Jill Family of Schools
20 First Cross Road, Twickenham,
Middlesex TW2 5QA
Tel: 03333 444630
Age range: B2–4 years G2–11 years

Lady Eleanor Holles (Junior Department)
Burlington House, 177 Uxbridge Road,
Hampton, Middlesex TW12 1BD
Tel: 020 8979 2173
Head of School: Mrs Paula Mortimer
Age range: G7–11 years

Newland House School
Waldegrave Park, Twickenham,
Middlesex TW1 4TQ
Tel: 020 8865 1234
Head of School: Mr Chris Skelton
Age range: 3–13 years
No. of pupils: 448

North London Collegiate School
Canons, Canons Drive,
Edgware, Middlesex HA8 7RJ
Tel: +44 (0)20 8952 0912
Headmistress: Vicky Bingham
Age range: G4–18 years
No. of pupils: 1080

Northwood College for Girls GDST
Maxwell Road, Northwood,
Middlesex HA6 2YE
Tel: 01923 825446
Head of School: Mrs Rebecca Brown
Age range: G3–18 years
No. of pupils: 844

Orley Farm School
South Hill Avenue, Harrow,
Middlesex HA1 3NU
Tel: 020 8869 7600
Headmaster: Mr Tim Calvey
Age range: 4–13 years

Quainton Hall School & Nursery
91 Hindes Road, Harrow,
Middlesex HA1 1RX
Tel: 020 8515 9500
Headmaster: S Ford BEd (Hons), UWE Bristol
Age range: 3–11 years
Fees: Day £11,850–£13,050

Radnor House
Pope's Villa, Cross Deep,
Twickenham, Middlesex TW1 4QG
Tel: +44 (0)20 8891 6264
Head: Mr Darryl Wideman MA Oxon, PGCE
Age range: 9–18 years

Reddiford School
36-38 Cecil Park, Pinner,
Middlesex HA5 5HH
Tel: 020 8866 0660
Headteacher: Mrs J Batt CertEd, NPQH
Age range: 3–11 years

Roxeth Mead School
Buckholt House, 25 Middle Road,
Harrow, Middlesex HA2 0HW
Tel: 020 8422 2092
Co-Headteachers: Mrs Suzanne Goodwin & Mrs Sarah Mackintosh
Age range: 0–7 years

St Catherine's Prep
Cross Deep, Twickenham,
Middlesex TW1 4QJ
Tel: 020 8891 2898
Headmistress: Mrs Johneen McPherson MA
Age range: G5–11 years
No. of pupils: 95
Fees: Day £13,395–£14,085

> **ST CATHERINE'S SCHOOL**
> *For further details see p. 58*
> Cross Deep, Twickenham,
> Middlesex TW1 4QJ
> Tel: 020 8891 2898
> Email: info@stcatherineschool.co.uk
> Website: www.stcatherineschool.co.uk
> Headmistress: Mrs Johneen McPherson MA
> Age range: G7–18 years
> No. of pupils: 405
> Fees: Day £15,285–£18,513

St Christopher's School
71 Wembley Park Drive,
Wembley, Middlesex HA9 8HE
Tel: 020 8902 5069
Head of School: Mr Jonathan Coke
Age range: 2–11 years

ENGLAND: Greater London

St Helen's College
Parkway, Hillingdon, Uxbridge, Middlesex UB10 9JX
Tel: 01895 234371
Head: Ms Shirley Drummond BA, PGCert, MLDP, FCCT
Age range: 2–11 years
No. of pupils: 380
Fees: Day £11,400–£14,250

St Helen's School
Eastbury Road, Northwood, Middlesex HA6 3AS
Tel: +44 (0)1923 843210
Headmistress: Mrs Alice Lucas
Age range: G3–18 years
No. of pupils: 1150

St John's School
Potter Street Hill, Pinner, Middlesex HA5 3ZF
Tel: 020 8866 0067
Headmaster: Mr Sean Robinson
Age range: B3–13 years

St Martin's School
40 Moor Park Road, Northwood, Middlesex HA6 2DJ
Tel: 01923 825740
Headmaster: Mr S Dunn BEd (Hons)
Age range: B3–13 years

Tashbar of Edgware
Mowbray Road, Edgware, Middlesex HA8 8JL
Age range: B3–11 years

The Eden SDA School
The Old Vicarage, High Street, Harmondsworth, Middlesex UB7 0AQ
Tel: 020 3627 5556
Head Teacher: Mrs Laura Osei
Age range: 2–18 years

The Hall Pre-Preparatory School & Nursery
The Grange Country House, Rickmansworth Road, Northwood, Middlesex HA6 2RB
Tel: 01923 822807
Headmistress: Mrs S M Goodwin
Age range: 0–7 years

The Mall School
185 Hampton Road, Twickenham, Middlesex TW2 5NQ
Tel: 0208 977 2523
Headmaster: Mr D C Price BSc, MA
Age range: B4–11 years

The St Michael Steiner School
Park Road, Hanworth Park, London, Middlesex TW13 6PN
Tel: 0208 893 1299
Age range: 3–18 years

Twickenham Preparatory School
Beveree, 43 High Street, Hampton, Middlesex TW12 2SA
Tel: 020 8979 6216
Headmaster: Mr Oliver Barrett
Age range: B4–13 years G4–11 years

Surrey

Al-Khair School
109-117 Cherry Orchard Road, Croydon, Surrey CR0 6BE
Tel: 020 8662 8664
Headteacher: Mrs Aisha Chaudhry
Age range: 2–16 years

Broomfield House School
Broomfield Road, Kew Gardens, Richmond, Surrey TW9 3HS
Tel: 020 8940 3884
Head of School: Ms Susie Byers
Age range: 3–11 years

Collingwood School
3 Springfield Road, Wallington, Surrey SM6 0BD
Tel: 020 8647 4607
Headmaster: Mr Leigh Hardie
Age range: 3–11 years

Croydon High School GDST
Old Farleigh Road, Selsdon, South Croydon, Surrey CR2 8YB
Tel: 02082 607543
Head: Ms Annabel Davies
Age range: G3–18 years

Cumnor House School for Boys
168 Pampisford Road, South Croydon, Surrey CR2 6DA
Tel: 020 8645 2614
Head of School: Miss Emma Edwards
Age range: B4–13 years
No. of pupils: 423
Fees: Day £3,880–£4,655

Cumnor House School for Girls
1 Woodcote Lane, Purley, Surrey CR8 3HB
Tel: 020 8668 0050
Head of School: Mrs Amanda McShane
Age range: G4–11 years

Date Valley School Trust
Mitcham Court, Cricket Green, Mitcham, Surrey CR4 4LB
Tel: +44 (0)20 8648 4647
Headteacher: Neena Lone
Age range: 3–11 years

Educare Small School
12 Cowleaze Road, Kingston upon Thames, Surrey KT2 6DZ
Tel: 020 8547 0144
Head Teacher: Mrs E Steinthal
Age range: 3–11 years

Elmhurst School
44-48 South Park Hill Road, South Croydon, Surrey CR2 7DW
Tel: 020 8688 0661
Head of School: Mrs Sara Marriott
Age range: 3–11 years
No. of pupils: 120
Fees: Day £2,669–£4,889

Hampton Court House
Hampton Court Road, Richmond upon Thames, London, Surrey KT8 9BS
Tel: 020 8614 0865
Headteacher: Katherine Vintiner
Age range: 2–18 years
No. of pupils: 300
Fees: Day £16,056–£23,475

HOLY CROSS PREPARATORY SCHOOL
For further details see p. 56
George Road, Kingston upon Thames, Surrey KT2 7NU
Tel: 020 8942 0729
Email: secretary@holycrossprep.com
Website: www.holycrossprepschool.co.uk
Headteacher: Mrs S. Hair BEd(Hons)
Age range: G3–11 years

Homefield Preparatory School
Western Road, Sutton, Surrey SM1 2TE
Tel: 02086 420965
Headmaster: Mr John Towers
Age range: B4–13 years

Kew College Prep
24-26 Cumberland Road, Kew, Surrey TW9 3HQ
Tel: 020 8940 2039
Head: Mrs Jane Bond BSc, MA(Ed), PGCE
Age range: 3–11 years
No. of pupils: 270

Kew Green Preparatory School
Layton House, Ferry Lane, Kew Green, Richmond, Surrey TW9 3AF
Tel: 020 8948 5999
Headteacher: Mrs Sasha Davies
Age range: 2–11 years
No. of pupils: 240

King's House School
68 King's Road, Richmond, Surrey TW10 6ES
Tel: 020 8940 1878
Head: Mr Mark Turner BA, PGCE, NPQH
Age range: B3–13 years G3–6 years
No. of pupils: 420
Fees: Day £2,870–£6,890

Laleham Lea School
29 Peaks Hill, Purley, Surrey CR8 3JJ
Tel: 020 8660 3351
Acting Head Teacher: Mrs Maria Reece
Age range: 3–11 years
No. of pupils: 136

Oakwood School
Coombe Road, Lloyd Park, Croydon, Surrey CR0 5RD
Tel: 02086 688080
Headmistress: Ms Debbie Morrison
Age range: 3–11 years

Old Palace of John Whitgift School
Old Palace Road, Croydon, Surrey CR0 1AX
Tel: 02086 882027
Head of School: Mrs Jane Burton
Age range: G3–18 years
No. of pupils: 650
Fees: Day £3,300–£5,536

Old Vicarage School
46-48 Richmond Hill, Richmond, Surrey TW10 6QX
Tel: 020 8940 0922
Headmistress: Mrs G D Linthwaite
Age range: G3–11 years
No. of pupils: 200
Fees: Day £5,200

Greater London: ENGLAND

Park Hill School
8 Queens Road, Kingston upon Thames, Surrey KT2 7SH
Tel: 020 8546 5496
Headmaster: Mr Alistair Bond
Age range: 2–11 years

Rokeby School
George Road, Kingston upon Thames, Surrey KT2 7PB
Tel: 020 8942 2247
Head: Mr J R Peck
Age range: B4–13 years

Royal Russell Junior School
Coombe Lane, Croydon, Surrey CR9 5BX
Tel: +44 (0)20 8657 4433
Junior School Headmaster: Mr John Evans
Age range: 3–11 years

Seaton House School
67 Banstead Road South, Sutton, Surrey SM2 5LH
Tel: 020 8642 2332
Headteacher: Mr Carl Bates
Age range: B3–5 years G3–11 years

Shrewsbury House School
107 Ditton Road, Surbiton, Surrey KT6 6RL
Tel: 020 8399 3066
Executive Head: Ms Joanna Hubbard MA BA(Hons) PGCE PGDipSEN
Age range: B7–13 years

St David's School
Woodcote Valley Road, Purley, Surrey CR8 3AL
Tel: 020 8660 0723
Headmistress: Cressida Mardell
Age range: 3–11 years

Staines Preparatory School
3 Gresham Road, Staines-upon-Thames, Surrey TW18 2BT
Tel: 01784 450909
Head of School: Ms Samantha Sawyer B.Ed (Hons), M.Ed, NPQH
Age range: 3–11 years
No. of pupils: 289
Fees: Day £11,975–£14,610

Sutton High School GDST
55 Cheam Road, Sutton, Surrey SM1 2AX
Tel: 020 8642 0594
Head of School: Ms Beth Dawson
Age range: G3–18 years

The Study School
57 Thetford Road, New Malden, Surrey KT3 5DP
Tel: 020 8942 0754
Headmaster: Mr Alistair Bond
Age range: 2–11 years

Unicorn School
238 Kew Road, Richmond, Surrey TW9 3JX
Tel: 020 8948 3926
Headteacher: Mrs Polly Fraley
Age range: 3–11 years

Westbury House
80 Westbury Road, New Malden, Surrey KT3 5AS
Tel: 020 8942 5885
Headteacher: Miss Clare King
Age range: 2–11 years

London

Central London D126
East London D126
North London D126
North-West London D127
South-East London D128
South-West London D129
West London D131

KEY TO SYMBOLS
- Boys' school
- Girls' school
- International school
- Tutorial or sixth form college
- A levels
- Boarding accommodation
- Bursaries
- International Baccalaureate
- Learning support
- Entrance at 16+
- Vocational qualifications
- Independent Association of Prep Schools
- The Headmasters' & Headmistresses' Conference
- Independent Schools Association
- Girls' School Association
- Boarding Schools' Association
- Society of Heads

Unless otherwise indicated, all schools are coeducational day schools. Single-sex and boarding schools will be indicated by the relevant icon.

ENGLAND: London

London

Central London

Charterhouse Square School
33-40 Charterhouse Square,
London EC1M 6EA
Tel: 020 7600 3805
Headteacher: Mrs Caroline Lloyd BEd (Hons)
Age range: 3–11 years

City Junior School
4 Gray's Inn Place, London WC1R 5EY
Tel: 020 3814 3506
Head: Ms Rachel Thompson
Age range: 7–11 years

Dallington School
8 Dallington Street, Islington, London EC1V 0BW
Tel: 020 7251 2284
Head of School: Mr James Griffiths
Age range: 3–11 years
No. of pupils: 81
Fees: Day £12,450–£15,660

École Jeannine Manuel - London
Bloomsbury, London WC1B 3DN
Tel: 020 3829 5970
Head of School: Pauline Prévot
Age range: 3–18 years
No. of pupils: 650
Fees: Day £23,970

St Paul's Cathedral School
2 New Change, London EC4M 9AD
Tel: 020 7248 5156
Head: Judith Fremont-Barnes MA (Hons), MEd
Age range: 4–13 years
No. of pupils: 287
Fees: Day £5,982–£6,440 FB £3,618

The Lyceum School
65 Worship Street, London EC2A 2DU
Tel: +44 (0)20 7247 1588
Headmaster: Mr Mike Stanley
Age range: 4–11 years

East London

Al-Falah Primary School
48 Kenninghall Road, Hackney, London E5 8BY
Tel: 020 8985 1059
Headteacher: Mr M A Hussain
Age range: 5–11 years

Al-Mizan School
46 Whitechapel Road, London E1 1JX
Tel: 020 7650 3070
Headteacher: Mr Mohammed Badr
Age range: B7–11 years

Azhar Academy Primary School
470 High Road, Leytonstone, London E11 3HN
Tel: 020 3327 1150
Headteacher: Ms Saima Ahmed
Age range: 3–11 years

Beis Trana Girls' School
186 Upper Clapton Road, London E5 9DH
Tel: 020 8815 8000
Age range: G3–16 years

Buttercup Primary School
181 Cannon Street Road, London E1 2LX
Tel: 020 3759 7408
Headteacher: Ms Rena Begum
Age range: 3–11 years

Chingford House Nursery
22 Marlborough Road, Waltham Forest, London E4 9AL
Tel: 02085 272902
Age range: 6 months–5 years

Daffodil Preparatory School
161-163 Commercial Road, Tower Hamlets, London E1 2DA
Tel: 020 4539 9737
Age range: 7–18 years

Faraday Prep School
Old Gate House, 7 Trinity Buoy Wharf, London E14 0JW
Tel: 020 8965 7374
Head Teacher: Lucas Motion
Age range: 4–11 years
No. of pupils: 108
Fees: Day £4,653

Forest School
College Place, Snaresbrook, London E17 3PY
Tel: 020 8520 1744
Warden: Mr Marcus Cliff Hodges
Age range: 4–18 years

Gatehouse School
Sewardstone Road, Victoria Park, London E2 9JG
Tel: 020 8980 2978
Headteacher: Mrs Sevda Korbay
Age range: 3–11 years

Grangewood Independent School
Chester Road, Forest Gate, London E7 8QT
Tel: 020 8472 3552
Headteacher: Mrs Beverley Roberts
Age range: 2–11 years

Hafs Academy
26 Maryland Road, Stratford, London E15 1JW
Tel: 020 8555 4260
Head of School: Mr Kazi Hussain
Age range: B7–16 years

Jasper City School
90A Lawson Close, London E16 3LU
Tel: 07957 163043
Head Teacher: Ms Michelle Kintu
Age range: 3–16 years

Lubavitch House School (Junior Boys)
135 Clapton Common, London E5 9AE
Tel: 020 8800 1044
Head: Mr R Leach
Age range: B5–11 years
No. of pupils: 101

Noor ul Islam Primary School
135 Dawlish Road, Leyton, London E10 6QW
Tel: 020 8558 0786
Interim Head Teacher: Aslam Hansa
Age range: 4–11 years

Normanhurst School
68-74 Station Road, Chingford, London E4 7BA
Tel: 020 8529 4307
Headmistress: Mrs Jacqueline Job
Age range: 2.5–16 years

Ohr Emes
148 Upper Clapton Road, London E5 9JZ
Tel: 020 8800 8932
Age range: B3–7 years

Pillar Box Montessori Nursery & Pre-Prep School
107 Bow Road, London E3 2AN
Tel: 020 8980 0700
Director: Lorraine Redknapp
Age range: 0–5 years
Fees: Day £12,000

Quwwat-ul-Islam Girls' School
16 Chaucer Road, Forest Gate, London E7 9NB
Tel: 020 8548 4736
Headteacher: Ms Shazia Member
Age range: G4–16 years

Snaresbrook Preparatory School
75 Woodford Road, South Woodford, London E18 2EA
Tel: 020 8989 2394
Headteacher: Mr Ralph Dalton
Age range: 3.5–11 years

Talmud Torah Machzikei Hadass School
1 Belz Terrace, Clapton, London E5 9SN
Tel: 020 8800 6599
Age range: B3–16 years

Walthamstow Montessori School
Penrhyn Hall, Penrhyn Avenue, Walthamstow, London E17 5DA
Tel: 020 8523 2968
Principal: Ms Lorna Mahoney
Age range: 2–6 years

Winston House Preparatory School
140 High Road, London E18 2QS
Tel: 020 8505 6565
Head Teacher: Mrs Marian Kemp
Age range: 3–11 years

North London

Annemount School
18 Holne Chase, Hampstead Garden Suburb, London N2 0QN
Tel: 020 8455 2132
Principal: Mrs G Maidment BA(Hons), MontDip
Age range: 2–7 years

Avenue Pre-Prep & Nursery School
2 Highgate Avenue, Highgate, London N6 5RX
Tel: 020 8348 6815
Head of School: Ms Sarah Tapp
Age range: 2–7 years

Beis Chinuch Lebonos Girls School
Woodberry Down Centre, Woodberry Down, London N4 2SH
Tel: 020 88097 737
Head of School: Mrs Leah Klein
Age range: G2–16 years

Beis Malka Girls School
93 Alkham Road, London N16 6XD
Tel: 020 8806 2070
Head of School: Mrs G Wind
Age range: G2–16 years

Beis Rochel D'Satmar Girls School
51-57 Amhurst Park, London N16 5DL
Tel: 020 8800 9060
Head of School: Mrs Elka Katz
Age range: G2–18 years

Bnois Jerusalem School
79-81 Amhurst Park, London N16 5DL
Tel: 020 8211 7136
Head of School: Mrs M Landau
Age range: G2–16 years

Bobov Primary School
87-90 Egerton Road, London N16 6UE
Tel: 020 8809 1025
Head of School: Mr Yossi Elzas
Age range: B2–13 years

Channing School
The Bank, Highgate, London N6 5HF
Tel: 020 8340 2328
Headmistress: Mrs Lindsey Hughes
Age range: G4–18 years

Dania Scandinavian School
Curran House, 3 Highbury Crescent, London N5 1RN
Tel: 07933 619674
Headteacher: Ms Katie Howard
Age range: 2–11 years

Dwight School London
6 Friern Barnet Lane, London N11 3LX
Tel: 020 8920 0600
Head: Chris Beddows
Age range: 2–18 years

Finchley & Acton Yochien School
6 Hendon Avenue, Finchley, London N3 1UE
Tel: 020 8343 2191
Head of School: Ms Junko Tanabe
Age range: 2–6 years

Grange Park Preparatory School
13 The Chine, Grange Park, Winchmore Hill, London N21 2EA
Tel: 020 8360 1469
Headteacher: Ms Flavia Rizzo
Age range: 3–11 years

Highgate Junior School
Cholmeley House, 3 Bishopswood Road, London N6 4PL
Tel: 020 8340 9193
Principal: Ms Philippa Studd
Age range: 7–11 years

London: ENGLAND

Highgate Pre-Preparatory School
7 Bishopswood Road, London N6 4PH
Tel: 020 8340 9196
Principal: Ms Sally Hancock
Age range: 4–7 years

Hyland House School
Holcombe Road, Tottenham, London N17 9AB
Tel: 0208 520 4186
Headteacher: Mr Errol Gayle
Age range: 2–11 years

Keble Prep
Wades Hill, Winchmore Hill, London N21 1BG
Tel: 020 8360 3359
Headmaster: Mr Perran Gill BA (Hons)
Age range: 3–13 years

Kerem School
Norrice Lea, Hampstead Garden Suburb, London N2 0RE
Tel: 020 8455 0909
Head Teacher: Ms Naomi Simon
Age range: 3–11 years

Norfolk House School
10 Muswell Avenue, Muswell Hill, London N10 2EG
Tel: +44 (0)2088 834584
Headteacher: Mr Tej Lander
Age range: 2–11 years

North London Grammar School
110 Colindeep Lane, Hendon, London NW9 6HB
Tel: 0208 205 0052
Headteacher: Mr Fatih Adak
Age range: 7–18 years

North London Rudolf Steiner School
1-3 The Campsbourne, London N8 7PN
Tel: 020 8341 3770
Age range: 0–6 years

Palmers Green High School
104 Hoppers Road, London N21 3LJ
Tel: 020 8886 1135
Head: Ms Sarah Proudlove
Age range: G4–16 years

Phoenix Academy
85 Bounces Road, Edmonton, London N9 8LD
Tel: 020 8807 6888
Head Teacher: Mr Paul Kelly
Age range: 5–18 years

Rosemary Works Independent School
1 Branch Place, London N1 5PH
Tel: 02077 393950
Headteacher: Ms Amanda Parker NPQH, MPhil
Age range: 3–11 years

Salcombe Preparatory School
Green Road, London N14 4AD
Tel: 020 8441 5356
Headmistress: Miss Nicola Sands
Age range: 3–11 years

Shakhsiyah School, London
1st Floor, 277 St Ann's Road, London N15 5RG
Tel: 020 8802 8651
Executive Headteacher: Mr Ziaur Rahman
Age range: 3–14 years

St Paul's Steiner School
1 St Paul's Road, Islington, London N1 2QH
Tel: 020 7226 4454
Head Teacher: Ms Anna Retsler
Age range: 3–14 years

Sunrise Nursery Stoke Newington
1 Cazenove Road, Stoke Newington, Hackney, London N16 6PA
Tel: 0208 8066279
Principal: Ms Didi Ananda Manika
Age range: 15 months–5 years

Talmud Torah Chaim Meirim School
26 Lampard Grove, London N16 6XB
Tel: 020 8806 0898
Age range: B5–13 years

Talmud Torah Yetev Lev School
111-115 Cazenove Road, London N16 6AX
Tel: 020 8806 3834
Age range: B3–11 years

Tayyibah Girls School
88 Filey Avenue, Hackney, London N16 6JJ
Tel: 020 8880 0085
Head Teacher: Mrs Sumeya Patel
Age range: G4–18 years

The Children's House Upper School
King Henry's Walk, London N1 4PB
Tel: 020 7249 6273
Headteacher: Ms Ellie Grunewald
Age range: 4–7 years

The Gower School Nursery
18 North Road, Islington, London N7 9EY
Tel: 020 7700 2445
Principal: Miss Emma Gowers
Age range: 3 months–5 years

The Gower School Primary
10 Cynthia Street, Barnsbury, London N1 9JF
Tel: 020 7278 2020
Principal: Miss Emma Gowers
Age range: 4–11 years

TTTYY School
14 Heathland Road, London N16 5NH
Tel: 020 8802 1348
Head of School: Rabbi Y.Y. Friesel
Age range: B2–13 years

Vita et Pax School
6a Priory Close, Green Road, Southgate, London N14 4AT
Tel: 020 8449 8336
Headteacher: Ms Allana Gay
Age range: 3–11 years

Yesodey Hatorah Senior Girls' School
Egerton Road, London N16 6UB
Tel: 020 8826 5500
Acting Head Teacher: Mrs C Neuberger
Age range: 3–16 years
No. of pupils: 920

North-West London

Al-Sadiq & Al-Zahra Schools
134 Salusbury Road, London NW6 6PF
Tel: 020 7372 7706
Heads: Mr Seyed Alireza Khoei & Mrs Zamina Rizvi
Age range: 3–16 years

Arnold House School
1 Loudoun Road, St John's Wood, London NW8 0LH
Tel: 020 7266 4840
Headmaster: Mr Giles F Tollit
Age range: B3–13 years

Barnet Hill Academy
10A Montagu Road, Hendon, London NW4 3ES
Tel: 020 3411 2660
Principal: Mr Alim Shaikh MA, PGCE, MPhil, NPQH
Age range: 3–11 years

Beis Soroh Schneirer
Arbiter House, Wilberforce Road, London NW9 6AX
Tel: 020 8201 7771
Head of School: Mrs Sonia Mossberg
Age range: G2–11 years

Belmont, Mill Hill Preparatory School
The Ridgeway, London NW7 4ED
Tel: 020 8906 7270
Head of School: Dr Susannah Abbott
Age range: 7–13 years
No. of pupils: 580
Fees: Day £26,835–£27,675

Broadhurst School
19 Greencroft Gardens, London NW6 3LP
Tel: 020 7328 4280
Headmistress: Mrs Zoe Sylvester
Age range: 2–5 years

Collège Français Bilingue de Londres (CFBL)
87 Holmes Road, Kentish Town, London NW5 3AX
Tel: 020 7993 7400
Head of School: Mr David Gassian
Age range: 3–15 years
No. of pupils: 700

Devonshire House Preparatory School
2 Arkwright Road, Hampstead, London NW3 6AE
Tel: 020 7435 1916
Headmistress: Mrs S. Piper BA(Hons)
Age range: B2.5–13 years G2.5–11 years
No. of pupils: 543
Fees: Day £9,870–£20,475

Goodwyn School
Hammers Lane, Mill Hill, London NW7 4DB
Tel: 020 8959 3756
Principal: Mr Struan Robertson
Age range: 3–11 years

Grimsdell, Mill Hill Pre-Preparatory School
Winterstoke House, Wills Grove, Mill Hill, London NW7 1QR
Tel: 020 8959 6884
Head: Mrs Kate Simon BA, PGCE
Age range: 3–7 years
No. of pupils: 221
Fees: Day £17,400–£22,785

Hampstead Hill School
St Stephen's Hall, Pond Street, Hampstead, London NW3 2PP
Tel: 020 7435 6262
Headteacher: Mr Ross Montague
Age range: 2–7+ years

Heathside School Hampstead
84a Heath Street, Hampstead, London NW3 1DN
Tel: +44 (0)20 3058 4011
Headteacher: Nadia Ward
Age range: 2–11 years
No. of pupils: 105
Fees: Day £19,665–£20,535

Hendon Prep School
20 Tenterden Grove, Hendon, London NW4 1TD
Tel: 020 8203 7727
Headteacher: Mrs Tushi Gorasia
Age range: 3–11 years
No. of pupils: 170

Hereward House School
14 Strathray Gardens, Hampstead, London NW3 4NY
Tel: 020 7794 4820
Headmaster: Mr Pascal Evans
Age range: B4–13 years
No. of pupils: 173
Fees: Day £19,350–£19,890

IRIS School
100 Carlton Vale, London NW6 5HE
Tel: 020 7372 8051
Headteacher: Mr Seyed Abbas Hosseini
Age range: 6–16 years

Ivy House School
Ivy House, 94-96 North End Road, London NW11 7SX
Tel: +44 (0)20 3869 3070
Headmaster: Mr Donal Brennan
Age range: 2–11 years
No. of pupils: 90

La Petite Ecole Bilingue Londres Kentish Town
22 Vicar's Road, London NW5 4NL
Tel: 020 7284 26 20
Head of Administration: Ms Natasha Henderson-Stewart
Age range: 3–11 years

Lyndhurst House Prep School
24 Lyndhurst Gardens, Hampstead, London NW3 5NW
Tel: 020 7435 4936
Head of School: Mr Andrew Reid MA (Oxon)
Age range: B4–13 years
No. of pupils: 125
Fees: Day £18,360–£20,790

ENGLAND: London

Maple Walk Prep School
62A Crownhill Road,
London NW10 4EB
Tel: 020 8963 3890
Head Teacher: Claire Murdoch
Age range: 4–11 years
No. of pupils: 174
Fees: Day £4,518

Maria Montessori School - Hampstead
26 Lyndhurst Gardens,
Hampstead, London NW3 5NW
Tel: 020 7435 3646
Age range: 2.5–12 years

Naima Jewish Preparatory School
21 Andover Place, London NW6 5ED
Tel: 020 7328 2802
Headmaster: Mr Bill Pratt
Age range: 2–11 years

Nancy Reuben Primary School
48 Finchley Lane, Hendon,
London NW4 1DJ
Tel: 020 8202 5646
Head Teacher: Mr Anthony Wolfson
Age range: 2–11 years

North Bridge House Nursery and Pre-Prep Hampstead
8 Netherhall Gardens,
London NW3 5RR
Tel: 020 7428 1520
Head of School: Mrs Christine McLelland
Age range: 2–7 years
No. of pupils: 190

North Bridge House Nursery and Pre-Prep West Hampstead
85-87 Fordwych Rd, London NW2 3TL
Tel: 020 7428 1520
Head of School: Mrs Christine McLelland
Age range: 2–7 years

North Bridge House Prep School Regent's Park
1 Gloucester Avenue,
London NW1 7AB
Tel: 020 7428 1520
Head of School: Mr Tom Le Tissier
Age range: 7–13 years
No. of pupils: 360
Fees: Day £21,810–£23,795

Rainbow Montessori School
13 Woodchurch Road,
Hampstead, London NW6 3PL
Tel: 020 7328 8986
Head Mistress: Maggy Miller MontDip
Age range: 2–5 years

Saint Christina's School
25 St Edmund's Terrace, St John's Wood, London NW8 7PY
Tel: 020 7722 8784
Headteacher: Mr Alastair Gloag
Age range: 3–11 years

Sarum Hall School
15 Eton Avenue, London NW3 3EL
Tel: 020 7794 2261
Headmistress: Miss Karen Coles BEd (Hons), Exon
Age range: G3–11 years
No. of pupils: 188

South Hampstead High School GDST
3 Maresfield Gardens,
London NW3 5SS
Tel: 020 7435 2899
Headmistress: Mrs Victoria Bingham MA (Oxon)
Age range: G4–18 years

Southbank International School - Hampstead
16 Netherhall Gardens,
London NW3 5TH
Tel: 020 3890 1969
Head of School: Stuart Bain
Age range: 2–11 years

St Christopher's School
32 Belsize Lane, Hampstead,
London NW3 5AE
Tel: 020 7435 1521
Head of School: Mr Mark Maddocks
Age range: G4–11 years

St Margaret's School
18 Kidderpore Gardens,
Hampstead, London NW3 7SR
Tel: 020 7435 2439
Principal: Mr Mark Webster BSc, PGCE
Age range: G4–16 years

St Martin's School
22 Goodwyn Avenue, Mill Hill, London NW7 3RG
Tel: 020 8959 1965
Headteacher: Mrs Samantha Mbah
Age range: 3–11 years

St Mary's School, Hampstead
47 Fitzjohn's Avenue, Hampstead,
London NW3 6PG
Tel: 020 7435 1868
Headteacher: Miss Charlotte Owen
Age range: G2 years 6 months–11 years
No. of pupils: 300
Fees: Day £3,345–£6,180

St Nicholas School
22 Salmon Street, London NW9 8PN
Tel: 020 8205 7153
Headmaster: Mr Matt Donaldson BA (Hons), PGCE, PGDip (Surv)
Age range: 3 months–11 years

St. Anthony's School for Boys
90 Fitzjohn's Avenue, Hampstead,
London NW3 6NP
Tel: 020 7431 1066
Head of School: Mr Richard Berlie MA (Cantab)
Age range: B2.5–13 years G2.5–4 years
No. of pupils: 275

The Academy School
3 Pilgrims Place, Rosslyn Hill,
Hampstead, London NW3 1NG
Tel: 020 7435 6621
Headteacher: Mr Garth Evans BA (Lond)
Age range: 6–13 years

The American School in London
One Waverley Place,
London NW8 0NP
Tel: +44 (0)20 7449 1200
Head of School: Ms Coreen R. Hester
Age range: 4–18 years

The Cavendish School
31 Inverness Street, Camden Town, London NW1 7HB
Tel: 020 7485 1958
Head of School: Mrs Taryn Lombard
Age range: G3–11 years

The Hall School
23 Crossfield Road, Hampstead,
London NW3 4NU
Tel: 020 7722 1700
Headmaster: Mr Chris Godwin
Age range: B4–13 years

The King Alfred School
North End Road, London NW11 7HY
Tel: 020 8457 5200
Head: Robert Lobatto MA (Oxon)
Age range: 4–18 years
No. of pupils: 670

The Mulberry House School
7 Minster Road, West Hampstead,
London NW2 3SD
Tel: 020 8452 7340
Headteacher: Ms Victoria Playford BA Hons, QTS
Age range: 2–7+ years

The Village Prep School
2 Parkhill Road, Belsize Park, London NW3 2YN
Tel: 020 7485 4673
Head of School: Mrs Kirstie Hampshire
Age range: G2–11 years

Torah Vodaas
Brent Park Road, West Hendon Broadway, London NW9 7AJ
Tel: 020 3670 4670
Head of School: Rabbi Y Feldman
Age range: B2–11 years

Trevor-Roberts School
55-57 Eton Avenue, London NW3 3ET
Tel: 020 7586 1444
Co-Heads: Simon & Amanda Trevor-Roberts
Age range: 5–13 years

University College School Hampstead (UCS) Junior
11 Holly Hill, Hampstead,
London NW3 6QN
Tel: 020 7435 3068
Headmaster: Mr Lewis Hayward
Age range: B7–11 years

University College School Hampstead (UCS) Pre-Prep
36 College Crescent,
Hampstead, London NW3 5LF
Tel: 020 7722 4833
Headmistress: Ms Zoe Dunn
Age range: B4–7 years

South-East London

Alleyn's School
Townley Road, Dulwich,
London SE22 8SU
Tel: 020 8557 1500
Head of School: Ms Jane Lunnon
Age range: 4–18 years

Blackheath High School GDST
Vanbrugh Park, Blackheath,
London SE3 7AG
Tel: 020 8853 2929
Acting Head: Ms Natalie Argile
Age range: G3–18 years

BLACKHEATH PREP
For further details see p. 61
4 St Germans Place,
Blackheath, London SE3 0NJ
Tel: 020 8858 0692
Email: info@blackheathprep.co.uk
Website: www.blackheathprep.co.uk
Head: Mr Alex Matthews
Age range: 3–11 years
No. of pupils: 388

Colfe's Junior School
Upwood Road, London SE12 8AA
Tel: 020 8463 8266
Head of School: Mrs M-C Gilfedder-Bonnar
Age range: 3–11 years

Dulwich College
Dulwich Common, London SE21 7LD
Tel: 020 8693 3601
Master: Dr J A F Spence
Age range: B6 months–18 years G6 months–7 years
Fees: Day £24,693 WB £48,324 FB £51,546

Dulwich College Kindergarten & Infants School
Eller Bank, 87 College Road,
London SE21 7HH
Tel: 020 8693 1538
Head: Mrs Miranda Norris
Age range: 3 months–7 years
No. of pupils: 251

Dulwich Prep London
42 Alleyn Park, Dulwich,
London SE21 7AA
Tel: 020 8766 5500
Head Master: Miss Louise Davidson
Age range: B3–13 years (boarding from 8) G3–5 years

Eltham College Junior School
Mottingham Lane, Mottingham,
London SE9 4RW
Tel: 020 8857 3457
Head of School: Mrs Vikki Meier
Age range: 7–11 years

Greenwich Steiner School
90 Mycenae Road, London SE3 7SE
Tel: 020 8858 4404
Executive Principal: Mr Allan Osborne
Age range: 3–18 years

London: ENGLAND

Heath House Preparatory School
37 Wemyss Road, Blackheath, London SE3 0TG
Tel: 020 8297 1900
Head Teacher: Mrs Sophia Laslett CertEd PGDE
Age range: 3–11 years

Herne Hill School
The Old Vicarage, 127 Herne Hill, London SE24 9LY
Tel: 020 7274 6336
Headteacher: Mrs Ngaire Telford
Age range: 2–7 years

James Allen's Girls' School
144 East Dulwich Grove, Dulwich, London SE22 8TE
Tel: 020 8693 1181
Head of School: Mrs Alex Hutchinson
Age range: G4–18 years

Kings Kids Christian School
100 Woodpecker Road, Newcross, London SE14 6EU
Tel: 020 8259 3659
Headteacher: Mrs M Okenwa
Age range: 3–11 years

London Christian School
40 Tabard Street, London SE1 4JU
Tel: 02031 306430
Head Teacher: Miss Nicola Collett-White
Age range: 3–11 years

Oakfield Preparatory School
125-128 Thurlow Park Road, West Dulwich, London SE21 8HP
Tel: 020 8670 4206
Head of School: Mrs Gemma Davies
Age range: 2–11 years
No. of pupils: 303

Octavia House School, Vauxhall
Vauxhall Street, London SE11 5LG
Tel: 020 3651 4396 (option 1)
Assistant Principal: Ms Ross
Age range: 5–11 years

Octavia House School, Walworth
Larcom Street, London SE17 1RT
Tel: 020 3651 4396 (option 2)
Assistant Principal: Mr Dickens
Age range: 11–14 years

Riverston School
63/69 Eltham Road, Lee, London SE12 8UF
Tel: 020 8318 4327
Headmaster: Mr David A T Ward MA
Age range: 9 months–19 years

Rosemead Preparatory School & Nursery, Dulwich
70 Thurlow Park Road, Dulwich, London SE21 8HZ
Tel: 020 8670 5865
Head of School: Mr Graeme McCafferty
Age range: 2.5–11 years

St Dunstan's College
Stanstead Road, London SE6 4TY
Tel: 020 8516 7200
Head of School: Mr Nick Hewlett
Age range: 3–18 years

St Olave's Preparatory School
106-110 Southwood Road, New Eltham, London SE9 3QS
Tel: 020 8294 8930
Headteacher: Miss Claire Holloway BEd, QTS
Age range: 3–11 years

Sydenham High School GDST
15 & 19 Westwood Hill, London SE26 6BL
Tel: 020 8557 7004
Head of School: Ms Antonia Geldeard
Age range: G4–18 years

The New School London
St. Mary's Lodge, 149 Central Hill, London SE19 1RT
Tel: 020 4513 0505
Co-Headteachers: Dhama Sangarabalan & Callie Sharma
Age range: 4–16 years

The Pointer School
19 Stratheden Road, Blackheath, London SE3 7TH
Tel: 020 8293 1331
Head of School: Ms Charlotte Crookes MA (Cantab), MA, PGCE
Age range: 3–11 years

The Villa School & Nursery
54 Lyndhurst Grove, Peckham, London SE15 5AH
Tel: 020 7703 6216
Head Teacher: Ms Louise Maughan
Age range: 2–7 years

South-West London

Bertrum House Nursery
290 Balham High Road, London SW17 7AL
Tel: 020 8767 4051
Age range: 2–5 years

Brighton College Prep Kensington
10-13 Prince's Gardens, London SW7 1ND
Tel: 0207 591 4622
Head of School: Mrs Lois Gaffney
Age range: 3–11 years

Broomwood Prep - Boys
26 Bolingbroke Grove, London SW11 6EL
Tel: 020 8682 8888
Head & Group Principal (from Sep 24): Mr Michael Hodge
Age range: B7–13 years
No. of pupils: 217
Fees: Day £7,535

Broomwood Prep - Girls
68-74 Nightingale Lane, London SW12 8NR
Tel: 020 8682 8810
Head: Mrs Louisa McCafferty
Age range: G7–13 years
No. of pupils: 217
Fees: Day £7,535

Broomwood Pre-Prep and Little Broomwood
192 Ramsden Road, London SW12 8RQ
Tel: 020 8682 8840
Head of School: Mrs Caron Mackay
Age range: 3–7 years
No. of pupils: 300

Cameron Vale School
4 The Vale, Chelsea, London SW3 6AH
Tel: 020 7352 4040
Headteacher: Ms Alison Melrose
Age range: 6 months–11 years
No. of pupils: 66

Dolphin School
106 Northcote Road, London SW11 6QW
Tel: 020 7924 3472
Head Teacher: Mr S Gosden
Age range: 2–11 years
No. of pupils: 162
Fees: Day £13,395–£14,670

Donhead Preparatory School
33 Edge Hill, Wimbledon, London SW19 4NP
Tel: 020 8946 7000
Headteacher: Catherine Hitchcock
Age range: 3–11 years

Eaton House Belgravia
3-5 Eaton Gate, London SW1W 9BA
Tel: 020 3917 5050
Headmaster: Mr Ross Montague
Age range: B2–11 years G2–4 years
No. of pupils: 180

Eaton House The Manor Boys' School
58 Clapham Common North Side, London SW4 9RU
Tel: 020 3917 5050
Head of Prep: Mrs Sarah Segrave
Age range: B2–13 years G2–4 years
No. of pupils: 430

Eaton House The Manor Girls' School
58 Clapham Common North Side, London SW4 9RU
Tel: 020 3917 5050
Headteacher: Mrs Claire Fildes
Age range: B2–4 years G2–11 years
No. of pupils: 220

Eaton Square Prep School
55-57 Eccleston Square, London SW1V 1PP
Tel: 0207 225 3131
Head of School: Ms Trish Watt
Age range: 4–11 years

Eveline Day School
Swan House, 207 Balham High Road, London SW17 7BQ
Tel: 020 8673 3188
Head Teacher: Ms Eveline Drut
Age range: 2–11 years

Evergreen Primary School
9 Swan Mews, Fulham, London SW6 4QT
Tel: 07429 112217
Headteacher: Ms Rena Begum
Age range: 3–11 years

Falcons School
11 Woodborough Road, Putney, London SW15 6PY
Tel: +44 (0)20 8992 5189
Headmistress: Mrs Sara Williams-Ryan
Age range: 2–11 years
No. of pupils: 134
Fees: Day £6,025

Falkner House
19 Brechin Place, South Kensington, London SW7 4QB
Tel: 02073 734501
Headteachers: Mrs Flavia Rogers & Mrs Eleanor Dixon
Age range: 2–11 years

Finton House School
171 Trinity Road, London SW17 7HL
Tel: 020 8682 0921
Head of School: Mr Ben Freeman
Age range: 4–11 years

Francis Holland Preparatory School
15 Manresa Road, London SW3 6NB
Tel: +44 (0)20 7352 7077
Head of School: Ms Suzy Dixon
Age range: 4–11 years

Francis Holland School, Sloane Square, SW1
39 Graham Terrace, London SW1W 8JF
Tel: 020 7730 2971
Head: Mrs Alexandra Haydon (MSc Oxon, BSc Durham)
Age range: G4–18 years

Garden House School
Turks Row, Chelsea, London SW3 4TW
Tel: 020 7730 1652/6652
Principals: Mr Christian Warland & Mrs Sophie Strafford
Age range: 3–11 years

Glendower Preparatory School
86/87 Queen's Gate, London SW7 5JX
Tel: 020 7370 1927
Head of School: Ms Claire Boyd
Age range: G3–11 years
No. of pupils: 290
Fees: Day £8,000–£8,600

Hall School Wimbledon Junior School
17, The Downs, Wimbledon, London SW20 8HF
Tel: 020 8879 9200
Headmaster: Mr. A Hammond
Age range: 5–11 years

Harrodian
Lonsdale Road, London SW13 9QN
Tel: 020 8748 6117
Headmaster: Mr James R Hooke
Age range: 4–18 years

Hill House
17 Hans Place, Chelsea, London SW1X 0EP
Tel: 020 7584 1331
Headmaster: Mr Richard Townend
Age range: 4–13 years

ENGLAND: London

Hornsby House School
Hearnville Road, Balham, London SW12 8RS
Tel: 020 8673 7573
Headmaster: Mr Edward Rees
Age range: 4–11 years

Hurlingham School
122 Putney Bridge Road, Putney, London SW15 2NQ
Tel: 020 8103 0823
Headmaster: Mr Simon Gould
Age range: 4–11 years

Ibstock Place School
Clarence Lane, Roehampton, London SW15 5PY
Tel: 020 8876 9991
Head of School: Mr Christopher J Wolsey
Age range: 4–18 years

Kensington Prep School
596 Fulham Road, London SW6 5PA
Tel: 0207 731 9300
Head of School: Mrs Caroline Hulme-McKibbin
Age range: G4–11 years
Fees: Day £6,954

Knightsbridge School
67 Pont Street, Knightsbridge, London SW1X 0BD
Tel: +44 (0)20 7590 9000
Head: Miss Shona Colaço
Age range: 3–16 years
No. of pupils: 400
Fees: Day £7,975

L'Ecole de Battersea
Trott Street, Battersea, London SW11 3DS
Tel: 020 7371 8350
Principal: Mrs F Brisset
Age range: 3–11 years
No. of pupils: 250
Fees: Day £5,625

L'Ecole des Petits
2 Hazlebury Road, Fulham, London SW6 2NB
Tel: 020 7371 8350
Principal: Mrs F Brisset
Age range: 3–6 years
No. of pupils: 120
Fees: Day £5,470

Lycée Français Charles de Gaulle de Londres
35 Cromwell Road, London SW7 2DG
Tel: 020 7584 6322
Headteacher: Catherine Bellus-Ferreira
Age range: 3–18 years
No. of pupils: 3450
Fees: Day £8,089–£16,923

Newton Prep
149 Battersea Park Road, London SW8 4BX
Tel: 020 7720 4091
Headmistress: Mrs Alison Fleming BA, MA Ed, PGCE
Age range: 3–13 years
No. of pupils: 646
Fees: Day £10,575–£22,395

Oliver House Preparatory School
7 Nightingale Lane, London SW4 9AH
Tel: 020 8772 1911
Headteacher: Mr Rob Farrell
Age range: 3–11 years
No. of pupils: 144
Fees: Day £6,600–£15,090

Parkgate House School
80 Clapham Common North Side, London SW4 9SD
Tel: +44 (0)20 7350 2461
Principal: Miss Catherine Shanley
Age range: 2.5–11 years

Parsons Green Prep School
1 Fulham Park Road, Fulham, London SW6 4LJ
Tel: 020 7371 9009
Head: Dr Pamela Edmonds
Age range: 4–11 years

Prospect House School
75 Putney Hill, London SW15 3NT
Tel: 020 8780 0456
Head of School: Mrs Kelly Gray BA (Leeds), PGCE
Age range: 3–11 years
No. of pupils: 287
Fees: Day £10,785–£23,695

Putney High School GDST
35 Putney Hill, London SW15 6BH
Tel: 020 8788 4886
Headmistress: Mrs Suzie Longstaff BA, MA, PGCE
Age range: G4–18 years

Queen's Gate School
133 Queen's Gate, London SW7 5LE
Tel: 020 7589 3587
Principal: Miss Amy Wallace MA MPhil (Cantab), PGCE (Oxon)
Age range: G4–18 years
No. of pupils: 469

Redcliffe Gardens School
47 Redcliffe Gardens, Chelsea, London SW10 9JH
Tel: 020 7352 9247
Head: Mrs Sarah Glencross
Age range: 2.5–11 years

Sinclair House Montessori Nursery
159 & 196 Munster Road, Fulham, London SW6 6AU
Tel: 0207 736 9182
Principal: Mrs Carlotta T M O'Sullivan

Sinclair House Preparatory School
59 Fulham High Street, Fulham, London SW6 3JJ
Tel: 0207 736 9182
Principal: Mrs Carlotta T M O'Sullivan
Age range: 2–11 years
No. of pupils: 120
Fees: Day £5,280–£17,025

St Paul's Juniors
St Paul's School, Lonsdale Road, London SW13 9JT
Tel: 020 8748 3461
Head of School: Mr Oliver Snowball
Age range: B7–13 years

St Philip's School
6 Wetherby Place, London SW7 4NE
Tel: 020 7373 3944
Head Master: Mr A Thomas
Age range: B7–13 years

Streatham & Clapham High School GDST
42 Abbotswood Road, London SW16 1AW
Tel: 020 8677 8400
Executive Head: Mrs Isabel Tobias MA (Cantab), PGCE
Age range: G3–18 years

Sussex House School
68 Cadogan Square, London SW1X 0EA
Tel: 020 7584 1741
Headmaster: Mr N P Kaye MA(Cantab), ACP, FRSA, FRGS
Age range: B8–13 years

Swedish School in London
82 Lonsdale Road, Barnes, London SW13 9JS
Tel: 020 8741 1751
Head of School: Ms. Jenny Abrahamsson
Age range: 3–18 years

The Merlin School
4 Carlton Drive, Putney, London SW15 2BZ
Tel: 020 8788 2769
Headteacher: Miss Violet McConville
Age range: 4–8 years
No. of pupils: 100
Fees: Day £6,315

The Montessori Pavilion - The Kindergarten School
Vine Road, Barnes, London SW13 0NE
Tel: 07554 277 746
Headmistress: Ms Georgina Dashwood
Age range: 3–8 years
No. of pupils: 50

The Norwegian School in London
28 Arterberry Road, Wimbledon, London SW20 8AH
Tel: 020 8947 6617
Headteacher: Ms Lise Meling Karlsen
Age range: 6–16 years

The Roche School
11 Frogmore, London SW18 1HW
Tel: 020 8877 0823
Headmaster: Mr Jonny Gilbert BA (Cantab.), MA (Cantab.)
Age range: 2–11 years
No. of pupils: 282
Fees: Day £19,770–£20,280

The Rowans School
19 Drax Avenue, Wimbledon, London SW20 0EG
Tel: 020 8946 8220
Head of School: Miss Elizabeth Spratt BMus PGCE Primary QTS
Age range: 3–7 years

The Study Preparatory School
Wilberforce House, Camp Road, Wimbledon Common, London SW19 4UN
Tel: 020 8947 6969
Interim Head: Ms Helen Lowe
Age range: G4–11 years

The White House Preparatory School & Woodentops Kindergarten
24 Thornton Road, Clapham, London SW12 0LF
Tel: 020 8674 9514
Headmaster: Mr. Tony Lewis
Age range: 3–11 years

Thomas's Academy
New King's Road, London SW6 4LY
Tel: 020 7736 2318
Head of School: Ms Suzanne Kelly
Age range: 4–11 years

Thomas's Battersea
28-40 Battersea High Street, London SW11 3JB
Tel: 020 7978 0900
Head of School: Mr Ben Thomas
Age range: 4–13 years

Thomas's Clapham
Broomwood Road, London SW11 6JZ
Tel: 020 7326 9300
Head of School: Mr Nathan Boller
Age range: 4–13 years

Thomas's Fulham
Hugon Road, London SW6 3ES
Tel: 020 7751 8200
Head of School: Ms Annette Dobson
Age range: 4–11 years

Thomas's Outdoors
Stroud Crescent, London SW15 3EQ
Tel: 020 7751 8200
Head of School: Mr Paul Wild
Age range: 4–18 years

Tower House School
188 Sheen Lane, East Sheen, London SW14 8LF
Tel: 020 8876 3323
Head of School: Mr Neill Lunnon
Age range: B4–13 years

Wandsworth Preparatory School
The Old Library, 2 Allfarthing Lane, London SW18 2PQ
Tel: +44 (0)2088 704133
Headteacher: Ms Laura Nike
Age range: 4–11 years

Westminster Abbey Choir School
Dean's Yard, Westminster, London SW1P 3NY
Tel: 020 7654 4918
Acting Headmaster: Mr Mark Mitchell
Age range: B8–13 years

Westminster Cathedral Choir School
Ambrosden Avenue, London SW1P 1QH
Tel: 020 7798 9081
Headmaster: Mr Neil McLaughlan
Age range: B4–13 years

London: ENGLAND

Westminster Under School
27 Vincent Square, London SW1P 2NN
Tel: 020 7821 5788
Master: Mrs C J Jefferson
Age range: B7–13 years

Wetherby Kensington
4 Wetherby Gardens, London SW5 0JN
Tel: 020 3910 9760
Executive Head: Mr Mark Snell
Age range: B4–8 years

Willington Independent Preparatory School
Worcester Road, Wimbledon, London SW19 7QQ
Tel: 020 8944 7020
Headmaster: Mr Keith Brown
Age range: 3–11 years

Wimbledon Common Preparatory School
113 Ridgway, Wimbledon, London SW19 4TA
Tel: 020 8946 1001
Head Teacher: Mr Andrew Forbes
Age range: B4–7 years

Wimbledon High School GDST
Mansel Road, Wimbledon, London SW19 4AB
Tel: 020 8971 0900
Head of School: Ms Fionnuala Kennedy
Age range: G4–18 years

West London

Avenue House School
70 The Avenue, Ealing, London W13 8LS
Tel: 020 8998 9981
Headteacher: Ravinder Nandra
Age range: 4–11 years

AZBUKA Russian-English Bilingual School
Studland Hall, Studland Street, Hammersmith, London W6 0JS
Tel: 020 8392 2286
Head Teacher: Ms Maria Gavrilova
Age range: 2–11 years

Bassett House School
60 Bassett Road, Notting Hill, London W10 6JP
Tel: 020 8969 0313
Head of School: Mr Chris Woodward
Age range: 3–11 years
No. of pupils: 131
Fees: Day £11,601–£23,940

Bute House Preparatory School for Girls
Bute House, Luxemburg Gardens, London W6 7EA
Tel: 020 7603 7381
Head of School: Ms Sian Bradshaw
Age range: G4–11 years

Chepstow House School
108a Lancaster Road, Notting Hill, London W11 1QS
Tel: 020 7243 0243
Headteacher: Ms Angela Barr
Age range: 2.5–11 years

Chiswick & Bedford Park Prep School
Priory House, Priory Avenue, London W4 1TX
Tel: 020 8994 1804
Head of School: Ms Henrietta Adams
Age range: B3–7+ years G3–11 years

Clifton Lodge School
8 Mattock Lane, Ealing, London W5 5BG
Tel: 020 8579 3662
Head of School: Mr Michael Belsito
Age range: 3–11 years
No. of pupils: 130
Fees: Day £14,400–£17,475

Connaught House School
47 Connaught Square, Westminster, London W2 2HL
Tel: 020 7262 8830
Principal: Ms Victoria Hampton
Age range: 4–11 years

Durston House
12-14 Castlebar Road, Ealing, London W5 2DR
Tel: 020 8991 6530
Headmaster: Mr Giles Entwisle
Age range: B3–13 years
No. of pupils: 389
Fees: Day £4,750–£6,180

Ecole Française de Londres Jacques Prévert
59 Brook Green, Hammersmith, London W6 7BE
Tel: 020 7602 6871
Director: Ms Sylvie Wanin
Age range: 4–11 years

Falcons Pre-Preparatory Chiswick
2 Burnaby Gardens, Chiswick, London W4 3DT
Tel: 020 8747 8393
Head: Ms Liz McLaughlin
Age range: B2–7 years G2–4 years

Fulham School
1-3 Chesilton Road, London SW6 5AA
Tel: 020 8154 6751
Executive Head of Fulham: Bex Tear
Age range: 3–18 years
No. of pupils: 600

Great Beginnings Montessori Nursery
39 Brendon Street, London W1H 5JE
Tel: 020 7258 1066
Head: Mrs Wendy Innes
Age range: 2–6 years

Greek Primary School of London
3 Pierrepoint Road, Acton, London W3 9JR
Tel: 020 8896 2118
Primary School Head Teacher: Ms Katerina Papagianni
Age range: 4–11 years

Harvington School
20 Castlebar Road, Ealing, London W5 2DS
Tel: 020 8997 1583
Headteacher: Mr Giles Entwisle
Age range: B3–7 years G3–11 years

Hawkesdown House School Kensington
27 Edge Street, Kensington, London W8 7PN
Tel: 020 7727 9090
Headmistress: Mrs S Gillam BEd (Cantab)
Age range: 2–8 years
No. of pupils: 100
Fees: Day £4,725–£21,120

Heathfield House School
Heathfield Gardens, Chiswick, London W4 4JU
Tel: 020 8994 3385
Headteacher: Ms Caroline Goodsman
Age range: 4–11 years

Holland Park Pre Prep School and Day Nursery
5, Holland Road, Kensington, London W14 8HJ
Tel: 020 7602 9066/020 7602 9266
Head Mistress: Mrs Kitty Mason
Age range: 3 months–8 years
No. of pupils: 39
Fees: Day £9,180–£18,120

ICS London
7B Wyndham Place, London W1H 1PN
Tel: +44 (0)20 729 88800
Head of School: Mona Taybi
Age range: 3–18 years
No. of pupils: 150
Fees: Day £22,440–£33,510

Instituto Español Vicente Cañada Blanch
317 Portobello Road, London W10 5SZ
Tel: +44 (0) 20 8969 2664
Head of School: Mr Antonio Simón Saiz
Age range: 3–18 years

International School of London (ISL)
139 Gunnersbury Avenue, London W3 8LG
Tel: +44 (0)20 8992 5823
Principal: Mr Richard Parker
Age range: 3–18 years
No. of pupils: 420
Fees: Day £23,000–£32,200

Kensington Wade School
Fulham Palace Road, London W6 9ER
Tel: 020 3096 2888
Headteacher: Mr Huw May
Age range: 3–11 years
No. of pupils: 100
Fees: Day £7,850

La Chouette School
17 The Mall, Ealing Broadway, London W5 2PJ
Tel: 020 8567 5323
Head of School: Ms Magali Amar
Age range: 2–6 years

La Petite Ecole Française
73 Saint Charles Square, London W10 6EJ
Tel: +44 (0)20 8960 1278
Age range: 3–11 years

Latymer Prep School
36 Upper Mall, Hammersmith, London W6 9TA
Tel: 020 7993 0061
Principal: Ms Andrea Rutterford
Age range: 7–11 years

Le Herisson
River Court Methodist Church, Rover Court Road, Hammersmith, London W6 9JT
Tel: 020 8563 7664
Director: Maria Frost
Age range: 2–6 years
Fees: Day £8,730–£8,970

L'Ecole Bilingue
St David's Welsh Church, St Mary's Terrace, London W2 1SJ
Tel: 020 7224 8427
Headteacher: Ms Veronique Ferreira
Age range: 3–11 years

Lloyd Williamson School Foundation
77 St Charles Square, London W10 6EB
Tel: 020 8962 0345
Co-Principals: Ms Lucy Meyer & Mr Aaron Williams
Age range: 4 months–16 years
Fees: Day £18,750

London Welsh School Ysgol Gymraeg Llundain
Hanwell Community Centre, Westcott Crescent, London W7 1PD
Tel: 020 8575 0237
Headteacher: Ms Tracey O'Brien
Age range: 3–11 years

Maria Montessori School - Bayswater
St Matthew's Church, St Petersburgh Place, Bayswater, London W2 4LA
Tel: 020 7435 3646
Age range: 2.5–12 years

Norland Place School
162-166 Holland Park Avenue, London W11 4UH
Tel: 020 7603 9103
Headmaster: Mr Patrick Mattar MA
Age range: 4–11 years

Notting Hill & Ealing High School GDST
2 Cleveland Road, West Ealing, London W13 8AX
Tel: (020) 8799 8400
Headmaster: Mr Matthew Shoults
Age range: G4–18 years

ENGLAND: London

Notting Hill Preparatory School
95 Lancaster Road, London W11 1QQ
Tel: 020 7221 0727
Head of School: Mrs Sarah Knollys
Age range: 4–13 years
No. of pupils: 444
Fees: Day £7,689

Orchard House School
16 Newton Grove, Bedford Park, London W4 1LB
Tel: 020 8742 8544
Headmistress: Mrs Henrietta Adams
Age range: 3–11 years
No. of pupils: 418
Fees: Day £11,331–£23,601

Pembridge Hall School
18 Pembridge Square, London W2 4EH
Tel: 020 7229 0121
Head: Mrs Sophie Banks
Age range: G4–11 years

Queen's College Preparatory School
61 Portland Place, London W1B 1QP
Tel: 020 7291 0660
Headmistress: Mrs Laura Hall
Age range: G4–11 years

Ravenscourt Park Preparatory School
16 Ravenscourt Avenue, London W6 0SL
Tel: 020 8846 9153
Headmaster: Mr Carl Howes MA (Cantab), PGCE (Exeter)
Age range: 4–11 years
No. of pupils: 420
Fees: Day £8,340

Southbank International School - Kensington
36-38 Kensington Park Road, London W11 3BU
Tel: 020 3890 1969
Head of School: David MacMorran
Age range: 2–18 years

St Augustine's Priory
Hillcrest Road, Ealing, London W5 2JL
Tel: 020 8997 2022
Headteacher: Mrs Sarah Raffray M.A., N.P.Q.H
Age range: B3–4 years G3–18 years

St Benedict's Junior School
5 Montpelier Avenue, Ealing, London W5 2XP
Tel: 020 8862 2050
Headmaster: Mr R G Simmons
Age range: 3–11 years

ST BENEDICT'S SCHOOL
For further details see p. 62
54 Eaton Rise, Ealing, London W5 2ES
Tel: 020 8862 2000
Email: admissions@stbenedicts.org.uk
Website: www.stbenedicts.org.uk
Headmaster: Mr Joe Smith
Age range: 3–18 years
No. of pupils: 1135

St James Preparatory School
Earsby Street, London W14 8SH
Tel: 02073 481794
Headmistress: Mrs Hilary Wyatt
Age range: 3–11 years

The Japanese School in London
87 Creffield Road, Acton, London W3 9PU
Tel: 020 8993 7145
Age range: 6–16 years

Thomas's Kensington
17-19 Cottesmore Gardens, London W8 5PR
Tel: 020 7361 6500
Head of School: Ms Kelly Miller
Age range: 4–11 years

Wetherby Notting Hill
11 Pembridge Square, London W2 4ED
Tel: 020 7727 9581
Headmaster: Mr Mark Snell
Age range: B2.5–8 years

Wetherby Preparatory School
Bryanston Square, London W1H 2EA
Tel: 020 7535 3520
Headmaster: Mr Mark White MA (Hons), PGCE
Age range: B8–13 years

North-East

Durham D134
Northumberland D134
Stockton-on-Tees D134
Tyne & Wear D134

KEY TO SYMBOLS
- Boys' school
- Girls' school
- International school
- Tutorial or sixth form college
- A levels
- Boarding accommodation
- Bursaries
- International Baccalaureate
- Learning support
- Entrance at 16+
- Vocational qualifications
- Independent Association of Prep Schools
- The Headmasters' & Headmistresses' Conference
- Independent Schools Association
- Girls' School Association
- Boarding Schools' Association
- Society of Heads

Unless otherwise indicated, all schools are coeducational day schools. Single-sex and boarding schools will be indicated by the relevant icon.

ENGLAND: North-East

Durham

Barnard Castle Preparatory School
Westwick Road, Barnard Castle, Durham DL12 8UW
Tel: +44 (0)1833 696032
Headmistress: Mrs Laura Turner
Age range: 4–11 years

Chorister School (Bow)
South Road, Durham DH1 3LS
Tel: +44 (0)191 731 9270
Head of School: Ms Sally Harrod
Age range: 3–7 years

Chorister School (Cathedral)
The College, Durham DH1 3EL
Tel: +44 (0)191 731 9270
Head of School: Ms Sally Harrod
Age range: 7–11 years

Durham High School for Girls
Farewell Hall, South Road, Durham DH1 3TB
Tel: 0191 384 3226
Headmistress: Mrs Simone Niblock
Age range: G3–18 years
No. of pupils: 347

The Independent Grammar School: Durham
Claypath, Durham DH1 1RH
Tel: 07984 619739
Principal: Mr Chris Gray
Age range: 4–13 years

Northumberland

Longridge Towers School
Longridge Towers, Berwick-upon-Tweed, Northumberland TD15 2XQ
Tel: 01289 307584
Headmaster: Mr Jonathan Lee
Age range: 3–19 years
No. of pupils: 350

Mowden Hall School
Newton, Stocksfield, Northumberland NE43 7TP
Tel: 01661 842147
Head: Ms Kate Martin
Age range: 3–13 years
No. of pupils: 200

Stockton-on-Tees

Red House School
36 The Green, Norton, Stockton-on-Tees TS20 1DX
Tel: 01642 553370
Head: Dr Rebecca Ashcroft
Age range: 3–16 years

Teesside High School
The Avenue, Eaglescliffe, Stockton-on-Tees TS16 9AT
Tel: 01642 782095
Head of School: Mrs K Mackenzie
Age range: 3–18 years

Yarm Preparatory School
Grammar School Lane, Yarm, Stockton-on-Tees TS15 9ES
Tel: 01642 781447
Headteacher: Mr William Sawyer
Age range: 3–11 years

Tyne & Wear

Argyle House School
19-20 Thornhill Park, Sunderland, Tyne & Wear SR2 7LA
Tel: 01915 100726
Headteacher: Mr. Chris Johnson
Age range: 3–16 years

Dame Allan's Junior School & Nursery
Hunters Road, Spital Tongues, Newcastle upon Tyne, Tyne & Wear NE2 4NG
Tel: 01912 750608
Headteacher: Mr Geoff Laidler
Age range: 3–11 years

Gateshead Jewish Primary School
18-22 Gladstone Terrace, Gateshead, Tyne & Wear NE8 4EA
Tel: 01914 772154
Age range: B5–11 years

Newcastle High School for Girls GDST
Tankerville Terrace, Jesmond, Newcastle upon Tyne, Tyne & Wear NE2 3BA
Tel: 01912 016511
Head: Mr Michael Tippett
Age range: G3–18 years

Newcastle Preparatory School
6 Eslington Road, Jesmond, Newcastle upon Tyne, Tyne & Wear NE2 4RH
Tel: 01912 811769
Head of School: Miss Gemma Strong
Age range: 3–11 years
No. of pupils: 286
Fees: Day £4,313

Newcastle School for Boys
30 West Avenue, Gosforth, Newcastle upon Tyne, Tyne & Wear NE3 4ES
Tel: 01912 559300
Headmaster: Mr David Tickner
Age range: B3–18 years

OneSchool Global UK York (Springwell) Campus
60 Peareth Hall Road, Springwell, Gateshead, Tyne & Wear NE9 7NT
Tel: 01904 663300
Age range: 7–18 years

Royal Grammar School
Eskdale Terrace, Newcastle upon Tyne, Tyne & Wear NE2 4DX
Tel: 01912 815711
Headmaster: Mr Geoffrey Stanford
Age range: 7–18 years

Westfield School
Oakfield Road, Gosforth, Newcastle upon Tyne, Tyne & Wear NE3 4HS
Tel: 01912 553980
Headmaster: Mr Neil Walker
Age range: G3–18 years

North-West

Cheshire D136
Cumbria D136
Greater Manchester D137
Isle of Man D138
Lancashire D138
Merseyshire D139

KEY TO SYMBOLS
- Boys' school
- Girls' school
- International school
- Tutorial or sixth form college
- A levels
- Boarding accommodation
- Bursaries
- International Baccalaureate
- Learning support
- Entrance at 16+
- Vocational qualifications
- Independent Association of Prep Schools
- The Headmasters' & Headmistresses' Conference
- Independent Schools Association
- Girls' School Association
- Boarding Schools' Association
- Society of Heads

Unless otherwise indicated, all schools are coeducational day schools. Single-sex and boarding schools will be indicated by the relevant icon.

ENGLAND: North-West

Cheshire

Abbey Gate College
Saighton Grange, Saighton,
Chester, Cheshire CH3 6EN
Tel: 01244 332077
Head: Mr Craig Jenkinson
Age range: 4–18 years

Alderley Edge School for Girls
Wilmslow Road, Alderley
Edge, Cheshire SK9 7QE
Tel: 01625 583028
Head of School: Ms Nicola Smillie
Age range: G2–18 years

Beech Hall School
Beech Hall Drive, Tytherington,
Macclesfield, Cheshire SK10 2EG
Tel: 01625 422192
Headmaster: Mr James Allen
Age range: 6 months–16 years

Bowdon Preparatory School for Girls
Ashley Road, Bowdon,
Altrincham, Cheshire WA14 2LT
Tel: 0161 928 0678
Headmistress: Mrs Helen Gee
Age range: G3–11 years

Brabyns Preparatory School
34-36 Arkwright Road, Marple,
Stockport, Cheshire SK6 7DB
Tel: 0161 427 2395
Headteacher: Mrs Cath Carrasco
Age range: 2–11 years

Cornerstone Academy
c/o Marlfields Primary Academy,
Waggs Road, Congleton,
Cheshire CW12 4BT
Tel: 01270 304094
Headteacher: Mr Damien Sweeney
Age range: 5–11 years

Cransley School
Belmont Hall, Belmont Road,
Great Budworth, Northwich,
Cheshire CW9 6HN
Tel: 01606 891747
Head of School: Mr Richard Pollock
LL.B, PGCE, PG Dip (RNCM)
Age range: 4–16 years

Green Meadow Independent School
Robson Way, Lowton, Warrington,
Cheshire WA3 2RD
Tel: 01942 671138
Head of School: Mrs S Green
Age range: 3–14 years

Greenbank Preparatory School
64 Heathbank Road, Cheadle
Hulme, Stockport, Cheshire SK8 6HU
Tel: 0161 485 3724
Head of School: Mr Malcolm Johnson
Age range: 6 months–11 years
No. of pupils: 283
Fees: Day £9,480

Hale Preparatory School
Broomfield Lane, Hale,
Cheshire WA15 9AS
Tel: 0161 928 2386
Headmaster: Mr J F Connor
Age range: 4–11 years

Lady Barn House School
Schools Hill, Cheadle,
Cheshire SK8 1JE
Tel: 0161 428 2912
Head of School: Ms Louise Higson
Age range: 3–11 years
No. of pupils: 479

OneSchool Global UK Northwich Campus
Hartford Manor, Greenbank Lane,
Northwich, Cheshire CW8 1HW
Tel: 01606 210320
Age range: 7–18 years

Pownall Hall School
Carrwood Road, Pownall Park,
Wilmslow, Cheshire SK9 5DW
Tel: 01625 523141
Headmaster: Mr David Goulbourn
Age range: 6 months–11 years

Terra Nova School
Jodrell Bank, Holmes Chapel,
Crewe, Cheshire CW4 8BT
Tel: 01477 571251
Headmaster: Mr Paul Campbell
Age range: 2.5–13 years
(boarding from 8)

The Firs School
45 Newton Lane, Upton,
Chester, Cheshire CH2 2HJ
Tel: 01244 322443
Head Teacher: Miss Rosemary Evans
Age range: 2–11 years

The Grange School
Bradburns Lane, Hartford,
Northwich, Cheshire CW8 1LU
Tel: 01606 668850
Senior Head: Dr Lorraine Earps
Age range: 4–18 years

The King's School in Macclesfield
Alderley Road, Prestbury,
Cheshire SK10 4SP
Tel: 01625 260000
Headmaster: Mr Jason Slack
Age range: 3–18 years

The King's School, Chester
Wrexham Road, Chester,
Cheshire CH4 7QL
Tel: 01244 689500
Headmaster: Mr George Hartley
Age range: 4–18 years

> **THE QUEEN'S SCHOOL**
> *For further details see p. 64*
> City Walls Road, Chester,
> Cheshire CH1 2NN
> **Tel:** 01244 312078
> **Email:**
> admissions@thequeensschool.co.uk
> **Website:**
> www.thequeensschool.co.uk
> **Headmistress:** Mrs Joanne Keville
> **Age range:** G4–18 years
> **No. of pupils:** 400

The Ryleys School
Ryleys Lane, Alderley Edge,
Cheshire SK9 7UY
Tel: 01625 583241
Headteacher: Mrs Julia Langford
Age range: 1–11 years

Wilmslow Preparatory School
Grove Avenue, Wilmslow,
Cheshire SK9 5EG
Tel: 01625 524246
Headteacher: Mr Bradley
Lavagna-Slater
Age range: 3–11 years

Cumbria

Austin Friars School
Etterby Scaur, Carlisle,
Cumbria CA3 9PB
Tel: 01228 528042
Headmaster: Mr Chris Hattam
Age range: 3–18 years

Casterton, Sedbergh Preparatory School
Casterton, Kirkby Lonsdale,
Cumbria LA6 2SG
Tel: 01524 279200
Headmaster: Mr Will Newman
BA(Ed) Hons MA
Age range: 3–13 years

Hunter Hall School
Frenchfield, Penrith,
Cumbria CA11 8UA
Tel: 01768 891291
Head Teacher: Mrs Donna Vinsome
Age range: 3–11 years

Lime House School
Holm Hill, Dalston, Carlisle,
Cumbria CA5 7BX
Tel: 01228 710225
Headteacher: Mr Michael John Smith
Age range: 7–18 years
No. of pupils: 168

Sedbergh School
Station Road, Sedbergh,
Cumbria LA10 5HG
Tel: 015396 20535
Headmaster: Mr Dan Harrison
Age range: 3–19 years

> **WINDERMERE SCHOOL, INFANT & JUNIOR SCHOOL**
> *For further details see p. 65*
> Browhead Campus,
> Patterdale Road, Windermere,
> Cumbria LA23 1NW
> **Tel:** 01539 446164
> **Email:**
> admissions@windermereschool.co.uk
> **Website:**
> www.windermereschool.co.uk
> **Head:** Mrs Jenny Davies
> **Age range:** 3–11 years
> **No. of pupils:** 72
> **Fees:** Day £7,125–£19,500

North-West: ENGLAND

Greater Manchester

Abbotsford Preparatory School
211 Flixton Road, Urmston, Manchester, Greater Manchester M41 5PR
Tel: 0161 748 3261
Head of School: Mrs Catherine Howard B.Ed(Hons)
Age range: 4 months–11 years

Afifah School
86 Clifton Street, Old Trafford, Manchester, Greater Manchester M16 9GN
Tel: 01618 721516
Principal: Mr Abdul Huy Malek
Age range: 2–16 years

Al-Huda Primary School
3 Hennon Street, Bolton, Greater Manchester BL1 3EH
Tel: 01204 841377
Headteacher: Zeinab Bhikha
Age range: 2–11 years

Altrincham Preparatory School
Marlborough Road, Bowdon, Altrincham, Greater Manchester WA14 2RR
Tel: 0161 928 3366
Headmaster: Mr N J Vernon
Age range: B2–11 years

Ateres Elisheva
Beis Menachem, Park Lane, Salford, Greater Manchester M7 4JD
Tel: 01612 587647
Age range: G2–9 years

Beech House School
184 Manchester Road, Rochdale, Greater Manchester OL11 4JQ
Tel: 01706 646309
Principal: Mr Kevin Sartain
Age range: 2–16 years

Beis Malka Girls school
399-401 Bury New Road, Salford, Greater Manchester M7 2BT
Tel: 01617 922323
Age range: G3–16 years

Beis Rochel Mcr Girls School
315-317 Great Clowes Street, Salford, Greater Manchester M7 2FZ
Tel: 01616 601001
Age range: G2–11 years

Beis Ruchel Girls School
87 Devonshire Street, Salford, Greater Manchester M7 4AE
Tel: 01617 951830
Age range: G2–16 years

Bnos Margulis Viznitz Girls' School
33 Northumberland Street, Salford, Greater Manchester M7 4DQ
Tel: 07807 099015
Age range: G3–11 years

Bnos Yisroel School
Leicester Road, Salford, Greater Manchester M7 4DA
Tel: 01617 923896
Headmaster: Rabbi R Spitzer
Age range: G3–16 years

Bolton School
Chorley New Road, Bolton, Greater Manchester BL1 4PA
Tel: 01204 840201
Head of Foundation: Philip Britton
Age range: 0–18 years
Fees: Day £10,380–£12,972

Branwood Preparatory School
Stafford Road, Monton, Eccles, Manchester, Greater Manchester M30 9HN
Tel: 0161 789 1054
Headmaster: Mr Andrew Whittell
Age range: 3–11 years

BRIDGEWATER SCHOOL
For further details see p. 63
Drywood Hall, Worsley Road, Worsley, Manchester, Greater Manchester M28 2WQ
Tel: 0161 794 1463
Email: admin@bwslive.co.uk
Website: www.bridgewater-school.co.uk
Head Teacher: Mrs J.A.T. Nairn CertEd(Distinction)
Age range: 3–18 years
No. of pupils: 471

Bury Grammar Schools
Tenterden Street, Bury, Greater Manchester BL9 0HN
Tel: 0161 696 8600
Headmistress: Mrs J Anderson
Age range: 3–18 years

Cheadle Hulme School
Claremont Road, Cheadle Hulme, Cheadle, Greater Manchester SK8 6EF
Tel: 0161 488 3330
Head: Mr Neil Smith
Age range: 3–18 years

Chetham's School of Music
Long Millgate, Manchester, Greater Manchester M3 1SB
Tel: 0161 834 9644
Joint Principals: Nicola Smith & Tom Redmond
Age range: 8–18 years
No. of pupils: 300

Clarendon Cottage School
Ivy Bank House, Half Edge Lane, Eccles, Manchester, Greater Manchester M30 9BJ
Tel: 0161 950 7868
Head of School: Miss E Bagnall
Age range: 3–11 years

Clevelands Preparatory School
425 Chorley New Road, Bolton, Greater Manchester BL1 5DH
Tel: 01204 843898
Head of School: Mr Keith Cahillane
Age range: 2–11 years

Covenant Christian School
The Hawthorns, 48 Heaton Moor Road, Stockport, Greater Manchester SK4 4NX
Tel: 0161 432 3782
Head: Dr Roger Slack
Age range: 5–16 years

Farrowdale House Preparatory School
Farrow Street, Shaw, Oldham, Greater Manchester OL2 7AD
Tel: 01706 844533
Headteacher: Miss Z. N. Campbell BA (Hons) PGCE
Age range: 3–11 years

Forest Park Preparatory School
Lauriston House, 27 Oakfield, Sale, Greater Manchester M33 6NB
Tel: 0161 973 4835
Headteacher: Mr Nick Tucker
Age range: 3–11 years

Forest Preparatory School & Nursery
Moss Lane, Timperley, Altrincham, Greater Manchester WA15 6LJ
Tel: 0161 980 4075
Headmaster: Mr Graeme Booth
Age range: 2–11 years

Hulme Hall Grammar School
Beech Avenue, Stockport, Greater Manchester SK3 8HA
Tel: 0161 485 3524
Headmaster: Mr Dean Grierson
Age range: 2–16 years
No. of pupils: 200
Fees: Day £2,840–£3,300

Kerem Shloime
Gloucester House, Back Duncan Street, Salford, Greater Manchester M7 2EY
Tel: 01617 927841
Head of School: Mr Rafael Brandies
Age range: B3–11 years

King of Kings School
142 Dantzic Street, Manchester, Greater Manchester M4 4DN
Tel: 0161 834 4214
Headteacher: Mrs Brenda Lewis
Age range: 3–18 years

Lord's School
Green Lane, Bolton, Greater Manchester BL3 2EF
Tel: 01204 523731
Headteacher: Mrs Anne Ainsworth
Age range: 7–18 years

Manchester High School for Girls
Grangethorpe Road, Manchester, Greater Manchester M14 6HS
Tel: 0161 224 0447
Head Mistress: Mrs Helen F Jeys
Age range: G4–18 years
No. of pupils: 1000

Manchester Junior Girls School
64 Upper Park Road, Salford, Greater Manchester M7 4JA
Tel: 0161 740 0566
Head of School: Mrs Hannah Ehrentreu
Age range: G3–13 years

Manchester Muslim Preparatory School
551 Wilmslow Road, Withington, Manchester, Greater Manchester M20 4BA
Tel: 0161 445 5452
Headteacher: Ms D Ghafori-Kanno
Age range: 3–11 years

Moor Allerton Preparatory School
131 Barlow Moor Road, West Didsbury, Manchester, Greater Manchester M20 2PW
Tel: 0161 445 4521
Headmistress: Ms Kathryn Unsworth
Age range: 6 months–11 years

Oholei Yosef Yitzchok (OYY) Lubavitch Boys School
4 Upper Park Road, Salford, Greater Manchester M7 4HL
Tel: 01617 400923
Head of School: Mendel Cohen
Age range: 5–16 years

Oholei Yosef Yitzchok (OYY) Lubavitch Girls School
460 Bury New Road, Park Lane, Salford, Greater Manchester M7 4LH
Tel: 01617 050483
Head of School: Mrs Avigail Di Veroli
Age range: G2–17 years

Oldham Hulme Grammar School
Chamber Road, Oldham, Greater Manchester OL8 4BX
Tel: 0161 624 4497
Principal: Mr CJD Mairs
Age range: 3–18 years

Prestwich Preparatory School
St Margaret's Building, 400 Bury Old Road, Prestwich, Manchester, Greater Manchester M25 1PZ
Tel: 0161 773 1223
Headmistress: Miss P Shiels
Age range: 2–11 years

ENGLAND: North-West

St Ambrose Preparatory School
Hale Barns, Altrincham, Greater Manchester WA15 0HF
Tel: 0161 903 9193
Headmaster: F J Driscoll
Age range: 3–11 years

St. Bede's College
Alexandra Park, Manchester, Greater Manchester M16 8HX
Tel: 0161 226 3323
Headteacher: Mrs Sandra Pike
Age range: 3–18 years
£

Stella Maris School
St. John's Road, Heaton Mersey, Stockport, Greater Manchester SK4 3BR
Tel: 0161 432 0532
Headteacher: Mrs N Johnson
Age range: 3–11 years

Stockport Grammar School
Buxton Road, Stockport, Greater Manchester SK2 7AF
Tel: 0161 456 9000
Headmaster: Dr Paul Owen
Age range: 3–18 years

Tashbar of Manchester
20 Upper Park Road, Salford, Greater Manchester M7 4HL
Tel: 01617 208254
Head of School: Rabbi David Hammond
Age range: B3–12 years

The Chadderton Preparatory Grammar School
Broadway, Chadderton, Oldham, Greater Manchester OL9 0AD
Tel: 0161 620 6570
Headteacher: Mrs Caroline Greenwood
Age range: 2–11 years

The Manchester Grammar School
Old Hall Lane, Fallowfield, Manchester, Greater Manchester M13 0XT
Tel: 0161 224 7201
High Master: Dr Martin Boulton
Age range: B7–18 years

Trinity Christian School
Birbeck Street, Off High Street, Stalybridge, Greater Manchester SK15 1SH
Tel: 0161 303 0674
Head: Mr Christopher O'Gorman
Age range: 3–16 years

Withington Girls' School
100 Wellington Road, Fallowfield, Manchester, Greater Manchester M14 6BL
Tel: 0161 224 1077
Headmistress: Mrs S J Haslam BA
Age range: G7–18 years

Isle of Man

The Buchan School
Westhill, Arbory Road, Castletown, Isle of Man IM9 1RD
Tel: +44 (0)1624 820110
Head of School: Mrs Janet Billingsley Evans
Age range: 2–11 years

Lancashire

AKS Lytham
Clifton Drive South, Lytham St Annes, Lancashire FY8 1DT
Tel: 01253 784100
Headmaster: Mr David Harrow
Age range: 0–18 years

Ashbridge Independent School
Lindle Lane, Hutton, Preston, Lancashire PR4 4AQ
Tel: 01772 619900
Headteacher: Ms Karen Mehta
Age range: 0–11 years

Highfield Priory School
58 Fulwood Row, Fulwood, Preston, Lancashire PR2 5RW
Tel: 01772 709624
Headteacher: Jeremy M Duke
Age range: 2–11 years
No. of pupils: 210
Fees: Day £8,370
£

Kirkham Grammar School
Ribby Road, Kirkham, Preston, Lancashire PR4 2BH
Tel: 01772 684264
Head of School: Mrs Deborah Parkinson
Age range: 3–18 years
No. of pupils: 820

Lancaster Steiner School
Lune Road, Lancaster, Lancashire LA1 5QU
Tel: 01524 381876
Principal: Patricia Williams
Age range: 0–11 years

Moorland School
Ribblesdale Avenue, Clitheroe, Lancashire BB7 2JA
Tel: 01200 423833
Headteacher: Mrs. Deborah Frost
Age range: 3 months–18 years (boarding from 7)

Oakhill School & Nursery
Wiswell Lane, Whalley, Clitheroe, Lancashire BB7 9AF
Tel: 01254 823546
Principal: Ms Jane Buttery BA (Hons) NPQH
Age range: 0–16 years

OneSchool Global UK Lancaster Campus
Melling Road, Hornby, Lancashire LA2 8LH
Tel: 01524 222159
Age range: 7–18 years

Rossall School
Broadway, Fleetwood, Lancashire FY7 8JW
Tel: +44 (0)1253 774201
Head: Mr Jeremy Quartermain
Age range: 0–18 years
No. of pupils: 843 VIth220
Fees: Day £9,435–£15,150 WB £16,050–£26,085 FB £23,865–£38,685

Scarisbrick Hall School
Southport Road, Scarisbrick, Ormskirk, Lancashire L40 9RQ
Tel: 01704 841151
Headmaster: Mr J Shaw
Age range: 0–18 years

St Joseph's Park Hill School
Padiham Road, Burnley, Lancashire BB12 6TG
Tel: 01282 455622
Headteacher: Mrs Maria Whitehead
Age range: 3–11 years

St Pius X Catholic Preparatory School
Oak House, 200 Garstang Road, Fulwood, Preston, Lancashire PR2 8RD
Tel: 01772 719937
Head of School: Mr Charlie Long
Age range: 2–11 years

St. Annes College Grammar School
293 Clifton Drive South, Lytham St Annes, Lancashire FY8 1HN
Tel: +44 (0)1253 725815
Head of School: S R Welsby
Age range: 2–18 years

Stonyhurst St Mary's Hall
Clitheroe, Lancashire BB7 9PH
Tel: 01254 826242
Headmaster: Mr Ian Murphy BA (Hons), PGCE Durham
Age range: 3–13 years

The Alternative School
Suite 4a, Ribble Court, 1 Mead Way, Padiham, Lancashire BB12 7NG
Tel: 01282 851800
Head of School: Ms Kirsty Swierkowski
Age range: 5–18 years

Westholme School
Wilmar Lodge, Meins Road, Blackburn, Lancashire BB2 6QU
Tel: 01254 506070
Principal: Dr Richard Robson
Age range: 4–18 years

North-West: ENGLAND

Merseyside

Auckland College
65-67 Parkfield Road, Aigburth,
Liverpool, Merseyside L17 4LE
Tel: 01517 270083
Headteacher: Miss Stephanie Boyd
Age range: 3–16 years

Avalon School
Caldy Road, West Kirby, Wirral,
Merseyside CH48 2HE
Tel: 01516 256993
Headteacher: Ms Joanna Callaway
Age range: 2–11 years

Birkenhead School
58 Beresford Road, Oxton,
Wirral, Merseyside CH43 2JD
Tel: 01516 524014
Headmaster: Mr Paul Vicars
Age range: 3 months–18 years

Carleton House Preparatory School
145 Menlove Avenue, Liverpool,
Merseyside L18 3EE
Tel: 01517 220756
Headteacher: Mrs Sandy Coleman
Age range: 3–11 years

Christian Fellowship School
Overbury Street, Edge Hill,
Liverpool, Merseyside L7 3HL
Tel: 01517 091642
Head Teacher: Mrs R Boulton
(BA Tons, PGCE)
Age range: 0–16 years

Prenton Preparatory School
12 Mount Pleasant, Oxton,
Wirral, Merseyside CH43 5SY
Tel: 01516 523182
Headteacher: Mr M Jones
BSC Hons, PGCE
Age range: 2–11 years

St. Mary's College
Everest Road, Crosby, Liverpool,
Merseyside L23 5TW
Tel: 01519 243926
Principal: Mr Michael
Kennedy Bsc, MA
Age range: 0–18 years

Stanfield Preparatory School
Liverpool Road, Crosby,
Liverpool, Merseyside L23 0QP
Tel: 01519 499400
Headmistress: Miss E Lynan
Age range: 4–11 years

The Belvedere Preparatory School
23 Belvidere Road, Princes Park,
Aigburth, Liverpool, Merseyside L8 3TF
Tel: 01514 711137
Headmistress: Miss Clare Burnham
Age range: 3–11 years

Tower College
Mill Lane, Rainhill, Prescot,
Merseyside L35 6NE
Tel: 01514 264333
Head of School: Ms Andrea Bingley
Age range: 3 months–16 years

South-East

Berkshire D142
Buckinghamshire D143
East Sussex D143
Hampshire D144
Isle of Wight D145
Kent D145
Portsmouth D146
Surrey D146
West Sussex D149

*See also Greater London (D119) for schools in Kent and Surrey

KEY TO SYMBOLS
- Boys' school
- Girls' school
- International school
- Tutorial or sixth form college
- A levels
- Boarding accommodation
- Bursaries
- International Baccalaureate
- Learning support
- Entrance at 16+
- Vocational qualifications
- (IAPS) Independent Association of Prep Schools
- (HMC) The Headmasters' & Headmistresses' Conference
- (ISA) Independent Schools Association
- (GSA) Girls' School Association
- (BSA) Boarding Schools' Association
- (S) Society of Heads

Unless otherwise indicated, all schools are coeducational day schools. Single-sex and boarding schools will be indicated by the relevant icon.

ENGLAND: South-East

Berkshire

Caversham Preparatory School
16 Peppard Road, Caversham, Reading, Berkshire RG4 8JZ
Tel: 01189 478 684
Head of School: Mrs Naomi Williams
Age range: 3–11 years

Claires Court Junior Boys
Ridgeway, The Thicket, Maidenhead, Berkshire SL6 3QE
Tel: 01628 327400
Head of Juniors: Ms Leanne Kirby
Age range: B4–11 years

Claires Court Nursery, Girls and Sixth Form
1 College Avenue, Maidenhead, Berkshire SL6 6AW
Tel: 01628 327500
Head of Juniors: Ms Leanne Kirby
Age range: B16–18 years G2–18 years

Crosfields School
Shinfield Road, Reading, Berkshire RG2 9BL
Tel: 0118 987 1810
Headmaster: Mr Craig Watson
Age range: 3–16 years

Darul Madinah Slough
50 Darvills Lane, Slough, Berkshire SL1 2PH
Tel: 01753 553841
Age range: 2–6 years

Deenway Montessori School & Unicity College
3-5 Sidmouth Street, Reading, Berkshire RG1 4QX
Tel: 0118 9574737
Headmaster: Mr Munawar Karim LL.B (Hons), M.A, Mont. Dip.
Age range: 3–18+ years

Dolphin School
Waltham Road, Hurst, Reading, Berkshire RG10 0FR
Tel: 0118 934 1277
Headmaster: Mr Adam Hurst
Age range: 3–13 years
No. of pupils: 209

Elstree School
Woolhampton Hill, Woolhampton, Reading, Berkshire RG7 5TD
Tel: 01189 713302
Headmaster: Mr Sid Inglis B.A. (Hons), P.G.C.E.
Age range: 3–13 years
No. of pupils: 270

Eton End School
35 Eton Road, Datchet, Slough, Berkshire SL3 9AX
Tel: 01753 541075
Head of School: Mrs Rachael Cox
Age range: 3–11 years
No. of pupils: 182
Fees: Day £12,162–£16,395

HERRIES PREPARATORY SCHOOL
For further details see p. 75
Dean Lane, Cookham Dean, Berkshire SL6 9BD
Tel: 01628 483350
Email: admissions@herries.org.uk
Website: www.herries.org.uk
Headteacher: Mr Robert Grosse
Age range: 2–11 years

Highfield Preparatory School
2 West Road, Maidenhead, Berkshire SL6 1PD
Tel: 01628 624918
Headteacher: Mrs Joanna Leach
Age range: B2–7 years G2–11 years

Holme Grange School
Heathlands Road, Wokingham, Berkshire RG40 3AL
Tel: 0118 978 1566
Headteacher: Mrs Claire Robinson
Age range: 2–16 years
No. of pupils: 638
Fees: Day £13,350–£18,960

Lambrook School
Winkfield Row, Nr Ascot, Berkshire RG42 6LU
Tel: 01344 882717
Headmaster: Mr Jonathan Perry
Age range: 3–13 years
No. of pupils: 600

Long Close School
Upton Court Road, Upton, Slough, Berkshire SL3 7LU
Tel: 01753 520095
Headteacher: Miss K Nijjar BA (Hons), Med, MA
Age range: 2–16 years
No. of pupils: 329

LUDGROVE
For further details see p. 78
Wokingham, Berkshire RG40 3AB
Tel: 0118 978 9881
Email: registrar@ludgroveschool.co.uk
Website: www.ludgrove.net
Head of School: Mr Simon Barber
Age range: B8–13 years
No. of pupils: 186

LVS Ascot
London Road, Ascot, Berkshire SL5 8DR
Tel: 01344 882770
Principal: Mrs Christine Cunniffe BA (Hons), MMus, MBA
Age range: 4–18 years
No. of pupils: 833
Fees: Day £12,315–£22,095 FB £30,915–£38,085

Newbold School
Popeswood Road, Binfield, Bracknell, Berkshire RG42 4AH
Tel: 01344 421088
Headteacher: Mrs Jaki Crissey MA, BA, PGCE Primary
Age range: 3–11 years

OneSchool Global UK Reading Campus (Primary)
401 Old Whitley Wood Lane, Reading, Berkshire RG2 8QA
Tel: 0118 931 2938
Age range: 7–11 years

Our Lady's Preparatory School
19 The Avenue, Crowthorne, Wokingham, Berkshire RG45 6PB
Tel: 01344 773394
Headmaster: Mr Michael Stone
Age range: 4–11 years
No. of pupils: 130
Fees: Day £8,748

Papplewick School
Windsor Road, Ascot, Berkshire SL5 7LH
Tel: 01344 621488
Headmaster: Mr Tom Bunbury
Age range: B6–13 years

Reddam House Berkshire
Bearwood Road, Sindlesham, Wokingham, Berkshire RG41 5BG
Tel: +44 (0)118 974 8300
Principal: Mr Rick Cross
Age range: 3 months–18 years
No. of pupils: 785
Fees: Day £13,026–£20,883 WB £32,769–£36,558 FB £34,578–£38,310

Shakhsiyah School, Slough
Cippenham Lodge, Cippenham Lane, Slough, Berkshire SL1 5AN
Tel: 01753 518000
Acting-Head Teacher: Ms Sajeada Ahmed
Age range: 3–11 years

St Andrew's School
Buckhold, Pangbourne, Reading, Berkshire RG8 8QA
Tel: 0118 974 4276
Head Master: Ed Graham
Age range: 3–13 years (boarding from 7)
Fees: Day £3,890–£6,525

St Bernard's Preparatory School
Hawtrey Close, Slough, Berkshire SL1 1TB
Tel: 01753 521821
Headteacher: Mrs A Verma
Age range: 2.5–11 years

St Edward's Prep
64 Tilehurst Road, Reading, Berkshire RG30 2JH
Tel: 0118 957 4342
Headteacher: Mr Jonathan Parsons
Age range: 3–11 years

St George's School Windsor Castle
Windsor Castle, Windsor, Berkshire SL4 1QF
Tel: 01753 865553
Head Master: Mr W Goldsmith BA (Hons), FRSA, FCCT
Age range: 3–13 years (boarding from 8)

St John's Beaumont Preparatory School
Priest Hill, Old Windsor, Berkshire SL4 2JN
Tel: 01784 494 053
Headmaster: Mr P Barr
Age range: B3–13 years G3–7 years
No. of pupils: 220
Fees: Day £3,788–£7,502 FB £3,807

St Joseph's College
Upper Redlands Road, Reading, Berkshire RG1 5JT
Tel: 0118 966 1000
Head of School: Mrs Laura Stotesbury
Age range: 3–18 years

St Piran's School
Gringer Hill, Maidenhead, Berkshire SL6 7LZ
Tel: 01628 594300
Headmaster: Mr Sebastian Sales
Age range: 2–11 years

Sunningdale School
Dry Arch Road, Sunningdale, Berkshire SL5 9PY
Tel: 01344 620159
Headmaster: Tom Dawson MA, PGCE
Age range: B7–13 years

The Abbey School
Kendrick Road, Reading, Berkshire RG1 5DZ
Tel: 0118 987 2256
Head: Mr Will le Fleming
Age range: G3–18 years
No. of pupils: 987
Fees: Day £13,500–£21,750

The King's House School, Windsor
King's House, 77A Frances Road, Windsor, Berkshire SL4 3AQ
Tel: 01753 834850
Headteacher: Mrs Lyndsey Harding
Age range: 3–11 years

The Marist Preparatory School
King's Road, Sunninghill, Ascot, Berkshire SL5 7PS
Tel: 01344 624291
Vice Principal Prep Phase: Mrs Jane Gow
Age range: G2–11 years

The Oratory Prep School
Great Oaks, Goring Heath, Reading, Berkshire RG8 7SF
Tel: 0118 984 4511
Headteacher: Mr Andrew De Silva
Age range: 2–13 years (boarding from 7)
No. of pupils: 300
Fees: Day £4,517–£7,775 FB £11,000

The Vine Christian School
Three Mile Cross Church, Basingstoke Road, Three Mile Cross, Reading, Berkshire RG7 1HF
Tel: 0118 988 6464
Head of School: Mrs René Esterhuizen
Age range: 3–18 years

South-East: ENGLAND

Trinity Christian School
62 London Road, Reading,
Berkshire RG1 5AS
Tel: 0118 336 0477
Headteacher: Ms Naomi Moorcroft
Age range: 4–11 years
Fees: Day £1,990

Upton House School
115 St Leonard's Road,
Windsor, Berkshire SL4 3DF
Tel: 01753 862610
Head: Mrs Rhian Thornton BA (Hons) NPQH LLE PGCE
Age range: 2–11 years
No. of pupils: 280
Fees: Day £2,842–£6,430

Waverley Preparatory School & Day Nursery
Waverley Way, Finchampstead, Wokingham, Berkshire RG40 4YD
Tel: 0118 973 1121
Principal: Mr Guy Shore
Age range: 3 months–11 years

WELLINGTON COLLEGE PREP
For further details see p. 82
Sandhurst, Berkshire GU47 8PH
Tel: 01344 772134
Email: info@wellingtoncollegeprep.org.uk
Website: www.wellingtoncollegeprep.org.uk
Head: Mr E. Venables
Age range: 3–13 years
No. of pupils: 385
Fees: Day £17,280–£27,090 FB £36,450

Buckinghamshire

Davenies
Station Road, Beaconsfield,
Buckinghamshire HP9 1AA
Tel: 01494 685400
Headmaster: Mr Alastair Thomas
Age range: B4–13 years
No. of pupils: 333
Fees: Day £14,130–£21,360

Gayhurst School
Bull Lane, Gerrards Cross,
Buckinghamshire SL9 8RJ
Tel: 01753 969538
Headmaster: Gareth R A Davies
Age range: 3–11 years

Maltman's Green School
Maltmans Lane, Gerrards Cross,
Buckinghamshire SL9 8RR
Tel: 01753 883022
Headmistress: Mrs Jill Walker BSc (Hons), MA Ed, PGCE
Age range: G2–11 years
No. of pupils: 315
Fees: Day £3,100–£6,975

St Mary's School
94 Packhorse Road, Gerrards Cross, Buckinghamshire SL9 8JQ
Tel: 01753 883370
Head of School: Mrs Patricia Adams
Age range: G3–18 years

Thorpe House School
Oval Way, Gerrards Cross,
Buckinghamshire SL9 8QA
Tel: 01753 882474
Headmaster: Mr Nicholas Pietrek
Age range: B4–16 years

East Sussex

Annan The Froebel School
Lewes Road, Easons Green,
Uckfield, East Sussex TN22 5RE
Tel: 01825 841410
Principal: Ms Debby Hunter
Age range: 2–11 years

Battle Abbey School
High Street, Battle, East
Sussex TN33 0AD
Tel: 01424 772385
Headmaster: Mr David Clark BA, M Phil (Cantab)
Age range: 3 months–18 years (boarding from 11)

Bede's Prep School
Duke's Drive, Eastbourne,
East Sussex BN20 7XL
Tel: 01323 356939
Head: Mrs Leigh-Anne Morris
Age range: 3 months–13 years (boarding from 9)
No. of pupils: 336
Fees: Day £3,660–£6,390 FB £2,990

Brighton & Hove Montessori School
67 Stanford Avenue, Brighton,
East Sussex BN1 6FB
Tel: 01273 702485
Headteacher: Mrs Daisy Cockburn AMI, MontDip
Age range: 2–12 years

Brighton College Prep School
Walpole Lodge, Walpole Road,
Brighton, East Sussex BN2 0EU
Tel: 01273 704343
Headmaster: Mr Ant Falkus
Age range: 3–13 years
No. of pupils: 510
Fees: Day £4,580–£8,400

Brighton Girls GDST
Montpelier Road, Brighton,
East Sussex BN1 3AT
Tel: 01273 280280
Head: Ms Rosie McColl
Age range: G4–18 years

Claremont Nursery & Prep School
Ebdens Hill, Baldslow, St Leonards-on-Sea, East Sussex TN37 7PW
Tel: 01424 751555
Head of Prep School: Mr Gavin Bunker
Age range: 3 months–13 years

Darvell School
Darvell, Brightling Road,
Robertsbridge, East Sussex TN32 5DR
Tel: 01580 883000
Age range: 6–14 years

Greenfields Independent Day & Boarding School
Priory Road, Forest Row,
East Sussex RH18 5JD
Tel: +44 (0)1342 822189
Executive Head: Mr. Jeff Smith
Age range: 2–18 years (boarding from 10)

Lancing Prep Hove
The Droveway, Hove,
East Sussex BN3 6LU
Tel: 01273 503452
Headmistress: Mrs Kirsty Keep BEd
Age range: 3–13 years

Lewes Old Grammar School
140 High Street, Lewes,
East Sussex BN7 1XS
Tel: 01273 472634
Headmaster: Mr Robert Blewitt
Age range: 3–18 years

Michael Hall School
Kidbrooke Park, Priory Road,
Forest Row, East Sussex RH18 5JA
Tel: 01342 822275
Head of School: Emmeline Hawker
Age range: 0–19 years

Sacred Heart School
Mayfield Lane, Durgates,
Wadhurst, East Sussex TN5 6DQ
Tel: 01892 783414
Headteacher: Ms Johanna Collyer
Age range: 2–11 years

Skippers Hill Manor Preparatory School
Five Ashes, Mayfield, East
Sussex TN20 6HR
Tel: 01825 830234
Headmaster: Mr Phillip Makhouli
Age range: 2–13 years

St Andrew's Prep
Meads Street, Eastbourne,
East Sussex BN20 7RP
Tel: +44 (0)1323 /33203
Headmaster: Tom Gregory BA(Hons), PGCE
Age range: 9 months–13 years
No. of pupils: 323

St Christopher's School
33 New Church Road, Hove,
East Sussex BN3 4AD
Tel: 01273 735404
Head of School: Ms Elizabeth Lyle
Age range: 4–13 years

The Brighton Waldorf School
Roedean Road, Brighton,
East Sussex BN2 5RA
Tel: 01273 386300
School Director: Mr Damian Mooncie
Age range: 0–16 years

The Drive Prep School
101 The Drive, Hove, East
Sussex BN3 6GE
Tel: 01273 738444
Head Teacher: Mrs S Parkinson CertEd, CertPerfArts
Age range: 7–16 years

The Montessori Place
45 Cromwell Road, Hove,
East Sussex BN3 3ER
Tel: 01273 773 764
Head of School: Mr Rob Gueterbock
Age range: 15 months–18 years

Vinehall
Robertsbridge, East Sussex TN32 5JL
Tel: 01580 880413
Headmaster: Joff Powis
Age range: 2–13 years
No. of pupils: 215
Fees: Day £11,850–£22,980 WB £28,545 FB £31,725

Windlesham School
190 Dyke Road, Brighton,
East Sussex BN1 5AA
Tel: 01273 553645
Headmaster: Mr John Ingrassia
Age range: 3–11 years

ENGLAND: South-East

Hampshire

BALLARD SCHOOL
For further details see p. 68
Fernhill Lane, New Milton,
Hampshire BH25 5SU
Tel: 01425 626900
Email: registrar@ballardschool.co.uk
Website: www.ballardschool.co.uk
Headmaster: Mr Andrew McCleave
Age range: 2–16 years
No. of pupils: 453
Fees: Day £3,455–£6,355

Bedales Prep, Dunhurst & Pre-Prep, Dunannie
Alton Road, Steep, Petersfield,
Hampshire GU32 2DR
Tel: 01730 300200 / 01730 300400
Head of Bedales Prep, Dunhurst: Mr Colin Baty
Age range: 3–13 years

Boundary Oak School
Roche Court, Wickham Road,
Fareham, Hampshire PO17 5BL
Tel: 01329 280955
Executive Headmaster: Mr James Polansky MA (Cantab) PGCE
Age range: 2–16 years
No. of pupils: 348
Fees: Day £9,195–£14,886 WB £16,155–£21,078 FB £18,144–£23,067

Charlton House Independent School
55-57 Midanbury Lane,
Southampton, Hampshire SO18 4DJ
Tel: 023 8067 1739
Head Teacher: Mrs Lea Pay
Age range: 9 months–11 years

Churcher's College
Petersfield, Hampshire GU31 4AS
Tel: 01730 263033
Headmaster: Mr Simon Williams , MA, BSc
Age range: 3–18 years
No. of pupils: 1317

Ditcham Park School
Ditcham Park, Petersfield,
Hampshire GU31 5RN
Tel: 01730 825659
Headmaster: Mr Graham Spawforth MA, MEd
Age range: 2–16 years
No. of pupils: 425
Fees: Day £3,593–£6,084

Durlston School
Becton Lane, Barton on-Sea, New
Milton, Hampshire BH25 7AQ
Tel: 01425 610010
Headmaster: Mr Richard May
Age range: 2–16 years
No. of pupils: 260

Embley
Embley Park, Romsey,
Hampshire SO51 6ZE
Tel: 01794 512206
Headteacher: Mr Cliff Canning
Age range: 2–18 years
No. of pupils: 600
Fees: Day £9,165–£17,004 WB £29,310 FB £9,598–£33,636

Farleigh School
Red Rice, Andover,
Hampshire SP11 7PW
Tel: 01264 710766
Headmaster: Fr Simon Everson
Age range: 3–13 years
No. of pupils: 460

Fitrah SIPS
55 Northumberland Road,
Southampton, Hampshire SO14 0EJ
Tel: 02380 570 849
Age range: 4–16 years

Forres Sandle Manor
Fordingbridge, Hampshire SP6 1NS
Tel: 01425 653131
Head of School: Mr Mark Howe
Age range: 2–16 years
No. of pupils: 210

Glenhurst School
16 Beechworth Road, Havant,
Hampshire PO9 1AX
Tel: 023 9248 4054
Age range: 3 months–5 years

Grantham Farm Montessori School & The Children's House
Grantham Farm, Baughurst,
Tadley, Hampshire RG26 5JS
Tel: 0118 981 5821
Head Teacher: Ms Emma Wetherley
Age range: 2–7 years

HIGHFIELD AND BROOKHAM SCHOOL
For further details see p. 76
Highfield Lane, Liphook,
Hampshire GU30 7LQ
Tel: 01428 728000
Email: admissions@highfieldandbrookham.co.uk
Website: www.highfieldandbrookham.co.uk
Headteacher: Mrs Suzannah Cryer BA (QTS)
Age range: 2–13 years
No. of pupils: 448

Hurst Lodge School
Yateley Hall, Firgrove Road,
Yateley, Hampshire GU46 6HJ
Tel: 01252 227002
Principal: Ms Victoria Smit
Age range: 4–19 years

Inwoods Small School
Brockwood Park, Bramdean,
Alresford, Hampshire SO24 0LQ
Tel: +44 (0)1962 771065
Age range: 5–11 years

King Edward VI Preparatory School
Highwood House, Highwood Lane,
Romsey, Hampshire SO51 9ZH
Tel: 01794 513231
Headmistress: Mrs Rebecca Smith
Age range: 2–11 years
Fees: Day £4,192–£6,949

Kingscourt School
182 Five Heads Road, Catherington,
Hampshire PO8 9NJ
Tel: 023 9259 3251
Headteacher: Ms Kerrie Daunter
Age range: 3–11 years

Mayville High School
35-37 St Simon's Road, Southsea,
Portsmouth, Hampshire PO5 2PE
Tel: 023 9273 4847
Head of School: Mrs Rebecca Parkyn
Age range: 2–16 years
No. of pupils: 500
Fees: Day £10,602–£17,394

Meoncross School
Burnt House Lane, Stubbington,
Fareham, Hampshire PO14 2EF
Tel: 01329 662182
Headmaster: Mr Mark Cripps
Age range: 2.5–16 years
No. of pupils: 405
Fees: Day £8,736–£12,576

Moyles Court School
Moyles Court, Ringwood,
Hampshire BH24 3NF
Tel: 01425 472856
Headmaster: Mr Richard Milner-Smith
Age range: 2–16 years

Portsmouth High School GDST
Kent Road, Southsea, Portsmouth,
Hampshire PO5 3EQ
Tel: 023 9282 6714
Headmistress: Mrs Jane Prescott BSc NPQH
Age range: G3–18 years
No. of pupils: 500
Fees: Day £2,574–£4,800

Prince's Mead School
Worthy Park House, Kings Worthy,
Winchester, Hampshire SO21 1AN
Tel: 01962 888000
Headmaster: Mr Peter Thacker
Age range: 3–11 years

Ringwood Waldorf School
Folly Farm Lane, Ashley, Ringwood,
Hampshire BH24 2NN
Tel: 01425 472664
Age range: 3–18 years

Rookwood School
Weyhill Road, Andover,
Hampshire SP10 3AL
Tel: 01264 325900
Headmaster: Mr Paul Robinson
Age range: 2–18 years (boarding from 7)

Sherborne House School
39 Lakewood Road, Chandlers Ford,
Eastleigh, Hampshire SO53 1EU
Tel: 02380 252440
Head of School: Mrs Cordelia Cripps
Age range: 6 months–11 years

Sherfield School
South Drive, Sherfield-on-Loddon,
Hook, Hampshire RG27 0HU
Tel: 01256 884800
Headmaster: TBC
Age range: 3 months–18 years (boarding from 9)
No. of pupils: 609

St Neot's School
St Neot's Road, Eversley,
Hampshire RG27 0PN
Tel: 0118 973 2118
Headmaster: Mr Jonathan Slot
Age range: 2–13 years

St Nicholas' School
Redfields House, Redfields
Lane, Church Crookham,
Fleet, Hampshire GU52 0RF
Tel: 01252 850121
Headmistress: Dr O Wright PhD, MA, BA Hons, PGCE
Age range: B3–7 years G3–16 years

ST SWITHUN'S PREP
For further details see p. 81
Alresford Road, Winchester,
Hampshire SO21 1HA
Tel: 01962 835750
Email: prepoffice@stswithuns.com
Website: www.stswithuns.com
Head of School: Mrs Liz Norris
Age range: B3–4 years G3–11 years
No. of pupils: 208

Stockton House School
Stockton Avenue, Fleet,
Hampshire GU51 4NS
Tel: 01252 616323
Early Years Manager: Mrs Jenny Bounds BA EYPS
Age range: 2–5 years

The Gregg Prep School
17-19 Winn Road, Southampton,
Hampshire SO17 1EJ
Tel: 023 8055 7352
Headteacher: Mr M Pascoe
Age range: 4–11 years

The King's School
Lakesmere House, Allington Lane,
Fair Oak, Eastleigh, Southampton,
Hampshire SO50 7DB
Tel: 023 8060 0986
Headteacher: Mrs Heather Bowden
Age range: 4–16 years

The New Forest Small School
1 Southampton Road, Lyndhurst,
Hampshire SO43 7BU
Tel: 02380 284415
Headteacher: Mr Alex James
Age range: 3–16 years

South-East: ENGLAND

The Pilgrims' School
3 The Close, Winchester,
Hampshire SO23 9LT
Tel: 01962 854189
Interim Head of School:
Mr Alistair Duncan
Age range: B4–13 years

The Portsmouth Grammar Junior School
High Street, Portsmouth,
Hampshire PO1 2LN
Tel: +44 (0)23 9236 4219
Age range: 2.5–11 years

Thorngrove School
The Mount, Highclere, Newbury,
Hampshire RG20 9PS
Tel: 01635 253172
Headmaster: Mr Adam King
Age range: 2.5–13 years

Twyford School
Twyford, Winchester,
Hampshire SO21 1NW
Tel: 01962 712269
Headmaster: Mr Andrew Harvey
Age range: 2–13 years

Walhampton
Walhampton, Lymington,
Hampshire SO41 5ZG
Tel: 01590 613300
Head: Mr Jonny Timms
Age range: 2–13 years
(boarding from 7)

Wellesley Prep School
Stratfield Turgis, Hook,
Hampshire RG27 0AR
Tel: 01256 882707
Headmaster: Mr Angus McDonald
Age range: 2–13 years
No. of pupils: 300

West Hill Park School
St Margaret's Lane, Titchfield,
Hampshire PO14 4BS
Tel: 01329 842356
Headmaster: Mr Chris Ward
Age range: 3–13 years

Yateley Manor School
51 Reading Road, Yateley,
Hampshire GU46 7UQ
Tel: 01252 405500
Headmaster: Mr Robert Upton
Age range: 3–13 years

Isle of Wight

Priory School of Our Lady of Walsingham
Beatrice Avenue, Whippingham,
Isle of Wight PO32 6LP
Tel: 01983 861222
Principal: Mr David EJJ Lloyd
Age range: 4–18 years
No. of pupils: 176
Fees: Day £6,690–£10,500

Ryde School with Upper Chine
Queen's Road, Ryde, Isle
of Wight PO33 3BE
Tel: 01983 562229
Headmaster: Mr Will Turner
Age range: 2–18 years
(boarding from 11)
No. of pupils: 720
Fees: Day £3,305–£5,850

Kent

Beech Grove School
Forest Drive, Nonington,
Dover, Kent CT15 4FB
Tel: 01304 843 707
Headteacher: Jeffrey Maendel
Age range: 6–18 years

Beechwood School
12 Pembury Road, Tunbridge
Wells, Kent TN2 3QD
Tel: 01892 532747
Headmaster: Mr Justin Foster-Gandey
Age range: 3–18 years

Bronte School
7 Pelham Road, Gravesend,
Kent DA11 0HU
Tel: 01474 533805
Headmistress: Ms Emma Wood
Age range: 4–11 years

Bryony School
Marshall Road, Rainham,
Gillingham, Kent ME8 0AJ
Tel: 01634 231511
Head of School: Mrs N Gee
Age range: 2–11 years

Chartfield School
45 Minster Road, Westgate
on Sea, Kent CT8 8DA
Tel: 01843 831716
Head & Proprietor: Miss L P Shipley
Age range: 3–11 years

Dover College
Effingham Crescent,
Dover, Kent CT17 9RH
Tel: 01304 205969
Head of School: Mr Simon Fisher
Age range: 3–18 years

Dulwich Cranbrook
Coursehorn, Cranbrook,
Kent TN17 3NP
Tel: 01580 712179
Head of School: Mrs Sophie Bradshaw
Age range: 2–16 years
No. of pupils: 436
Fees: Day £5,097–£8,682

Gad's Hill School
Gravesend Road, Higham,
Rochester, Kent ME3 7PA
Tel: 01474 822366
Headmaster: Mr Paul Savage
Age range: 3–16 years

Haddon Dene School
57 Gladstone Road,
Broadstairs, Kent CT10 2HY
Tel: 01843 861176
Headmistress: Mrs Joanne Parpworth
Age range: 3–11 years

Hilden Grange School
Dry Hill Park Road, Tonbridge,
Kent TN10 3BX
Tel: 01732 352706
Headmaster: Mr M Gough
BA, LLB (Rhodes), LLM (Cape
Town), PGCE (OU)
Age range: 2.5–13 years
No. of pupils: 294

Hilden Oaks Preparatory School & Nursery
38 Dry Hill Park Road,
Tonbridge, Kent TN10 3BU
Tel: 01732 353941
Head of School: Mrs Sharon Wade
Age range: 3 months–11 years

Holmewood House School
Barrow Lane, Langton Green,
Tunbridge Wells, Kent TN3 0EB
Tel: 01892 860000
Head of School: Mrs Ruth O'Sullivan
Age range: 3–13 years
No. of pupils: 450

KENT COLLEGE JUNIOR SCHOOL
For further details see p. 77
Harbledown, Canterbury,
Kent CT2 9AQ
Tel: 01227 762436
Email: admissions@kentcollege.co.uk
Website: kentcollege.com/junior-school
Head: Mr Simon James
Age range: 0–11 years
No. of pupils: 220

Kent College Pembury
Old Church Road, Pembury,
Tunbridge Wells, Kent TN2 4AX
Tel: +44 (0)1892 822006
Head of School: Miss Katrina Handford
Age range: B3–11 years G3–18 years (boarding from 8)
No. of pupils: 500
Fees: Day £22,575 WB
£28,200 FB £35,700

King's School Rochester Preparatory
St Nicholas House, King Edward
Road, Rochester, Kent ME1 1UB
Tel: 01634 888577
Head of School: Mr Tom Morgan
Age range: 8–13 years

King's School Rochester Pre-Preparatory & Nursery
Chadlington House, Lockington
Grove, Rochester, Kent ME1 1RH
Tel: 01634 888566
Head of School: Mrs Kellie Crozer
Age range: 3–8 years

Lorenden Preparatory School
Painter's Forstal, Faversham,
Kent ME13 0EN
Tel: 01795 590030
Head of School: Mr Richard McIntosh
Age range: 3–11 years
No. of pupils: 122

Maple Tree Primary School
162 Ramsgate Road,
Broadstairs, Kent CT10 2EW
Tel: 01843 317080
Acting Head: Ms Laura Stubbs
Age range: 7–11 years

Marlborough House School
High Street, Hawkhurst, Kent TN18 4PY
Tel: 01580 753555
Head: Mr Eddy Newton
Age range: 2.5–13 years
No. of pupils: 250
Fees: Day £9,165–£18,690

Northbourne Park School
Betteshanger, Deal, Kent CT14 0NW
Tel: 01304 611215
Headmaster: Mr Mark Hammond
BA (Hons), PGCE, MA
Age range: 2–13 years
(boarding from 7)
No. of pupils: 161
Fees: Day £3,397–£6,470 WB
£8,143 FB £9,429–£9,890

ENGLAND: South-East

OneSchool Global UK Maidstone Campus
Heath Road, Maidstone, Kent ME17 4HT
Tel: 03000 700 507
Age range: 7–18 years

Radnor House, Sevenoaks
Combe Bank Drive, Sevenoaks, Kent TN14 6AE
Tel: 01959 563720
Head of School: Mr Fraser Halliwell
Age range: 2–18 years

Rose Hill School
Coniston Avenue, Tunbridge Wells, Kent TN4 9SY
Tel: 01892 525591
Head: Ms Emma Neville
Age range: 3–13 years

Russell House School
Station Road, Otford, Sevenoaks, Kent TN14 5QU
Tel: 01959 522352
Headmaster: Mr Craig McCarthy
Age range: 2–11 years

Saint Ronan's School
Water Lane, Hawkhurst, Kent TN18 5DJ
Tel: 01580 752271
Headmaster: Mr William Trelawny-Vernon BSc(Hons)
Age range: 3–13 years

Sevenoaks Preparatory School
Godden Green, Sevenoaks, Kent TN15 0JU
Tel: 01732 762336
Headmaster: Mr Luke Harrison
Age range: 2–13 years

Solefield School
Solefields Road, Sevenoaks, Kent TN13 1PH
Tel: 01732 452142
Headmistress: Ms Helen McClure
Age range: 3–13 years

Somerhill
Tonbridge, Kent TN11 0NJ
Tel: 01732 352124
Principal: Mr Duncan Sinclair
Age range: 2–13 years

SPRING GROVE SCHOOL
For further details see p. 80
Harville Road, Wye, Kent TN25 5EZ
Tel: 01233 812337
Email: office@springgroveschool.co.uk
Website: www.springgroveschool.co.uk
Head of School: Mrs Therésa Jaggard
Age range: 2–11 years
No. of pupils: 201
Fees: Day £11,088–£17,242

St Andrew's School
24-28 Watts Avenue, Rochester, Medway, Kent ME1 1SA
Tel: 01634 843479
Principal: Mrs E Steinmann-Gilbert
Age range: 2.5–11 years

St Edmund's Junior School
St Thomas Hill, Canterbury, Kent CT2 8HU
Tel: 01227 475600
Head of School: Mr Andrew De Silva
Age range: 2–13 years (boarding from 11)

St Faith's Prep
5 The Street, Ash, Canterbury, Kent CT3 2HH
Tel: 01304 813409
Headmaster: Mr Lawrence Groves
Age range: 2–11 years

St Helens Montessori School
Lower Road, East Farleigh, Maidstone, Kent ME15 0JT
Tel: 01622 721731
Headteacher: Miss Jeannelle Dening-Smitherman
Age range: 2–11 years

St Lawrence College
College Road, Ramsgate, Kent CT11 7AE
Tel: 01843 572931
Head of College: Mr Barney Durrant
Age range: 3–18 years
No. of pupils: 501
Fees: Day £9,255–£22,860
FB £30,927–£42,945

St Michael's Preparatory School
Otford Court, Row Dow, Otford, Sevenoaks, Kent TN14 5RY
Tel: 01959 522137
Head: Mr Nik Pears
Age range: 2–13 years

Steephill School
Off Castle Hill, Fawkham, Longfield, Kent DA3 7BG
Tel: 01474 702107
Head: Mr John Abbott
Age range: 3–11 years

Sutton Valence Preparatory School
Church Road, Chart Sutton, Maidstone, Kent ME17 3RF
Tel: 01622 842117
Head: Miss C Corkran
Age range: 2–11 years

The Annex School
New Ash Green, Longfield, Kent DA3 8JF
Tel: 01474 871999
Director of Education: Ms Jane Parish
Age range: 6–16 years

The Granville School
2 Bradbourne Park Road, Sevenoaks, Kent TN13 3LJ
Tel: 01732 453039
Headmistress: Mrs Louise Lawrance B. Prim. Ed. (Hons)
Age range: B3–4 years G3–11 years

The Junior King's School, Canterbury
Milner Court, Sturry, Canterbury, Kent CT2 0AY
Tel: 01227 714000
Head of School: Ms Emma Károlyi
Age range: 3–13 years

The Mead School
16 Front Road, Tunbridge Wells, Kent TN2 5SN
Tel: 01892 525837
Headmistress: Ms Catherine Openshaw
Age range: 3–11 years

The New Beacon School
Brittains Lane, Sevenoaks, Kent TN13 2PB
Tel: 01732 452131
Head of School: Mrs Sarah Brownsdon
Age range: B3–13 years
No. of pupils: 350

Walthamstow Hall Pre-Prep and Junior School
Bradbourne Park Road, Sevenoaks, Kent TN13 3LD
Tel: 01732 453815
Headmistress: Miss Stephanie Ferro
Age range: G3–11 years

Wellesley House
114 Ramsgate Road, Broadstairs, Kent CT10 2DG
Tel: 01843 862991
Headmaster: Mr G D Franklin
Age range: 2–13 years

Portsmouth

Madani Academy
Merefield House, Nutfield Place, , Portsmouth PO1 4JZ
Tel: 02392 830764
Headteacher: Mr Luthfur Rahman
Age range: 4–16 years

Surrey

ABERDOUR SCHOOL
For further details see p. 66
Brighton Road, Burgh Heath, Tadworth, Surrey KT20 6AJ
Tel: +44 (0)1737 354119
Email: enquiries@aberdourschool.co.uk
Website: www.aberdourschool.co.uk
Headmaster: Mr Phillip Makhouli
Age range: 2–11 years
No. of pupils: 330
Fees: Day £7,785–£22,032

ACS Cobham International School
Heywood, Portsmouth Road, Cobham, Surrey KT11 1BL
Tel: +44 (0) 1932 867251
Head of School: Mr Barnaby Sandow
Age range: 2–18 years

ACS Egham International School
London Road, Egham, Surrey TW20 0HS
Tel: +44 (0) 1784 430800
Head of School: Mr Jeremy Lewis
Age range: 4–18 years

Aldro School
Lombard Street, Shackleford, Godalming, Guildford, Surrey GU8 6AS
Tel: 01483 810266
Headmaster: Mr Chris Carlier
Age range: 7–13 years

South-East: ENGLAND

Amesbury School
Hazel Grove, Hindhead,
Surrey GU26 6BL
Tel: 01428 604322
Head of School: Mr Jonathan Whybrow
Age range: 2–13 years

Banstead Preparatory School
Sutton Lane, Banstead,
Surrey SM7 3RA
Tel: 01737 363601
Head of School: Mr Jon Chesworth
Age range: 2–11 years

Barfield School
Guildford Road, Runfold,
Farnham, Surrey GU10 1PB
Tel: 01252 782271
Headmaster: Mr Andy Boyle
Age range: 2–11 years

BARROW HILLS SCHOOL
For further details see p. 67
Roke Lane, Witley, Godalming,
Surrey GU8 5NY
Tel: +44 (0)1428 683639
Email: info@barrowhills.org
Website: www.barrowhills.org
Headmaster: Mr John Towers
Age range: 2–13 years
No. of pupils: 200

Bishopsgate School
Bishopsgate Road, Englefield Green, Egham, Surrey TW20 0YJ
Tel: 01784 432109
Headmaster: Mr R Williams
Age range: 3–13 years
No. of pupils: 370

Caterham School
Harestone Valley Road,
Caterham, Surrey CR3 6YA
Tel: 01883 343028
Headmaster: Mr C. W. Jones MA(Cantab)
Age range: 3–18 years

Chinthurst School
52 Tadworth Street, Tadworth,
Surrey KT20 5QZ
Tel: 01737 812011
Head: Miss Catherine Trundle
Age range: 3–11 years

City of London Freemen's School
Ashtead Park, Ashtead,
Surrey KT21 1ET
Tel: +44 (0)1372 822400
Headmaster: Mr Roland J. Martin
Age range: 7–18 years

Claremont Fan Court School
Claremont Drive, Esher,
Surrey KT10 9LY
Tel: 01372 473794
Head: Mr William Brierly
Age range: 2.5–18 years
No. of pupils: 1100

COWORTH FLEXLANDS SCHOOL
For further details see p. 70
Chertsey Road, Chobham,
Surrey GU24 8TE
Tel: 01276 855707
Email: secretary@coworthflexlands.co.uk
Website: www.coworthflexlands.co.uk
Head of School: Miss Nicola Cowell
Age range: 2.5–11 years
No. of pupils: 150

Cranleigh Preparatory School
Horseshoe Lane, Cranleigh,
Surrey GU6 8QH
Tel: 01483 542058
Headmaster: Mr Neil Brooks BA(Hons) (QTS)
Age range: 7–13 years

Cranmore School
Epsom Road, West Horsley,
Surrey KT24 6AT
Tel: 01483 280340
Headmaster: Mr Barry Everitt
Age range: 2–18 years

DANES HILL SCHOOL
For further details see p. 71
Leatherhead Road,
Oxshott, Surrey KT22 0JG
Tel: 01372 842509
Email: registrar@daneshill.surrey.sch.uk
Website: www.daneshillschool.co.uk
Head of School: Mr Colin Baty
Age range: 2–13 years
No. of pupils: 630

Danesfield Manor School
Rydens Avenue, Walton-on-Thames, Surrey KT12 3JB
Tel: 01932 220930
Head Teacher: Mrs Jo Smith
Age range: 2–11 years

Downsend School
1 Leatherhead Road,
Leatherhead, Surrey KT22 8TJ
Tel: 01372 372197
Headmaster: Mr Ian Thorpe
Age range: 7–16 years

Duke of Kent School
Peaslake Road, Ewhurst,
Surrey GU6 7NS
Tel: 01483 277313
Head: Mrs Sue Knox BA(Hons) MBA MEd
Age range: 3–16 years
No. of pupils: 316
Fees: Day £2,740–£6,540

EDGEBOROUGH
For further details see p. 72
84 Frensham Road, Frensham,
Farnham, Surrey GU10 3AH
Tel: 01252 792495
Email: office@edgeborough.co.uk
Website: www.edgeborough.co.uk
Headmaster: Mr Daniel Cox
Age range: 2–13 years (boarding from 7)
No. of pupils: 360

Essendene Lodge School
Essendene Road, Caterham,
Surrey CR3 5PB
Tel: 01883 348349
Headteacher: Mrs K Ali
Age range: 2–11 years

Ewell Castle School
Church Street, Ewell, Epsom,
Surrey KT17 2AW
Tel: 020 8393 1413
Principal: Mr Silas Edmonds
Age range: 4–18 years
No. of pupils: 650

FELTONFLEET SCHOOL
For further details see p. 73
Byfleet Road, Cobham,
Surrey KT11 1DR
Tel: 01932 862264
Email: admissions@feltonfleet.co.uk
Website: www.feltonfleet.co.uk
Headmistress: Mrs Shelley Lance
Age range: 3–13 years (boarding from 7)
No. of pupils: 494

Frensham Heights
Rowledge, Farnham, Surrey GU10 4EA
Tel: 01252 792561
Head: Mr Andrew Fisher
Age range: 3–18 years (boarding from 11)

Glenesk School
Ockham Road North, East Horsley, Surrey KT24 6NS
Tel: 01483 282329
Headmistress: Mrs Sarah Bradley
Age range: 2–7 years

Greenfield School
Old Woking Road, Woking,
Surrey GU22 8HY
Tel: 01483 772525
Headmistress: Mrs. Tania Botting MEd
Age range: 6 months–11 years
No. of pupils: 347

Guildford High School
London Road, Guildford,
Surrey GU1 1SJ
Tel: 01483 561440
Headmistress: Mrs F J Boulton BSc, MA
Age range: G4–18 years

Hall Grove School
London Road, Bagshot,
Surrey GU19 5HZ
Tel: 01276 473059
Principal: Mr Alastair Graham
Age range: 3–13 years (boarding from 8)

Halstead St Andrew's School (Lower)
Woodham Rise, Woking,
Surrey GU21 4EE
Tel: 01483 772682
Head of School: Mr Andrew Ward
Age range: 2–8 years
Fees: Day £1,425–£4,580

Halstead St Andrew's School (Upper)
Church Hill House, Wilson Way,
Horsell, Woking, Surrey GU21 4QW
Tel: 01483 760943
Head of School: Mr Andrew Ward
Age range: 8–13 years (16 from Sept 2026)
Fees: Day £5,420–£6,135

HAZELWOOD SCHOOL
For further details see p. 74
Wolf's Hill, Limpsfield,
Oxted, Surrey RH8 0QU
Tel: 01883 712194
Email: schoolsec@hazelwoodschool.com
Website: www.hazelwoodschool.co.uk
Head: Mrs Lindie Louw
Age range: 9 months–13 years
No. of pupils: 572
Fees: Day £13,770–£22,626

Hoe Bridge School
Hoe Place, Old Woking Road,
Woking, Surrey GU22 8JE
Tel: 01483 760018
Headmaster: Mr C Webster MA BSc (Hons) PGCE
Age range: 2–16 years

Kingswood House School
56 West Hill, Epsom, Surrey KT19 8LG
Tel: 01372 723590
Headmaster: Mr Duncan Murphy BA (Hons), MEd, FRSA
Age range: 4–16 years
No. of pupils: 250

Lingfield College
St Piers Lane, Lingfield, Surrey RH7 6PN
Tel: 01342 832407
Headmaster: Mr Richard Bool
Age range: 0–18 years
No. of pupils: 940
Fees: Day £3,500–£6,810

Little Downsend Ashtead
Ashtead Lodge, 22 Oakfield Road, Ashtead, Surrey KT21 2RE
Tel: 01372 385439
Age range: 6 months–4 years

Little Downsend Epsom
Epsom Lodge, 6 Norman Avenue, Epsom, Surrey KT17 3AB
Tel: 01372 385438
Age range: 2–7 years

ENGLAND: South-East

Little Downsend Leatherhead
13 Epsom Road, Leatherhead, Surrey KT22 8ST
Tel: 01372 385437
Age range: 2–7 years

Longacre School
Hullbrook Lane, Shamley Green, Guildford, Surrey GU5 0NQ
Tel: 01483 893225
Head of School: Mr Matthew Bryan MA(Cantab.), MA(Oxon.), MSc, FRSA
Age range: 2–11 years

Lyndhurst School
36 The Avenue, Camberley, Surrey GU15 3NE
Tel: 01276 22895
Head: Mr Andrew Rudkin
Age range: 3–11 years

Manor House School, Bookham
Manor House Lane, Little Bookham, Leatherhead, Surrey KT23 4EN
Tel: 01372 457077
Headteacher: Ms Tracey Fantham BA (Hons) MA NPQH
Age range: B2–6 years G2–16 years
No. of pupils: 280
Fees: Day £10,980–£20,634

Micklefield School
10 Somers Road, Reigate, Surrey RH2 9DU
Tel: 01737 224212
Head: Mr R Ardé
Age range: 3–11 years
No. of pupils: 250

MILBOURNE LODGE SCHOOL
For further details see p. 79
Arbrook Lane, Esher, Surrey KT10 9EG
Tel: 01372 462737
Email: registrar@milbournelodge.co.uk
Website: www.milbournelodge.co.uk
Head: Mrs Judy Waite
Age range: 4–13 years
No. of pupils: 245
Fees: Day £17,418–£23,700

Notre Dame School
Cobham, Surrey KT11 1HA
Tel: 01932 869990
Head of Seniors: Mrs Anna King MEd, MA (Cantab), PGCE
Age range: B2–7 years G2–18 years

Oakhyrst Grange School
160 Stanstead Road, Caterham, Surrey CR3 6AF
Tel: 01883 343344
Headmaster: Mr Alex Gear
Age range: 4–11 years

OneSchool Global UK Hindhead Campus
Tilford Road, Hindhead, Surrey GU26 6SJ
Tel: 01428 601800
Age range: 7–18 years

OneSchool Global UK Kenley Campus
Victor Beamish Avenue, Kenley, Surrey CR3 5FX
Tel: 01883 338634
Age range: 7–18 years

Parkside School
The Manor, Stoke d'Abernon, Cobham, Surrey KT11 3PX
Tel: 01932 862749
Headteacher: Ms Nicole Janssen
Age range: B2–13 years G2–4 years
No. of pupils: 270

Reigate St Mary's Prep & Choir School
Chart Lane, Reigate, Surrey RH2 7RN
Tel: 01737 244880
Headmaster: Mr Marcus Culverwell MA
Age range: 2–11 years

RGS Guildford Prep
Maori Road, Guildford, Surrey GU1 2EL
Tel: 01483 880650
Head of School: Mr Toby Freeman-Day
Age range: B3–11 years

Ripley Court School
Rose Lane, Ripley, Surrey GU23 6NE
Tel: 01483 225217
Headmistress: Ms Aislinn Clarke
Age range: 3–11 years

Rowan Preparatory School
6 Fitzalan Road, Claygate, Esher, Surrey KT10 0LX
Tel: 01372 462627
Headmistress: Ms Sarah Raja
Age range: G2–11 years

Rydes Hill Preparatory School
Rydes Hill House, Aldershot Road, Guildford, Surrey GU2 8BP
Tel: 01483 563160
Headmistress: Mrs Sarah Norville
Age range: B3–7 years G3–11 years

Shrewsbury House Pre-Preparatory School
22 Milbourne Lane, Esher, Surrey KT10 9EA
Tel: 01372 462781
Head: Mr Jon Akhurst BA (Hons) PGCE
Age range: 3–7 years

St Catherine's, Bramley
Station Road, Bramley, Guildford, Surrey GU5 0DF
Tel: 01483 899609
Headmistress: Ms Alice Phillips
Age range: G4–18 years (boarding from 11)

St Christopher's School
6 Downs Road, Epsom, Surrey KT18 5HE
Tel: 01372 721807
Headteacher: Bronia Grehan
Age range: 3–7 years

St George's Junior School
Thames Street, Weybridge, Surrey KT13 8NL
Tel: 01932 839400
Headmaster: Mr Antony Hudson
Age range: 3–11 years

St Hilary's School
Holloway Hill, Godalming, Surrey GU7 1RZ
Tel: 01483 416551
Headmistress: Mrs Jane Whittingham BEdCert, ProfPracSpLD
Age range: 2–11 years

St Ives School
Three Gates Lane, Haslemere, Surrey GU27 2ES
Tel: 01428 643734
Head Teacher: Kay Goldsworthy
Age range: 2–11 years

St Teresa's Effingham (Preparatory School)
Effingham, Surrey RH5 6ST
Tel: 01372 453456
Headteacher: Ms Sarah Conrad
Age range: B2–4 years G2–11 years

St. Edmund's School
Portsmouth Road, Hindhead, Surrey GU26 6BH
Tel: 01428 604808
Headmaster: Mr A J Walliker MA(Cantab), MBA, PGCE
Age range: 2–16 years

Surbiton Preparatory School
3 Avenue Elmers, Surbiton, Surrey KT6 4SP
Tel: 02084 391400
Principals: Mrs Louise McCabe-Arnold & Mrs Tracey Chong
Age range: 4–11 years

TASIS England
Coldharbour Lane, Thorpe, Surrey TW20 8TE
Tel: +44 (0)1932 582316
Head of School: Mr Bryan Nixon
Age range: 3–18 years (boarding from 13)
No. of pupils: 650
Fees: Day £13,880–£35,740 FB £66,970

The Hawthorns School
Pendell Court, Bletchingley, Redhill, Surrey RH1 4QJ
Tel: 01883 743048
Headmaster: Mr Adrian Floyd
Age range: 2–13 years

The Royal Junior School
Portsmouth Road, Hindhead, Surrey GU26 6BW
Tel: 01428 607977
Director: Dr Annalisa Alexander
Age range: 6 weeks–9 years

Tormead School
Cranley Road, Guildford, Surrey GU1 2JD
Tel: 01483 575101
Head of School: Mr David Boyd
Age range: G4–18 years

Warlingham Park School
Chelsham Common, Warlingham, Surrey CR6 9PB
Tel: 01883 626844
Head of School: Ms Annie Ingrassia
Age range: 2–11 years

Weston Green School
Weston Green Road, Thames Ditton, Surrey KT7 0JN
Tel: 020 8398 2778
Head Teacher: Mrs Sarah Evans BA Hons, NPQH
Age range: 2–11 years
No. of pupils: 179

Woodcote House School
Snows Ride, Windlesham, Surrey GU20 6PF
Tel: 01276 472115
Headmaster: Mr D.M.K. Paterson
Age range: B7–13 years (boarding from 7)

Yehudi Menuhin School
Stoke Road, Stoke d'Abernon, Cobham, Surrey KT11 3QQ
Tel: 01932 864739
Headmaster: Mr Ben Gudgeon
Age range: 8–19 years

South-East: ENGLAND

West Sussex

Ardingly College Preparatory School
College Road, Haywards Heath, West Sussex RH17 6SQ
Tel: +44 (0)1444 893320
Head of Prep School: Mr Harry Hastings
Age range: 2.5–13 years

Brambletye
Brambletye, East Grinstead, West Sussex RH19 3PD
Tel: 01342 321004
Headmaster: Mr Will Brooks
Age range: 2–13 years

Burgess Hill Girls
Keymer Road, Burgess Hill, West Sussex RH15 0EG
Tel: 01444 241050
Head of School (Interim): Heather Cavanagh
Age range: B2.5–4 years G2.5–18 years
No. of pupils: 503 VIth59
Fees: Day £11,010–£24,855 FB £38,745–£44,595

Copthorne Prep School
Effingham Lane, Copthorne, West Sussex RH10 3HR
Tel: 01342 712311
Headmaster: Mr Nathan Close
Age range: 2–13 years

Cottesmore School
Buchan Hill, Pease Pottage, West Sussex RH11 9AU
Tel: 01293 520648
Head of School: Mr Tom Rogerson
Age range: 4–13 years

Cumnor House Sussex
London Road, Danehill, Haywards Heath, West Sussex RH17 7HT
Tel: 01825 790347
Headmaster: Mr Fergus Llewellyn
Age range: 2–13 years
(boarding from 11)

Dorset House School
The Manor, Church Lane, Bury, Pulborough, West Sussex RH20 1PB
Tel: 01798 831456
Headmaster: Mr Matt Thomas Med BA Ed (Hons) (Exeter) FRGS
Age range: 4–13 years
(boarding from 9)
No. of pupils: 140
Fees: Day £9,315–£18,945 WB £1,258–£4,488

Great Ballard School
Eartham House, Eartham, Nr Chichester, West Sussex PO18 0LR
Tel: 01243 814236
Head of School: Mr Matt King
Age range: 2.5–16 years
No. of pupils: 220
Fees: Day £9,300–£17,500

Great Walstead School
East Mascalls Lane, Lindfield, Haywards Heath, West Sussex RH16 2QL
Tel: 01444 483528
Headmaster: Mr Chris Calvey
Age range: 2.5–13 years
No. of pupils: 345
Fees: Day £3,098–£5,938

Handcross Park School
London Road, Handcross, Haywards Heath, West Sussex RH17 6HF
Tel: 01444 400526
Headmaster: Mr Richard Brown
Age range: 2–13 years
(boarding from 8)

Hurst College Prep School
Chalker's Lane, Hurstpierpoint, West Sussex BN6 9JS
Tel: 01273 834975
Head of School: Mr Ian Pattison
Age range: 4–13 years

Lancing Prep Worthing
Broadwater Road, Worthing, West Sussex BN14 8HU
Tel: 01903 201123
Head: Mrs Heather Beeby
Age range: 2–13 years

Oakwood Preparatory School
Chichester, West Sussex PO18 9AN
Tel: 01243 575209
Headteacher: Mrs Clare Bradbury
Age range: 2.5–11 years
No. of pupils: 310
Fees: Day £3,450–£5,520

Our Lady of Sion School
Gratwicke Road, Worthing, West Sussex BN11 4BL
Tel: 01903 204063
Headmaster: Mr Steven Jeffery
Age range: 3–18 years

Pennthorpe School
Church Street, Horsham, West Sussex RH12 3HJ
Tel: 01403 822391
Hea: Ms Lydia Waller
Age range: 2–13 years

Seaford College
Lavington Park, Petworth, West Sussex GU28 0NB
Tel: 01798 867392
Headmaster: J P Green MA BA
Age range: 5–18 years
No. of pupils: 943 VIth264
Fees: Day £12,720–£26,355 WB £26,475–£35,685 FB £40,740

Shoreham College
St Julian's Lane, Shoreham-by-Sea, West Sussex BN43 6YW
Tel: 01273 592681
Principal: Mrs Sarah Bakhtiari
Age range: 3–16 years

Slindon College
Slindon House, Top Road, Slindon, Arundel, West Sussex BN18 0RH
Tel: 01243 814320
Headteacher: Mrs Sotiria Vlahodimou
Age range: B8–18 years
(boarding from 11)
No. of pupils: 107
Fees: Day £5,505 FB £10,760

Sompting Abbotts Preparatory School
Church Lane, Sompting, West Sussex BN15 0AZ
Tel: 01903 235960
Headmaster: Mr Stuart Douch
Age range: 2–13 years

The Prebendal School
52-55 West Street, Chichester, West Sussex PO19 1RT
Tel: 01243 772220
Head: Ms Alison Napier
Age range: 3–13 years
(boarding from 7)

Westbourne House School
Coach Road, Chichester, West Sussex PO20 2BH
Tel: 01243 782739
Headmaster: Mr Martin Barker
Age range: 2.5–13 years
(boarding from 7)

Windlesham House School
London Road, Washington, Pulborough, West Sussex RH20 4AY
Tel: 01903 874700
Headmaster: Mr Ben Evans
Age range: 4–13 years
(boarding from 7)

South-West

Bath & North-East Somerset D152
Bristol D152
Cornwall D153
Devon D153
Dorset D154
Somerset D154

KEY TO SYMBOLS
- Boys' school
- Girls' school
- International school
- Tutorial or sixth form college
- A levels
- Boarding accommodation
- Bursaries
- International Baccalaureate
- Learning support
- Entrance at 16+
- Vocational qualifications
- Independent Association of Prep Schools
- The Headmasters' & Headmistresses' Conference
- Independent Schools Association
- Girls' School Association
- Boarding Schools' Association
- Society of Heads

Unless otherwise indicated, all schools are coeducational day schools. Single-sex and boarding schools will be indicated by the relevant icon.

ENGLAND: South-West

Bath & North-East Somerset

King Edward's Junior School
North Road, Bath, Bath & North-East Somerset BA2 6JA
Tel: 01225 464218
Head of School: Mr Greg Taylor
Age range: 7–11 years

King Edward's Pre-Prep & Nursery School
Weston Lane, Bath, Bath & North-East Somerset BA1 4AQ
Tel: 01225 421681
Head of School: Ms Jayne Gilbert
Age range: 3–7 years

Kingswood School
Lansdown Road, Bath, Bath & North-East Somerset BA1 5RG
Tel: 01225 734200
Headmaster: Mr Andrew Gordon-Brown
Age range: 9 months–18 years

Monkton Prep School
Church Road, Combe Down, Bath, Bath & North-East Somerset BA2 7ET
Tel: 01225 831200
Head: Mrs Catherine Winchcombe
Age range: 2–13 years (boarding from 7)
No. of pupils: 280

Royal High Bath
Lansdown Road, Bath, Bath & North-East Somerset BA1 5SZ
Tel: +44 (0)1225 313877
Head: Ms Heidi-Jayne Boyes
Age range: G3–18 years (boarding from 11)
No. of pupils: 580
Fees: Day £6,592 WB £13,549 FB £15,073

The Paragon School
Lyncombe House, Lyncombe Vale, Bath, Bath & North-East Somerset BA2 4LT
Tel: 01225 310837
Head of School: Ms Rosie Allen
Age range: 3–11 years

Bristol

Badminton Junior School
Westbury Road, Westbury-on-Trym, Bristol BS9 3BA
Tel: 0117 905 5200
Head of Junior School: Ms Heidi Welch
Age range: G3–11 years (boarding from 9)

Bristol Grammar School
University Road, Bristol BS8 1SR
Tel: 0117 973 6006
Headmaster: Mr Jaideep Barot
Age range: 4–18 years

Bristol Steiner School
Redland Hill House, Redland, Bristol BS6 6UX
Tel: 0117 933 9990
Head of School: Angela Cogan
Age range: 3–11 years
No. of pupils: 128
Fees: Day £7,977

Cleve House School
254 Wells Road, Knowle, Bristol BS4 2PN
Tel: 0117 9777218
Head of School: Ms Clare Fraser
Age range: 2–11 years

Clifton College Preparatory School
The Avenue, Clifton, Bristol BS8 3HE
Tel: +44 (0)117 315 7502
Head of Preparatory School: Mr Jim Walton
Age range: 2–13 years (boarding from 8)

Clifton High School
College Road, Clifton, Bristol BS8 3JD
Tel: 0117 973 0201
Head of School: Mr Luke Goodman
Age range: 3–18 years
No. of pupils: 779
Fees: Day £3,295–£5,840

Collegiate School, Bristol
Stapleton, Bristol BS16 1BJ
Tel: 0117 965 5207
Headmaster: Mr Jeremy McCullough
Age range: 3–18 years
No. of pupils: 816
Fees: Day £8,055–£14,625

Fairfield School
Fairfield Way, Backwell, Bristol BS48 3PD
Tel: 01275 462743
Headmistress: Mrs Lesley Barton
Age range: 2–11 years

Queen Elizabeth's Hospital
Berkeley Place, Clifton, Bristol BS8 1JX
Tel: 0117 930 3040
Head: Mr Rupert Heathcote
Age range: B7–18 years G16–18 years

Redmaids' High Junior School
Grange Court Road, Westbury-on-Trym, Bristol BS9 4DP
Tel: 0117 962 9451
Headteacher: Mrs Lisa Brown BSc (Hons)
Age range: G7–11 years

The Downs Preparatory School
Wraxall, Bristol BS48 1PF
Tel: 01275 852008
Head: Ms Debbie Isaachsen
Age range: 4–13 years

Tockington Manor School
Washingpool Hill Road, Tockington, Bristol BS32 4NY
Tel: 01454 613229
Headteacher: Mr Stephen Symonds
Age range: 2–13 years
No. of pupils: 264

Torwood House School
8 Durdham Park, Redland, Bristol BS6 6XA
Tel: 0117 736620
Head Teacher: Mrs Dionne Seagrove B.Ed, M.Ed
Age range: 0–11 years

South-West: ENGLAND

Cornwall

Polwhele House School
Truro, Cornwall TR4 9AE
Tel: 01872 273011
Head of School: Mrs Hilary Mann
Age range: 3–13 years

St Joseph's School
15 St Stephen's Hill, Launceston,
Cornwall PL15 8HN
Tel: 01566 772580
Head Teacher: Mr Oliver Scott
Age range: 4–16 years

The Cornwall Independent School
14 Trelissick Road, Hayle,
Cornwall TR27 4HY
Tel: 01736 752612
Headteacher: Ms Louise Adams
Age range: 4–16 years

Truro High School for Girls
Falmouth Road, Truro,
Cornwall TR1 2HU
Tel: 01872 272830
Headmistress: Mrs Sarah Matthews
Age range: G4–18 years
(boarding from 9)

Truro School
Trennick Lane, Truro, Cornwall TR1 1TH
Tel: 01872 272763
Head of School: Mr Andy Johnson
Age range: 3–18 years

Devon

Abbey School
Hampton Court, St Marychurch,
Torquay, Devon TQ1 4PR
Tel: 01803 327868
Head of School: Ms Fleur Greinig BA (Hons), MSc
Age range: 0–11 years

Blundell's Preparatory School
Milestones House, Blundell's Road,
Tiverton, Devon EX16 4NA
Tel: 01884 252393
Head Master: Mr Andrew Southgate BA Ed (Hons)
Age range: 3–11 years

Exeter Cathedral School
The Chantry, Palace Gate,
Exeter, Devon EX1 1HX
Tel: 01392 255298
Headmaster: James Featherstone
Age range: 3–13 years
(boarding from 8)
No. of pupils: 271
Fees: Day £2,992–£4,900 FB £2,886

Exeter Pre-Prep School
The Avenue, Exminster,
Exeter, Devon EX6 8AT
Tel: 01392 496122
Head: Mr Daniel Ayling
Age range: 3–7 years

Exeter School
Victoria Park Road, Exeter,
Devon EX2 4NS
Tel: 01392 307080
Head: Ms Louise Simpson
Age range: 3–18 years
No. of pupils: 1021
Fees: Day £3,120–£5,845

Fletewood School
88 North Road East, Plymouth,
Devon PL4 6AN
Tel: 01752 663782
Headteacher: Mrs R Gray
Age range: 3–11 years

King's School
Hartley Road, Mannamead,
Plymouth, Devon PL3 5LW
Tel: 01752 771789
Head of School: Mrs Clare Page
Age range: 8 months–11 years

Kingsley School
Northdown Road, Bideford,
Devon EX39 3LY
Tel: 01237 426200
Headteacher: Mr Robert Pavis
Age range: 0–18 years
(boarding from 9)
No. of pupils: 395
Fees: Day £5,220 WB £8,370

Mount Kelly
Parkwood Road, Tavistock,
Devon PL19 0HZ
Tel: +44 (0)1822 813100
Head of School: Mr. Guy Ayling
Age range: 4–18 years

OneSchool Global UK Plymouth Campus
Foulston Avenue, Plymouth,
Devon PL5 1HL
Tel: 01752 363290
Age range: 7–18 years

Park School
Park Road, Dartington Hall,
Totnes, Devon TQ9 6EQ
Tel: 01803 864588
Headteacher: Laura Hare
Age range: 3–12 years

Plymouth College
Ford Park, Plymouth, Devon PL4 6RN
Tel: 01752 505100
Headteacher: Mrs Jo Hayward
Age range: 3–18 years
No. of pupils: 569

Shebbear College
Shebbear, Beaworthy,
Devon EX21 5HJ
Tel: 01409 282000
Head: Ms Caroline Kirby
Age range: 4–18 years

South Devon Steiner School
Hood Manor, Buckfastleigh Road,
Dartington, Totnes, Devon TQ9 6AB
Tel: 01803 897377
Education Manager: Jeff van Zyl
Age range: 3–19 years

St Christopher's Prep School & Nursery
Mount Barton, Staverton,
Devon TQ9 6PF
Tel: 01803 762202
Headmistress: Mrs Alexandra Cottell
Age range: 3–11 years

St John's School
Broadway, Sidmouth,
Devon EX10 8RG
Tel: 01395 513984
Head of School: Mr Bryan Kane
Age range: 2–18 years
(boarding from 8)

St Peter's Preparatory School
Harefield, Lympstone,
Exmouth, Devon EX8 5AU
Tel: 01395 272148
Head: Mrs Charlotte Johnston
Age range: 3–13 years

St Wilfrid's School
25-29 St David's Hill, Exeter,
Devon EX4 4DA
Tel: 01392 276171
Headteacher: Mr Ross Bovingdon
Age range: 3–16 years

Stover School
Stover, Newton Abbot,
Devon TQ12 6QG
Tel: +44 (0)1626 354505
Headmaster: Mr R W D Notman
Age range: 3–18 years

The Maynard School
Denmark Road, Exeter, Devon EX1 1SJ
Tel: 01392 273417
Headmistress: Mrs Liz Gregory
Age range: G4–18 years

Trinity School
Buckeridge Road, Teignmouth,
Devon TQ14 8LY
Tel: 01626 774138
Headteacher: Mr Robert Robinson
Age range: 3–18 years
(boarding from 9)

West Buckland School
Barnstaple, Devon EX32 0SX
Tel: 01598 760000
Headmaster: Mr Phillip Stapleton
Age range: 3–18 years

ENGLAND: South-West

Dorset

Bournemouth Collegiate School (BCS Prep)
40 St. Osmund's Road, Lower Parkstone, Poole, Dorset BH14 9JY
Tel: 01202 714110
Head of Prep: Mrs Karen Wyborn
Age range: 3–11 years

Bryanston Prep
Durweston, Blandford, Dorset DT11 0PY
Tel: 01258 452065
Head of School: Mr Will Lockett
Age range: 3–13 years

Castle Court School
Knoll Lane, Corfe Mullen, Wimborne, Dorset BH21 3RF
Tel: 01202 694438
Head of School: Mr Andrew Pilkington
Age range: 2–13 years

Clayesmore Preparatory School
Blandford Road, Iwerne Minster, Dorset DT11 8LL
Tel: 01747 811707
Head of School: Mr Jonathon Anderson
Age range: 3–13 years

Dumpton School
Deans Grove House, Deans Grove, Wimborne, Dorset BH21 7AF
Tel: 01202 883818
Headmaster: Mr Christian Saenger
Age range: 2–13 years

HANFORD SCHOOL
For further details see p. 84
Child Okeford, Blandford Forum, Dorset DT11 8HN
Tel: 01258 860219
Email: office@hanford.dorset.sch.uk
Website: www.hanfordschool.co.uk
Head of School: Hilary Phillips
Age range: G7–13 years (boarding from 7)

Leweston Prep School
Sherborne, Dorset DT9 6EN
Tel: 01963 210790
Head of School: Ms Alanda Phillips
Age range: 0–11 years

Park School
43 Queens Park South Drive, Bournemouth, Dorset BH8 9BJ
Tel: 01202 396640
Headteacher: Mrs Melanie Dowler
Age range: 3 months–11 years
No. of pupils: 356

Port Regis
Motcombe Park, Shaftesbury, Dorset SP7 9QA
Tel: 01747 857800
Headmaster: Mr Titus Mills
Age range: 2–13 years (boarding from 7)

Sherborne Preparatory School
Acreman Street, Sherborne, Dorset DT9 3NY
Tel: 01935 812097
Head: Ms Natalie Bone
Age range: 3–13 years (boarding from 7)

St Martin's School
15 Stokewood Road, Bournemouth, Dorset BH3 7NA
Tel: 01202 292011
Headteacher: Kerri Male
Age range: 4–11 years

Sunninghill Preparatory School
South Court, South Walks Road, Dorchester, Dorset DT1 1EB
Tel: 01305 262306
Headmaster: Mr David Newberry
Age range: 3–13 years

Talbot Heath
Rothesay Road, Talbot Woods, Bournemouth, Dorset BH4 9NJ
Tel: 01202 761881
Senior School Head: Mrs A Holloway MA (Oxon) PGCE
Age range: G3–18 years (boarding from 11)

Talbot House Preparatory School
8 Firs Glen Road, Talbot Park, Bournemouth, Dorset BH9 2LR
Tel: 01202 510348
Headteacher: Mrs Emma Haworth
Age range: 3–11 years

Yarrells School & Nursery
Yarrells House, Upton, Poole, Dorset BH16 5EU
Tel: 01202 622229
Head: Mrs Sally Moulton
Age range: 2–11 years
No. of pupils: 257

Somerset

All Hallows Preparatory School
Cranmore Hall, Shepton Mallet, Somerset BA4 4SF
Tel: 01749 881600
Headmaster: Dr Trevor Richards
Age range: 3–13 years

Chard School
Fore Street, Chard, Somerset TA20 1QA
Tel: 01460 63234
Head of School: Ms Becky Pielesz
Age range: 4–11 years

HAZLEGROVE PREP SCHOOL
For further details see p. 86
Hazlegrove House, Sparkford, Somerset BA22 7JA
Tel: 01963 442606
Email: admissions@hazlegrove.co.uk
Website: www.hazlegrove.co.uk
Headmaster: Mr Ed Benbow BA MEd PGCE
Age range: 2–13 years
No. of pupils: 372
Fees: Day £4,025–£8,161
FB £9,468–£12,080

King's College Prep School
Kingston Road, Taunton, Somerset TA2 8AA
Tel: 01823 285920
Head: Mr Justin Chippendale
Age range: 2–13 years
No. of pupils: 300
Fees: Day £9,600–£20,400

MILLFIELD PREPARATORY SCHOOL
For further details see p. 87
Edgarley Hall, Glastonbury, Somerset BA6 8LD
Tel: 01458 832446
Email: prepadmissions@millfieldschool.com
Website: www.millfieldschool.com/prep
Headmaster: Dan Thornburn
Age range: 2–13 years
No. of pupils: 472

Perrott Hill
North Perrott, Crewkerne, Somerset TA18 7SL
Tel: 01460 72051
Headmaster: Mr Alex McCullough
Age range: 3–13 years

Queen's College
Trull Road, Taunton, Somerset TA1 4QS
Tel: +44 (0)1823 272559
Head of College: Mr Julian Noad
Age range: 3 months–18 years

Sidcot School
Oakridge Lane, Winscombe, Somerset BS25 1PD
Tel: 01934 843102
Head of School: James Jones
Age range: 3–18 years (boarding from 11)
No. of pupils: 620
Fees: Day £3,335–£7,766
FB £12,512–£14,958

Springmead Preparatory School & Nursery
13 Castle Corner, Beckington, Frome, Somerset BA11 6TA
Tel: 01373 831555
Headteacher: Ms Sally Cox
Age range: 3–11 years

Taunton School
Staplegrove Road, Taunton, Somerset TA2 6AD
Tel: +44 (0)1823 703703
Headmaster, Taunton School: Mr. James Johnson
Age range: 0–18 years
No. of pupils: 1182

Wellington Prep School
South Street, Wellington, Somerset TA21 8NT
Tel: 01823 668700
Head of School: Ms Victoria Richardson
Age range: 3–11 years

Wells Cathedral School
The Liberty, Wells, Somerset BA5 2ST
Tel: +44 (0)1749 834200
Head Master: Mr Alastair Tighe
Age range: 2–18 years

West Midlands

Herefordshire D156
Shropshire D156
Staffordshire D156
Warwickshire D157
West Midlands D157
Worcestershire D158

KEY TO SYMBOLS

- Boys' school
- Girls' school
- International school
- Tutorial or sixth form college
- A levels
- Boarding accommodation
- £ Bursaries
- IB International Baccalaureate
- Learning support
- 16+ Entrance at 16+
- Vocational qualifications
- IAPS Independent Association of Prep Schools
- HMC The Headmasters' & Headmistresses' Conference
- ISA Independent Schools Association
- GSA Girls' School Association
- BSA Boarding Schools' Association
- S Society of Heads

Unless otherwise indicated, all schools are coeducational day schools. Single-sex and boarding schools will be indicated by the relevant icon.

ENGLAND: West Midlands

Herefordshire

Hereford Cathedral Junior School
28 Castle Street, The Cathedral Close, Hereford, Herefordshire HR1 2NW
Tel: 01432 363511
Headteacher: Mrs Helen Hoffmann
Age range: 3–11 years

Lucton School
Lucton, Herefordshire HR6 9PN
Tel: 01568 782000
Headmaster: Mr David Bicker-Caarten
Age range: 6 months–18 years (boarding from 7)
No. of pupils: 300
Fees: Day £7,500–£14,250 WB £24,345–£28,695 FB £35,130

Shropshire

Adcote School for Girls
Little Ness, Shrewsbury, Shropshire SY4 2JY
Tel: 01939 260202
Head of School: Mrs Nicola Tribe
Age range: G7–18 years (boarding from 7)

Bedstone College
Bedstone, Bucknell, Shropshire SY7 0BG
Tel: 01547 530303
Headmaster: Mr Toby Mullins
Age range: 4–18 years

Birchfield School
Albrighton, Wolverhampton, Shropshire WV7 3AF
Tel: 01902 372534
Headmistress: Sarah Morris
Age range: 4–16 years
No. of pupils: 142
Fees: Day £7,500–£11,000

Castle House School
Chetwynd End, Newport, Shropshire TF10 7JE
Tel: 01952 567600
Headteacher: Mr Ian Sterling
Age range: 2–11 years

Ellesmere College
Ellesmere, Shropshire SY12 9AB
Tel: 01691 622321
Acting Head: Mrs Vicky Pritt-Roberts
Age range: 7–18 years (boarding from 12)
No. of pupils: 600
Fees: Day £4,725–£7,710 WB £9,490–£10,010 FB £11,235–£14,020

MOOR PARK
For further details see p. 88
Richards Castle, Ludlow, Shropshire SY8 4DZ
Tel: 01584 876 061
Email: registrar@moorpark.org.uk
Website: www.moorpark.org.uk
Head of School: Mr James Duffield
Age range: 0–13 years
No. of pupils: 202
Fees: Day £3,156–£8,742 FB £10,829–£12,936

Moreton Hall Prep
Weston Rhyn, Oswestry, Shropshire SY11 3EW
Tel: 01691 776028
Head: Mrs Deborah Speakman
Age range: 6 months–11 years
No. of pupils: 140
Fees: Day £11,535–£16,380 FB £26,550

Oswestry School
Upper Brook Street, Oswestry, Shropshire SY11 2TL
Tel: +44 (0)1691 655711
Headmaster: Mr Peter Middleton
Age range: 4–18 years

Packwood Haugh School
Ruyton XI Towns, Shrewsbury, Shropshire SY4 1HX
Tel: 01939 260217
Headmaster: Mr Robert Fox
Age range: 4–13 years

Prestfelde Preparatory School
London Road, Shrewsbury, Shropshire SY2 6NZ
Tel: 01743 245400
Head of School: Mrs F Orchard
Age range: 3–13 years

Shrewsbury High School GDST
32 Town Walls, Shrewsbury, Shropshire SY1 1TN
Tel: 01743 494000
Headteacher: Ms Jo Sharrock
Age range: G4–18 years

St Winefride's RC Independent School
Belmont, Shrewsbury, Shropshire SY1 1TE
Tel: 01743 369883
Headteacher: Mrs E Devey
Age range: 3–11 years

The Old Hall School
Stanley Road, Wellington, Shropshire TF1 3LB
Tel: 01952 223117
Head of School: Mrs Anna Karacan
Age range: 4–11 years
No. of pupils: 222
Fees: Day £10,770–£16,890

Staffordshire

Abbotsholme School
Rocester, Uttoxeter, Staffordshire ST14 5BS
Tel: 01889 590217
Head of School: Mr Simon Ruscoe-Price
Age range: 2–18 years
No. of pupils: 285
Fees: Day £8,985–£22,485 WB £18,525–£27,450 FB £24,585–£33,750

Chase Grammar School
Convent Close, Cannock, Staffordshire WS11 0UR
Tel: +44 (0)1543 501800
Principal: Mrs Moira Simpson
Age range: 2–19 years

Denstone College Preparatory School
Smallwood Manor, Uttoxeter, Staffordshire ST14 8NS
Tel: 01889 562083
Head of School: Mrs Tracey Davies
Age range: 4–13 years (boarding from 7)
No. of pupils: 100
Fees: Day £3,669–£4,719

Edenhurst Preparatory School
Westlands Avenue, Newcastle-under-Lyme, Staffordshire ST5 2PU
Tel: 01782 619348
Headteacher: Mrs Emma Mousley
Age range: 3 months–11 years

Lichfield Cathedral School
The Palace, The Close, Lichfield, Staffordshire WS13 7LH
Tel: 01543 306170
Head: Mrs Susan E Hannam BA (Hons) MA PGCE
Age range: 2.5–18 years

Newcastle under Lyme School
Mount Pleasant, Newcastle-under-Lyme, Staffordshire ST5 1DB
Tel: 01782 631197
Headmaster: Mr Michael Getty BA, NPQH
Age range: 3–18 years
No. of pupils: 879 VIth152
Fees: Day £3,152–£4,330

St. Dominic's Grammar School
32 Bargate Street, Brewood, Staffordshire ST19 9BA
Tel: 01902 850248
Headmaster: Mr Peter McNabb BSc Hons, PGCE
Age range: 4–18 years

St. Dominic's Priory School Stone
37 Station Road, Stone, Staffordshire ST15 8ER
Tel: +44 (0)1785 814181
Headteacher: Mrs Rebecca Harrison
Age range: 3–16 years

Stafford Grammar School
Burton Manor, Burton Manor Road, Stafford, Staffordshire ST18 9AT
Tel: 01785 249752
Headmaster: Mr W P N Pietrek
Age range: 4–18 years
No. of pupils: 380
Fees: Day £4,065–£5,310

Yarlet School
Yarlet, Stafford, Staffordshire ST18 9SU
Tel: 01785 286568
Headmaster: Mr I Raybould BEd(Hons)
Age range: 2–13 years

West Midlands: ENGLAND

Warwickshire

Arnold Lodge School
15-17 Kenilworth Road, Leamington Spa, Warwickshire CV32 5TW
Tel: 01926 778050
Headmaster: Mr David Preston
Age range: 4–18 years

Bilton Grange Preparatory School
Dunchurch, Rugby, Warwickshire CV22 6QU
Tel: 01788 810217
Headmaster: Mr Gareth Jones
Age range: 3–13 years (boarding from 8)

Crackley Hall School
St Joseph's Park, Kenilworth, Warwickshire CV8 2FT
Tel: 01926 514444
Headmaster: Mr Rob Duigan
Age range: 4–11 years

OneSchool Global UK Atherstone Campus
Long Street, Atherstone, Warwickshire CV9 1AE
Tel: 01827 721751
Age range: 7–18 years

Stratford Preparatory School
Church House, Old Town, Stratford-upon-Avon, Warwickshire CV37 6BG
Tel: 01789 297993
Head of School: Ms Tracey Woodcock
Age range: 2–11 years

The Crescent School
Bawnmore Road, Bilton, Rugby, Warwickshire CV22 7QH
Tel: 01788 521595
Headmaster: Mr J.P. Thackway B.A.Hons, P.G.C.E.
Age range: 4–11 years

The Croft Preparatory School
Alveston Hill, Loxley Road, Stratford-upon-Avon, Warwickshire CV37 7RL
Tel: 01789 293795
Headmaster: Mr Marcus Cook
Age range: 3–11 years

The Kingsley School
Beauchamp Hall, Beauchamp Avenue, Leamington Spa, Warwickshire CV32 5RD
Tel: 01926 425127
Headteacher: Mr James Mercer-Kelly
Age range: B3–11 years G3–18 years

Twycross House Pre-Preparatory School (The Hollies)
The Green, Twycross (Near Atherstone), Warwickshire CV9 3PQ
Tel: 01827 880725
Age range: 4–8 years

Twycross House School
The Green, Twycross (Near Atherstone), Warwickshire CV9 3PQ
Tel: 01827 880651
Headmaster: Mr S D Assinder
Age range: 8–18 years

Warwick Preparatory School
Banbury Road, Warwick, Warwickshire CV34 6PL
Tel: 01926 491545
Headmistress: Ms Hellen Dodsworth
Age range: B3–7 years G3–11 years

Warwick School
Myton Road, Warwick, Warwickshire CV34 6PP
Tel: 01926 776400
Head Master: Mr James Barker
Age range: B7–18 years

West Midlands

Abu Bakr Boys School
154 Wednesbury Road, Walsall, West Midlands WS1 4JJ
Tel: 01922 724149
Head of School: Monzoor Hussain
Age range: B4–16 years

Abu Bakr Girls School
Shelly Campus, Scarborough Road, Walsall, West Midlands WS2 9TY
Tel: 01922 612361
Headteacher: Mrs Hasina Varachia
Age range: G4–16 years

Al Ameen Primary School
Stanfield House, 447 Warwick Way, Tyseley, Birmingham, West Midlands B11 2JR
Tel: 0121 706 3322
Head Teacher: Maulana Mohammed Aminur Rahman
Age range: 3–11 years

Al-Furqan Primary School
Reddings Lane, Tyseley, Birmingham, West Midlands B11 3EY
Tel: 01217 772222
Executive Head Teacher: Ms Susan Barratt
Age range: 4–11 years

Bablake Junior School
Coundon Road, Coventry, West Midlands CV1 4AU
Tel: 02476 271260
Headmaster: Mr Warren Honey
Age range: 7–11 years

Bablake Pre-Prep
The Grange, Brownshill Green Road, Coventry, West Midlands CV6 2EG
Tel: 02476 271285
Head of Pre Prep: Mrs Tracy Horton
Age range: 3–7 years

Edgbaston High School for Girls
Westbourne Road, Edgbaston, Birmingham, West Midlands B15 3TS
Tel: 01214 545831
Headmistress: Mrs Clare Macro
Age range: G2.5–18 years
No. of pupils: 880
Fees: Day £3,106–£4,695

Elmfield Rudolf Steiner School
14 Love Lane, Stourbridge, West Midlands DY8 2EA
Tel: 01384 394633
Age range: 3–17 years

Emmanuel School (Walsall)
36 Wolverhampton Road, Walsall, West Midlands WS2 8PR
Tel: 01922 635810
Head Teacher: Mr Jonathan Swain BA PGCE
Age range: 3–16 years

Eversfield Preparatory School
Warwick Road, Solihull, West Midlands B91 1AT
Tel: 0121 705 0354
Headmaster: Mr Robert A Yates MA, BA, PGCE, LPSH
Age range: 3–11 years
No. of pupils: 335
Fees: Day £9,708–£15,762

Greenfields Primary School
472 Coventry Road, Small Heath, Birmingham, West Midlands B10 0UG
Tel: 01217 724567
Headteacher: Mr Matthew Williams
Age range: 5–11 years

Hallfield School
48 Church Road, Edgbaston, Birmingham, West Midlands B15 3SJ
Tel: 0121 454 1496
Head Master: Mr Keith Morrow
Age range: 3 months–13 years
No. of pupils: 520
Fees: Day £4,770–£5,980

Hamd House School
The Custard House, 29-43 Blake Lane, Birmingham, West Midlands B9 5QT
Tel: +44 (0)1217 713030
Age range: 5–16 years

Highclare School
10 Sutton Road, Erdington, Birmingham, West Midlands B23 6QL
Tel: 01213 737400
Headmaster: Dr Richard Luker
Age range: 2–18 years

Hydesville Tower School
25 Broadway North, Walsall, West Midlands WS1 2QG
Tel: 01922 624374
Headteacher: Mrs Raj Samra
Age range: 3–16 years

King Henry VIII Preparatory School
Warwick Road, Coventry, West Midlands CV3 6AQ
Tel: 02476 271160
Headmaster: Mr J. Holtby
Age range: 3–11 years

Kingswood School
St James Place, Shirley, Solihull, West Midlands B90 2BA
Tel: 01217 447883
Headmaster: Mr Rob Luckham BSc(Hons), PGCE
Age range: 2–16 years

Lambs Christian School
113 Soho Hill, Hockley, Birmingham, West Midlands B19 1AY
Tel: 01215 543790
Headteacher: Mrs Patricia Ekhuenelo
Age range: 3–11 years

Lote Tree Primary
643 Foleshill Road, Coventry, West Midlands CV6 5JQ
Tel: 02476 261803
Headteacher: Ms Mariam Ashique
Age range: 2–11 years

Mayfield Preparatory School
Sutton Road, Walsall, West Midlands WS1 2PD
Tel: 01922 624107
Headmaster: Mr Matthew Draper
Age range: 2–11 years

Newbridge Preparatory School
51 Newbridge Crescent, Tettenhall, Wolverhampton, West Midlands WV6 0LH
Tel: 01902 751088
Headmistress: Mrs Sarah Fisher
Age range: B2–7 years G2–11 years

Norfolk House School
4 Norfolk Road, Edgbaston, Birmingham, West Midlands B15 3PS
Tel: 01214 547021
Susannah: Ms Susannah Palmer
Age range: 3–11 years

Pattison School
86-90 Binley Road, Coventry, West Midlands CV3 1FQ
Tel: 024 7645 5031
Head of School: Mr Graeme Delaney
Age range: 2–18 years

Priory School
39 Sir Harry's Road, Edgbaston, Birmingham, West Midlands B15 2UR
Tel: 0121 440 4103
Headmaster: Mr J Cramb
Age range: 6 months–18 years

ENGLAND: West Midlands

Ruckleigh School
17 Lode Lane, Solihull, West Midlands B91 2AB
Tel: 01217 052773
Headmaster: Mr Dominic Smith
Age range: 3–11 years

Solihull Preparatory School
Malvern Hall, Brueton Avenue, Solihull, West Midlands B91 3EN
Tel: 01217 051265
Head of School: Mr Mark P Penney
Age range: 3–11 years

St George's School, Edgbaston
31 Calthorpe Road, Edgbaston, Birmingham, West Midlands B15 1RX
Tel: 01216 250398
Head of School: Mr Gary Neal BEd (Hons)
Age range: 3–18 years

Tettenhall College
Wood Road, Tettenhall, Wolverhampton, West Midlands WV6 8QX
Tel: 01902 751119
Headteacher: Mr Christopher McAllister
Age range: 2–18 years (boarding from 10)
No. of pupils: 521

The Blue Coat School
Somerset Road, Edgbaston, Birmingham, West Midlands B17 0HR
Tel: 01214 106800
Headmaster: Mr N G Neeson
Age range: 3–11 years

The Royal School, Wolverhampton
Penn Road, Wolverhampton, West Midlands WV3 0EG
Tel: +44 (0)1902 341230
Principal: Mr Tom Macdonald
Age range: 4–19 years (boarding from 11)
No. of pupils: 1486
Fees: FB £16,740

The Shrubbery School
Walmley Ash Road, Walmley, Sutton Coldfield, West Midlands B76 1HY
Tel: 01213 511582
Head Teacher: Mrs Amanda Lees
Age range: 3–11 years

West House School
24 St James's Road, Edgbaston, Birmingham, West Midlands B15 2NX
Tel: 0121 440 4097
Headmaster: Mr Alistair M J Lyttle BA(Hons), PGCE, NPQH
Age range: B6 months–11 years G6 months–4 years
No. of pupils: 350
Fees: Day £2,200–£4,226

Wolverhampton Grammar School
Compton Road, Wolverhampton, West Midlands WV3 9RB
Tel: 01902 421326
Head of School: Mr Nic Anderson
Age range: 4–18 years

Worcestershire

Bowbrook House School
Main Street, Peopleton, Pershore, Worcestershire WR10 2EE
Tel: 01905 841242
Headmaster: Mr C D Allen BSc(Hons)
Age range: 3.5–16 years

Bromsgrove Preparatory School
Old Station Road, Bromsgrove, Worcestershire B60 2BU
Tel: 01527 579679
Headmaster: Mr Mike Marie
Age range: 7–13 years (boarding from 7)

Bromsgrove Pre-preparatory & Nursery School
Avoncroft House, Hanbury Road, Bromsgrove, Worcestershire B60 4JS
Tel: 01527 579679 (Ext:204)
Headmaster: Mr Mike Marie
Age range: 2–7 years

Heathfield Knoll School
Wolverley, Kidderminster, Worcestershire DY10 3QE
Tel: 01562 850204
Head of School: Mr. L. G. Collins B.Sc.(Hons), M.A.,P.G.C.E.
Age range: 3 months–18 years
No. of pupils: 243
Fees: Day £10,113–£15,975

King's Hawford
Lock Lane, Claines, Worcester, Worcestershire WR3 7SD
Tel: 01905 451292
Acting Head: Ms Caroline Knight
Age range: 2–11 years
No. of pupils: 270
Fees: Day £2,661–£4,789

King's St Alban's
Mill Street, Worcester, Worcestershire WR1 2NJ
Tel: 01905 354906
Head of School: Mr Richard Chapman
Age range: 2–11 years
No. of pupils: 182
Fees: Day £2,538–£4,593

Malvern St James Girls' School
15 Avenue Road, Great Malvern, Worcestershire WR14 3BA
Tel: 01684 892288
Headteacher: Mrs Olivera Raraty BA PGCE
Age range: G3–18 years (boarding from 7)

RGS Dodderhill
Dodderhill Road, Droitwich Spa, Worcestershire WR9 0BE
Tel: 01905 778290
Headmistress: Mrs Sarah Atkinson
Age range: B2–11 years G2–16 years

RGS Springfield
Springfield, Britannia Square, Worcester, Worcestershire WR1 3DL
Tel: 01905 24999
Headmistress: Mrs Laura Brown
Age range: 2–11 years

RGS The Grange
Grange Lane, Claines, Worcester, Worcestershire WR3 7RR
Tel: 01905 451205
Headmaster: Mr Gareth Hughes
Age range: 2–11 years

The Downs Malvern
Brockhill Road, Malvern, Worcestershire WR13 6EY
Tel: 01684 544100
Headmaster: Mr Andy Nuttall
Age range: 3–13 years (boarding from 7)

The Elms
Colwall, Malvern, Worcestershire WR13 6EF
Tel: 01684 540344
Interim Co-Headmasters: Mr Jonathan Bungard & Mr David Pearce
Age range: 3–13 years

The River School
Oakfield House, Rose Bank, Worcester, Worcestershire WR3 7ST
Tel: 01905 457047
Headteacher: Mr Adrian Parsonage
Age range: 2–16 years

Winterfold House School
Chaddesley Corbett, Kidderminster, Worcestershire DY10 4PW
Tel: 01562 777234
Headmistress: Mrs Denise Toms BA (Hons) QTS, NPQH
Age range: 3 months–13 years

Yorkshire & Humberside

East Riding of Yorkshire D160
North Yorkshire D160
North-East Lincolnshire D160
South Yorkshire D161
West Yorkshire D161

KEY TO SYMBOLS
- Boys' school
- Girls' school
- International school
- Tutorial or sixth form college
- (A) A levels
- Boarding accommodation
- (£) Bursaries
- (IB) International Baccalaureate
- Learning support
- (16+) Entrance at 16+
- Vocational qualifications
- (IAPS) Independent Association of Prep Schools
- (HMC) The Headmasters' & Headmistresses' Conference
- (ISA) Independent Schools Association
- (GSA) Girls' School Association
- (BSA) Boarding Schools' Association
- (S) Society of Heads

Unless otherwise indicated, all schools are coeducational day schools. Single-sex and boarding schools will be indicated by the relevant icon.

ENGLAND: Yorkshire & Humberside

East Riding of Yorkshire

Froebel House School
5 Marlborough Avenue,
Kingston upon Hull, East Riding
of Yorkshire HU5 3JP
Tel: 01482 342272
Head Teacher: Mr A Roberts
M.Ed BA Hons PGCE
Age range: 4–11 years

Hessle Mount School
Jenny Brough Lane, Hessle, East
Riding of Yorkshire HU13 0JZ
Tel: 01482 643371
Principal: Miss Sarah Cutting
Age range: 3–8 years

Hymers College
Hymers Avenue, Kingston upon Hull,
East Riding of Yorkshire HU3 1LW
Tel: 01482 343555
Headmaster: Mr Justin Stanley
Age range: 8–18 years
(A) (£)

Tranby
Tranby Croft, Anlaby, Kingston upon
Hull, East Riding of Yorkshire HU10 7EH
Tel: 01482 657016
Headmistress: Mrs Alex Wilson BA
(Surrey) PGCE (Cantab) MA (London)
Age range: 3–18 years
No. of pupils: 576
(A) (£)

North Yorkshire

Ashville College
Green Lane, Harrogate,
North Yorkshire HG2 9JP
Tel: +44 (0)1423 566358
Head: Mrs Rhiannon Wilkinson
Age range: 2–18 years

Aysgarth School
Newton le Willows, Bedale,
North Yorkshire DL8 1TF
Tel: 01677 450240
Head of School: Mr Rob Morse
Age range: B3–13 years
(boarding from 8) G3–8 years

Belmont Grosvenor School
Swarcliffe Hall, Birstwith, Harrogate,
North Yorkshire HG3 2JG
Tel: 01423 771029
Headmaster: Mr Nathan Sadler
Age range: 3 months–11 years

Bootham Junior School
Rawcliffe Lane, York, North
Yorkshire YO30 6NP
Tel: 01904 655021
Head: Mrs Helen Todd
Age range: 3–11 years
Fees: Day £2,475–£3,700

Brackenfield School
128 Duchy Road, Harrogate,
North Yorkshire HG1 2HE
Tel: 01423 508558
Headteacher: Mr Joe Masterson
Age range: 2–11 years

Chapter House Preparatory School
Thorpe Underwood Hall, Ouseburn,
York, North Yorkshire YO26 9SS
Tel: 01423 33 33 30
Head Teacher: Mrs Karen Kilkenny BSc
Age range: 3 months–10 years

Cundall Manor School
Cundall, North Yorkshire YO61 2RW
Tel: 01423 360200
Headmaster: Mr Simon Weale
Age range: 2–16 years
(boarding from 7)
Fees: Day £10,785–£17,805
WB £22,395–£23,115

Fyling Hall School
Robin Hood's Bay, Whitby,
North Yorkshire YO22 4QD
Tel: 01947 880353
Headmaster: Mr. Steven Allen
Age range: 4–18 years

Giggleswick School
Settle, North Yorkshire BD24 0DE
Tel: 01729 893000
Headmaster: Mr Sam Hart
Age range: 2–18 years
(boarding from 8)

Highfield Prep School
Clarence Drive, Harrogate,
North Yorkshire HG1 2QG
Tel: 01423 537060
Head: Mr James Savile
Age range: 2–11 years

Pocklington School
West Green, Pocklington, York,
North Yorkshire YO42 2NJ
Tel: 01759 321200
Head of School: Ms Becky Lovelock
Age range: 2–18 years
No. of pupils: 741 VIth165
Fees: Day £19,692 WB
£32,079 FB £38,034

Queen Ethelburga's Collegiate
Thorpe Underwood Estate, York,
North Yorkshire YO26 9SS
Tel: +44 (0)1423 33 33 30
Principal: Daniel Machin
Age range: 3 months–19
years (boarding from 7)
No. of pupils: 1300

Queen Mary's School
Baldersby Park, Topcliffe, Thirsk,
North Yorkshire YO7 3BZ
Tel: 01845 575000
Head: Carole Cameron
Age range: B4–7 years G4–16
years (boarding from 7)

Scarborough College
Filey Road, Scarborough,
North Yorkshire YO11 3BA
Tel: +44 (0)1723 360620
Headmaster: Mr Guy Emmett
Age range: 3–18 years
(boarding from 11)
No. of pupils: 528
Fees: Day £9,852–£20,712
FB £27,168–£44,844

St Peter's 2-8
Clifton, York, North
Yorkshire YO30 6AB
Tel: 01904 527361
Head of School: Mr Phil Hardy
Age range: 2–8 years

St Peter's 8-13
Queen Anne's Road, York,
North Yorkshire YO30 7AA
Tel: 01904 527416
Head of School: Mr Andy Falconer
Age range: 8–13 years

Terrington Hall
Terrington, York, North
Yorkshire YO60 6PR
Tel: 01653 648227
Headmaster: Mr. Simon Kibler
Age range: 3–13 years

The Mount Junior School
Dalton Terrace, York, North
Yorkshire YO24 4DD
Tel: 01904 667500
Head of School: Ms Rachel Capper
Age range: G3–11 years

The Read School
Drax, Selby, North Yorkshire YO8 8NL
Tel: 01757 618248
Head: Ms Ruth Ainley
Age range: 4–18 years
(boarding from 8)

Wharfedale Montessori School
Bolton Abbey, Skipton, North
Yorkshire BD23 6AN
Tel: 01756 710452
Age range: 6 months–11 years

York Steiner School
Danesmead, Fulford Cross, York,
North Yorkshire YO10 4PB
Tel: 01904 654983
Headteacher: Ms Annabel Gibb
Age range: 0–14 years

North-East Lincolnshire

OneSchool Global UK Ridgeway Campus
Ridge Way, Scunthorpe, North-
East Lincolnshire DN17 1BS
Tel: 03300 552611
Age range: 7–18 years

St Martin's Preparatory School
63 Bargate, Grimsby, North-
East Lincolnshire DN34 5AA
Tel: 01472 878907
Headmaster: Mr Joel Jackson
Age range: 2–11 years

The Children's House
Station Road, Stallingborough,
North-East Lincolnshire DN41 8AJ
Tel: 01472 886000
Headteacher: Ms Theresa Ellerby
Age range: 4–11 years

Yorkshire & Humberside: ENGLAND

South Yorkshire

Bethany School
Finlay Street, Sheffield,
South Yorkshire S3 7PS
Tel: 0114 272 6994
Head of School: Mr David Charles B.Eng. (Hons) (Sheffield) PGCE
Age range: 4–16 years

Birkdale School
4 Oakholme Road, Sheffield,
South Yorkshire S10 3DH
Tel: 01142 668408
Head of School: Mr Peter Harris
Age range: 4–18 years

Hill House School
6th Avenue, Auckley, Doncaster,
South Yorkshire DN9 3GG
Tel: +44 (0)1302 776300
Headmaster: Mr David Holland
Age range: 3–18 years

Mylnhurst Preparatory School & Nursery
Button Hill, Woodholm Road, Ecclesall, Sheffield,
South Yorkshire S11 9HJ
Tel: 0114 2361411
Headmaster: Mr Michael Hibbert
Age range: 3–11 years

Sheffield Girls' GDST
10 Rutland Park, Sheffield,
South Yorkshire S10 2PE
Tel: 01142 660324
Head: Mrs Nina Gunson
Age range: G4–18 years

Sycamore Hall Preparatory School
1 Hall Flat Lane, Balby, Doncaster,
South Yorkshire DN4 8PT
Tel: 01302 856800
Headmistress: Miss Jane Spencer
Age range: 3–11 years

Westbourne School
60 Westbourne Road, Sheffield,
South Yorkshire S10 2QT
Tel: 01142 660374
Headmaster: Mr Chris Hattam
Age range: 3–16 years

West Yorkshire

ACKWORTH SCHOOL
For further details see p. 89
Pontefract Road, Ackworth,
Pontefract, West Yorkshire WF7 7LT
Tel: 01977 233600
Email: admissions@ackworthschool.com
Website: www.ackworthschool.com
Headteacher: Mr Martyn Beer
Age range: 2.5–18 years (boarding from 11)
No. of pupils: 430
Fees: Day £4,440–£6,959
FB £14,214–£15,584

Al Mu'min Primary School
Clifton Street, Bradford,
West Yorkshire BD8 7DA
Tel: 01274 488593
Headteacher: Mr M M Azam
Age range: 3–18 years

Al-Furqaan Preparatory School
Drill Hall House, Bath Street,
Dewsbury, West Yorkshire WF13 2JR
Tel: 01924 453661
Head of School: Ms Shaheda Ughratdar
Age range: 2–11 years

Bradford Christian School
Livingstone Road, Bolton Woods,
Bradford, West Yorkshire BD2 1BT
Tel: 01274 532649
Head Teacher: Ms Jane Prothero
Age range: 4–16 years

Bradford Grammar School
Keighley Road, Bradford,
West Yorkshire BD9 4JP
Tel: 01274 542492
Headmaster: Dr Simon Hinchliffe
Age range: 4–18 years

Brontë House School
Apperley Bridge, Bradford,
West Yorkshire BD10 0NR
Tel: 0113 250 2811
Age range: 2–11 years

Crystal Gardens Primary School
38-40 Greaves Street, Bradford,
West Yorkshire BD5 7PE
Tel: 01274 573004
Headteacher: Ms Rashta Bibi
Age range: 4–11 years

Fulneck School
Fulneck, Pudsey, Leeds,
West Yorkshire LS28 8DS
Tel: +44 (0)113 257 0235
Headmaster: Mr Devin Cassidy
Age range: 3–18 years (boarding from 11)
No. of pupils: 245 VIth22
Fees: Day £5,745–£18,752 FB £40,095

Gateways School
Leeds Road, Harewood, Leeds,
West Yorkshire LS17 9LE
Tel: 0113 2886345
Head: Dr Tracy Johnson
Age range: B2–15 years G2–18 years
No. of pupils: 430
Fees: Day £9,270–£14,865

Ghyll Royd School and Pre-School
Greystone Manor, Ilkley Road, Burley in Wharfedale,
West Yorkshire LS29 7HW
Tel: 01943 865575
Headteacher: Mr David Martin BA MA PGCE
Age range: 2–11 years
No. of pupils: 100
Fees: Day £3,200

Heathfield Preparatory School
308 Oldham Road, Rishworth,
West Yorkshire HX6 4QF
Tel: +44 (0)1422 822217
Age range: 3–11 years

Huddersfield Grammar School
Royds Mount, Luck Lane, Marsh,
Huddersfield, West Yorkshire HD1 4QX
Tel: 01484 424549
Headmaster: Mr Stuart Rees
Age range: 3–16 years
No. of pupils: 516
Fees: Day £11,550–£16,317

Islamic Tarbiyah Preparatory School
Ambler Street, Bradford,
West Yorkshire BD8 8AW
Tel: 01274 490462
Headteacher: Mr S A Nawaz
Age range: 3–11 years

Lady Lane Park School
College Road, Bingley, West Yorkshire BD16 4AP
Tel: 01274 551168
Headmaster: Mr Nigel Saunders
Age range: 2–11 years

Leeds Menorah School
399 Street Lane, Leeds, West Yorkshire LS17 6HQ
Tel: 0113 2697709
Head Teacher: Mrs Ethel Refson
Age range: 3–11 years

Madni Academy
40-42 Scarborough Street,
Savile Town, Dewsbury, West Yorkshire WF12 9AY
Tel: 01924 500335
Headteacher: Mrs Shakora A Mirza
Age range: G2–16 years

Moorfield School
Wharfedale Lodge, 11 Ben Rhydding Road, Ilkley, West Yorkshire LS29 8RL
Tel: 01943 607285
Headmistress: Mrs Tina Herbert
Age range: 2–11 years
No. of pupils: 110
Fees: Day £10,395

Moorlands School
Foxhill Drive, Weetwood Lane,
Leeds, West Yorkshire LS16 5PF
Tel: 0113 2785286
Head of School: Ms Jacqueline Atkinson
Age range: 2–11 years

OneSchool Global UK York Campus
Bishopthorpe Road, York,
West Yorkshire YO23 2QA
Tel: 01904 663300
Age range: 7–18 years

Paradise Primary School
1 Bretton Street, Dewsbury,
West Yorkshire WF12 9BB
Tel: 01924 439803
Head of School: Mrs A Patel
Age range: 2–11 years

Queen Elizabeth Grammar School (Junior Section)
158 Northgate, Wakefield,
West Yorkshire WF1 3QY
Tel: 01924 373821
Director of Junior Section: Mr Richard Thompson BA (Hons), PGCE
Age range: B7–11 years

Queenswood School
Queen Street, Morley, Leeds,
West Yorkshire LS27 9EB
Tel: 01132 534033
Headteacher: Mrs Julie Tanner MMus, BA, FTCL, ARCO
Age range: 4–11 years

Richmond House School
168-170 Otley Road, Leeds,
West Yorkshire LS16 5LG
Tel: 0113 2752670
Headteacher: Mrs Sharon Young BA (Hons), PGCE, MEd
Age range: 3–11 years

Silcoates School
Wrenthorpe, Wakefield,
West Yorkshire WF2 0PD
Tel: 01924 291614
Headmaster: Mr Chris Wainman MA
Age range: 3–18 years

ENGLAND: Yorkshire & Humberside

The Branch Christian School
Dewsbury Revival Centre,
West Park Street, Dewsbury,
West Yorkshire WF13 4LA
Tel: +44 (0)1924 452511
Head Teacher: Mrs Jill Holt
Age range: 3–18 years

THE FROEBELIAN SCHOOL
For further details see p. 90
Clarence Road, Horsforth,
Leeds, West Yorkshire LS18 4LB
Tel: 0113 2583047
Email: office@froebelian.co.uk
Website: www.froebelian.com
Head Teacher: Mrs Anna Coulson
Age range: 2–11 years
No. of pupils: 132
Fees: Day £5,430–£10,095

The Gleddings School
Birdcage Lane, Savile Park,
Halifax, West Yorkshire HX3 0JB
Tel: 01422 354605
Head Teacher: Ms Jill Wilson
Age range: 3–11 years

The Grammar School at Leeds
Alwoodley Gates, Harrogate Road,
Leeds, West Yorkshire LS17 8GS
Tel: 0113 2291552
Principal: Mrs Sue Woodroofe
Age range: 3–18 years

The Mount School
3 Binham Road, Edgerton,
Huddersfield, West Yorkshire HD2 2AP
Tel: 01484 426432
Head Teacher: Mr Euan Burton-Smith
Age range: 3–11 years

Wakefield Girls' High School (Junior Section)
2 St. John's Square, Wakefield,
West Yorkshire WF1 2QX
Tel: 01924 374577
Director of Junior Section: Mr S Rowley BSc (Hons), PGCE, MSc
Age range: G7–11 years

Wakefield Grammar Pre-Preparatory School
Margaret Street, Wakefield,
West Yorkshire WF1 2DG
Tel: 01924 231618
Head: Mrs Emma Gill
Age range: 3–7 years

Wakefield Independent School
The Nostell Centre, Doncaster Road, Nostell, Wakefield,
West Yorkshire WF4 1QG
Tel: 01924 865757
Headmistress: Mrs K E Caryl
Age range: 3–16 years

Westville House School
Carter's Lane, Middleton, Ilkley,
West Yorkshire LS29 0DQ
Tel: 01943 608053
Head of School: Fran Colman
Age range: 2–11 years

WOODHOUSE GROVE SCHOOL
For further details see p. 91
Apperley Bridge, Bradford,
West Yorkshire BD10 0NR
Tel: 0113 250 2477
Email: admissions@woodhousegrove.co.uk
Website: www.woodhousegrove.co.uk
Headmaster: Mr James Lockwood
Age range: 2–18 years (boarding from 11)
No. of pupils: 1048 VIth212
Fees: Day £11,625–£18,882 FB £41,724–£41,958

Northern Ireland

County Antrim D164
County Armagh D164
County Down D164
County Londonderry D164
County Tyrone D164

KEY TO SYMBOLS
- Boys' school
- Girls' school
- International school
- Tutorial or sixth form college
- A levels
- Boarding accommodation
- Bursaries
- International Baccalaureate
- Learning support
- Entrance at 16+
- Vocational qualifications
- Independent Association of Prep Schools
- The Headmasters' & Headmistresses' Conference
- Independent Schools Association
- Girls' School Association
- Boarding Schools' Association
- Society of Heads

Unless otherwise indicated, all schools are coeducational day schools. Single-sex and boarding schools will be indicated by the relevant icon.

NORTHERN IRELAND

County Antrim

Ballymoney Independent Christian School
55 Market Street, Ballymoney,
County Antrim BT53 6ED
Tel: 028 2766 3402
Principal: Mrs J Boyd
Age range: 3–11 years

Campbell College Junior School
Belmont Road, Belfast,
County Antrim BT4 2ND
Tel: 028 9076 3076
Head of Junior School: Miss Andrea Brown
Age range: B3–11 years G3–4 years

Inchmarlo
Cranmore Park, Belfast,
County Antrim BT9 6JR
Tel: 028 9038 1454
Headteacher: Mrs A Morwood
Age range: B4–11 years

Methodist College
1 Malone Road, Belfast,
County Antrim BT9 6BY
Tel: 028 9020 5205
Principal: Mr Scott Naismith
Age range: 4–18 years

Newtownabbey Independent Christian school
307-309 Ballyclare Road,
Glengormley, Newtownabbey,
County Antrim BT36 4TQ
Tel: 028 9084 4937
Principal: Mrs L McClung
Age range: 4–18 years

Victoria College Belfast
2A Cranmore Park, Belfast,
County Antrim BT9 6JA
Tel: 028 9066 1506
Principal: Mrs Karen Quinn
Age range: G3–19 years

County Armagh

Portadown Independent Christian School
Levaghery Gardens, Portadown,
County Armagh BT63 5EQ
Tel: 028 3833 6733
Principal: Miss Diane Haffey
Age range: 3–16 years

The Royal School, Armagh
College Hill, Armagh, County
Armagh BT61 9DH
Tel: 02837 522807
Headmaster: Mr Graham G W Montgomery
Age range: 4–18 years
(boarding from 8)

County Down

Bangor Independent Christian School
277A Clandeboye Road, Bangor,
County Down BT19 1AA
Tel: 028 9145 0240
Headteacher: Miss Anna Priestley
Age range: 3–16 years

Harmony Christian School
17-19 Main Street, Ballynahinch,
County Down BT24 8DH
Tel: 028 9756 3487
Principal: Mrs Leanne Woods
Age range: 4–18 years

Holywood Steiner School
34 Croft Road, Holywood,
County Down BT18 0PR
Tel: 028 9042 8029
Headteacher: Mr Peter Chambers
Age range: 3–17 years

Mourne Independent Christian School
5 Carrigenagh Road, Kilkeel,
County Down BT34 4NE
Tel: 028 417 62712
Principal: Mrs H Campbell
Age range: 4–16 years

OneSchool Global UK Newry Campus
22 Rampart Road, Newry,
County Down BT34 2QU
Tel: 02830 260777
Age range: 7–18 years

Rockport School
15 Rockport Road, Craigavad,
Holywood, County Down BT18 0DD
Tel: 028 9042 8372
Headmaster: Mr George Vance
Age range: 3–18 years

County Londonderry

OneSchool Global UK Knockloughrim Campus
23 Rocktown Road, Knockloughrim,
County Londonderry BT45 8QE
Tel: 02879 645191
Age range: 7–18 years

County Tyrone

Clogher Valley Independent Christian School
150 Ballagh Road, Fivemiletown,
County Tyrone BT75 0QP
Tel: 028 89521851
Principal: Mrs R Carscadden
Age range: 4–16 years

Kilskeery Independent Christian School
19 Old Junction Road, Kilskeery,
Omagh, County Tyrone BT78 3RN
Tel: 028 89 561 560
Principal: Mrs Pamela Foster
Age range: 4–18 years

Scotland

Aberdeen D166
Aberdeenshire D166
Angus D166
Argyll & Bute D166
Borders D166
Clackmannanshire D166
Dundee D166
East Lothian D166
Edinburgh D166
Fife D166
Glasgow D166
Moray D167
Perth & Kinross D167
Renfrewshire D167
South Ayrshire D167
South Lanarkshire D167
Stirling D167

KEY TO SYMBOLS
- Boys' school
- Girls' school
- International school
- Tutorial or sixth form college
- A levels
- Boarding accommodation
- Bursaries
- International Baccalaureate
- Learning support
- Entrance at 16+
- Vocational qualifications
- Independent Association of Prep Schools
- The Headmasters' & Headmistresses' Conference
- Independent Schools Association
- Girls' School Association
- Boarding Schools' Association
- Society of Heads

Unless otherwise indicated, all schools are coeducational day schools. Single-sex and boarding schools will be indicated by the relevant icon.

SCOTLAND

Aberdeen

Albyn School
17-23 Queen's Road,
Aberdeen AB15 4PB
Tel: 01224 322408
Headmaster: Mr Stefan Horsman
Age range: 2–18 years

International School of Aberdeen
Pitfodels House, North Deeside Road,
Pitfodels, Cults, Aberdeen AB15 9PN
Tel: 01224 730300
Head of School: Mr Nick Little
Age range: 3–18 years

Robert Gordon's College
Schoolhill, Aberdeen AB10 1FE
Tel: 01224 646346
Head of College: Mr Robin Macpherson
Age range: 3–18 years

St Margaret's School for Girls
17 Albyn Place, Aberdeen AB10 1RU
Tel: +44 (0)1224 584466
Headmistress: Miss Anna Tomlinson
Age range: B3–5 years G3–18 years

Aberdeenshire

OneSchool Global UK Caledonia (North) Campus
Millden, Balmedie,
Aberdeenshire AB23 8YY
Tel: 01259 303030
Age range: 7–18 years

Angus

Lathallan School
Brotherton Castle, Johnshaven,
Montrose, Angus DD10 0HN
Tel: 01561 362220
Headmaster: Mr Richard Toley
Age range: 6 months–18 years

Argyll & Bute

Lomond School
10 Stafford Street, Helensburgh,
Argyll & Bute G84 9JX
Tel: +44 (0)1436 672476
Principal: Mrs Claire Chisholm
Age range: 3–18 years
No. of pupils: 320

Borders

St. Mary's School
Abbey Park, Melrose, Borders TD6 9LN
Tel: 01896 822517
Headmaster: Mr Liam Harvey
Age range: 2–13 years

Clackmannanshire

Dollar Academy
Dollar, Clackmannanshire FK14 7DU
Tel: 01259 742511
Rector: Mr Ian Munro
Age range: 4–18 years (boarding from 10)
No. of pupils: 1340
Fees: Day £10,899–£14,571 WB £28,197–£31,869 FB £30,051–£33,723

OneSchool Global UK Caledonia (South) Campus
The Pavillions, Stirling Road, Alloa,
Clackmannanshire FK10 1TA
Tel: 01259 303030
Age range: 7–18 years

Dundee

High School of Dundee
Euclid Crescent, Dundee DD1 1HU
Tel: 01382 202921
Rector: Mrs Lise Hudson
Age range: 3–18 years
No. of pupils: 1000
Fees: Day £9,618–£13,650

East Lothian

Belhaven Hill School
Belhaven Road, Dunbar,
East Lothian EH42 1NN
Tel: 01368 862785
Headmaster: Mr. Olly Langton
Age range: 5–13 years

Loretto Junior School
North Esk Lodge, 1 North High Street,
Musselburgh, East Lothian EH21 6JA
Tel: 0131 653 4570
Headmaster: Mr Andrew Dickenson
Age range: 3–12 years

The Compass School
West Road, Haddington,
East Lothian EH41 3RD
Tel: 01620 822642
Headmaster: Mr Mark Becher MA(Hons), PGCE
Age range: 3–12 years

Edinburgh

Cargilfield School
45 Gamekeeper's Road,
Edinburgh EH4 6HU
Tel: 0131 336 2207
Headmaster: Mr. Robert Taylor
Age range: 3–13 years

Clifton Hall School
Newbridge, Edinburgh EH28 8LQ
Tel: 0131 333 1359
Headmaster: Mr R Grant
Age range: 3–18 years

Edinburgh Montessori Arts School
18N Liberton Brae,
Edinburgh EH16 6AE
Tel: 0131 600 0123
Principal: Ms Emma Rattigan
Age range: 1–18 years

Edinburgh Steiner School
60-64 Spylaw Road,
Edinburgh EH10 5BR
Tel: 0131 337 3410
Age range: 2–18 years
No. of pupils: 380

ESMS Junior School
11 Queensferry Terrace,
Edinburgh EH4 3EQ
Tel: +44 (0)131 311 1111
Head of School: Mr Mike Kane
Age range: 3–11 years

Fettes College Preparatory School
East Fettes Avenue,
Edinburgh EH4 1DL
Tel: 0131 332 2976
Headmaster: Mr Charlie Minogue
Age range: 5–13 years

George Heriot's School
Lauriston Place, Edinburgh EH3 9EQ
Tel: 0131 229 7263
Principal: Mr Gareth Warren
Age range: 3–18 years

George Watson's College
69-71 Colinton Road,
Edinburgh EH10 5EG
Tel: 0131 446 6000
Principal: Mr Melvyn Roffe
Age range: 3–18 years

Mannafields Christian School
Unit B12, St Margaret's House, 151
London Road, Edinburgh EH7 6AE
Tel: 131516 3221
Age range: 5–14 years

MERCHISTON CASTLE SCHOOL
For further details see p. 94
294 Colinton Road,
Edinburgh EH13 0PU
Tel: 0131 312 2200
Email: admissions@merchiston.co.uk
Website: www.merchiston.co.uk
Headmaster: Mr Jonathan Anderson
Age range: B3–18 years (boarding 12–18) G3–11 years
No. of pupils: 380
Fees: Day £18,000–£30,430 FB £30,240–£42,255

Regius School
69a Whitehill Street, Newcraighall,
Edinburgh EH21 8QZ
Tel: 07932 801780
Head of School: Mr James Steward
Age range: 5–14 years

St George's School for Girls
Garscube Terrace,
Edinburgh EH12 6BG
Tel: 0131 311 8000
Head: Mrs Alex Hems
Age range: B3–5 years G3–18 years (boarding from 10)

St Mary's Music School
Coates Hall, 25 Grosvenor
Crescent, Edinburgh EH12 5EL
Tel: 0131 538 7766
Headteacher: Dr Kenneth Taylor BSc Hons, PhD, PGCE, PG Dip
Age range: 9–19 years

The Edinburgh Academy
42 Henderson Row,
Edinburgh EH3 5BL
Tel: 0131 556 4603
Rector: Barry Welsh
Age range: 2–18 years

Fife

St Leonards School
South Street, St Andrews, Fife KY16 9QJ
Tel: 01334 472126
Head: Mr Simon Brian
Age range: 5–18 years (boarding from 10)
No. of pupils: 570
Fees: Day £12,168–£19,704 FB £29,814–£46,446

Glasgow

Belmont House School
Sandringham Avenue, Newton
Mearns, Glasgow G77 5DU
Tel: 0141 639 2922
Principal: Mr Melvyn D Shanks BSc, DipEd, MInstP, CPhys, SQH
Age range: 3–18 years

Fernhill School
Fernbrae Avenue, Burnside,
Rutherglen, Glasgow G73 4SG
Tel: 01416 342674
Head Teacher: Mr Mark Donnelly
Age range: 3–18 years
No. of pupils: 230
Fees: Day £8,900–£13,500

Hutchesons' Grammar School
21 Beaton Road, Glasgow G41 4NW
Tel: 0141 423 2933
Rector: Mr Colin Gambles BSc (Hons) PGCE
Age range: 3–18 years

Kelvinside Academy
33 Kirklee Road, Glasgow G12 0SW
Tel: 0141 357 3376
Rector: Mr Daniel J Wyatt BA (Ed) Hons
Age range: 3–18 years

SCOTLAND

Olivewood Primary School
81 Lister Street, Glasgow G4 0BZ
Age range: 5–11 years

St Aloysius' College
45 Hill Street, Glasgow G3 6RJ
Tel: 0141 332 3190
Head Master: Mr Matthew Bartlett MA (Cantab), PGCE, NLE, NPQH
Age range: 3–18 years
£ ✎

The Glasgow Academy, Kelvinbridge
Colebrooke Street, Kelvinbridge, Glasgow G12 8HE
Tel: 0141 334 8558
Rector: Mr Matthew K Pearce BA (Dunelm)
Age range: 3–18 years
£ ✎

The Glasgow Academy, Milngavie
Mugdock Road, Milngavie, Glasgow G62 8NP
Tel: 0141 956 3758
Rector: Mr Matthew K Pearce BA (Dunelm)
Age range: 3–8 years

The Glasgow Academy, Newlands
54 Newlands Road, Newlands, Glasgow G43 2JG
Tel: 0141 632 0736
Rector: Mr Matthew K Pearce BA (Dunelm)
Age range: 3–8 years

The High School of Glasgow
637 Crow Road, Glasgow G13 1PL
Tel: 0141 954 9628
Rector: Mr John O'Neill
Age range: 3–18 years
£ ✎

Moray

Drumduan School
Clovenside Road, Forres, Moray IV36 2RD
Tel: + 44 (0)1309 676300
Principal Teacher: Krzysztof Zajaczkowski
Age range: 3–18 years

Gordonstoun
Elgin, Moray IV30 5RF
Tel: 01343 837837
Principal: Ms Lisa Kerr BA
Age range: 4.5–18 years (Boarding from age 8)
No. of pupils: 546
Fees: Day £5,149–£12,865 WB £11,220 FB £11,220–£17,705

Perth & Kinross

Ardvreck School
Crieff, Perth & Kinross PH7 4EX
Tel: 01764 653112
Headmistress: Mrs Ali Kinge
Age range: 3–13 years (boarding from 7)

Craigclowan School & Nursery
Edinburgh Road, Perth, Perth & Kinross PH2 8PS
Tel: 01738 626310
Head of School: Liz Henderson
Age range: 3–13 years
No. of pupils: 219
Fees: Day £5,330

Morrison's Academy
Ferntower Road, Crieff, Perth & Kinross PH7 3AN
Tel: 01764 653885
Rector: Mr A J McGarva
Age range: 2–18 years

Renfrewshire

Al-Qalam Primary & High School
Ben Nevis Road, Paisley, Renfrewshire PA2 7LA
Tel: 014123 72236
Executive Head: Mr Shoeb Sarguroh
Age range: 5–14 years

St Columba's School
Duchal Road, Kilmacolm, Renfrewshire PA13 4AU
Tel: 01505 872238
Rector: Ms Victoria J. Reilly
Age range: 3–18 years

South Ayrshire

Wellington School
Carleton Turrets, 1 Craigweil Road, Ayr, South Ayrshire KA7 2XH
Tel: 01292 269321
Head: Mr S Johnson MA (Cantab) PGCE
Age range: 3–18 years

South Lanarkshire

Hamilton College
Bothwell Road, Hamilton, South Lanarkshire ML3 0AY
Tel: 01698 282700
Headteacher: Mr Richard Charman
Age range: 2–18 years
No. of pupils: 400
Fees: Day £8,985–£12,588

Stirling

Fairview International School, Bridge of Allan
52 Kenilworth Road, Bridge of Allan, Stirling FK9 4RY
Tel: +44 (0)1786 231952
Headteacher: Mrs. Victoria Gamble
Age range: 5–18 years
No. of pupils: 86

Wales

Carmarthenshire D170
Clwyd D170
Denbighshire D170
Glamorgan D170
Gwynedd D170
Monmouthshire D170
Pembrokeshire D170
Powys D170

KEY TO SYMBOLS
- Boys' school
- Girls' school
- International school
- Tutorial or sixth form college
- A levels
- Boarding accommodation
- Bursaries
- International Baccalaureate
- Learning support
- Entrance at 16+
- Vocational qualifications
- Independent Association of Prep Schools
- The Headmasters' & Headmistresses' Conference
- Independent Schools Association
- Girls' School Association
- Boarding Schools' Association
- Society of Heads

Unless otherwise indicated, all schools are coeducational day schools. Single-sex and boarding schools will be indicated by the relevant icon.

WALES

Carmarthenshire

Llandovery College
Queensway, Llandovery,
Carmarthenshire SA20 0EE
Tel: +44(0)1550 723000
Warden: Mr Dominic Findlay
Age range: 3–18 years

St. Michael's School
Bryn, Llanelli, Carmarthenshire
SA14 9TU
Tel: 01554 820325
Headmaster: Mr Benson Ferrari
Age range: 3–18 years

Clwyd

Rydal Penrhos Preparatory School
Pwllycrochan Avenue, Colwyn
Bay, Clwyd LL29 7BT
Tel: +44 (0)1492 530 381
Head of School: Mrs Lucy Davies
Age range: 2–11 years

Denbighshire

Fairholme Preparatory School
The Mount, Mount Road, St.
Asaph, Denbighshire LL17 0DH
Tel: 01745 583 505
Principal: Mrs E Perkins MA(Oxon)
Age range: 3–11 years

Myddelton College
Peakes Lane, Denbigh,
Denbighshire LL16 3EN
Tel: +44 174 547 2201
Head Teacher: Mr Andrew Allman
Age range: 4–18 years

Glamorgan

Cardiff Montessori School
Golden Gate, 73 Ty Glas
Avenue, Llanishen, Cardiff,
Glamorgan CF14 5DX
Tel: 02920 567311
Head of School: Ms Esma Izzidien
Age range: 2–12 years

Cardiff Muslim Primary School
Merthyr Street, Cathays, Cardiff,
Glamorgan CF24 4JL
Tel: 029 2034 2040
Headteacher: Sakhawat Ali
Age range: 4–11 years

Cardiff Steiner School
Hawthorn Road West, Llandaff
North, Cardiff, Glamorgan CF14 2FL
Tel: 029 2056 7986
Age range: 3–18 years

Ely Presbyterian Church School
4-6 Archer Road, Cardiff,
Glamorgan CF5 4FR
Tel: 02920 596410
Headteachers: Mrs Julia Haines
& Stephanie Williams
Age range: 3–16 years

Howell's School, Llandaff GDST
Cardiff Road, Llandaff, Cardiff,
Glamorgan CF5 2YD
Tel: 029 2056 2019
Principal: Mrs Sally Davis BSc
Age range: B16–18 years G3–18 years

Kings Monkton School
6 West Grove, Cardiff,
Glamorgan CF24 3XL
Tel: 02920 482854
Principal: Mr Paul Norton
Age range: 3–18 years

Oakleigh House School
38 Penlan Crescent, Uplands,
Swansea, Glamorgan SA2 0RL
Tel: 01792 298537
Headteacher: Mrs Nikki Hill
Age range: 2.5–11 years
Fees: Day £3,125–£4,313

OneSchool Global UK Swansea Campus
Sway Road, Morriston, Swansea,
Glamorgan SA6 6JA
Tel: 01792 581221
Age range: 7–18 years

St Clare's School
Newton, Porthcawl,
Glamorgan CF36 5NR
Tel: 01656 782509
Head of School: Helen Hier
Age range: 2.5–18 years
No. of pupils: 250
Fees: Day £6,753–£11,799

St John's College, Cardiff
College Green, Old St Mellons,
Cardiff, Glamorgan CF3 5YX
Tel: 029 2077 8936
Headteacher: Mr Shaun
Moody BA (Hons) PGCE
Age range: 3–18 years

The Cathedral School, Llandaff
Cardiff Road, Llandaff, Cardiff,
Glamorgan CF5 2YH
Tel: 029 2056 3179
Head: Ms Clare Sherwood
Age range: 3–18 years

Ummul Mumineen Academy
142 Penarth Road, Grangetown,
Cardiff, Glamorgan CF11 6NJ
Tel: 02920 220 383
Age range: 8–16 years

Westbourne School
Hickman Road, Penarth,
Glamorgan CF64 2AJ
Tel: 029 2070 5705
Headteacher: Dr GW Griffiths
BSc, PhD, ARCS, PGCE
Age range: 2–18 years
No. of pupils: 382
Fees: Day £9,192–£16,152
FB £38,950–£40,620

Gwynedd

ST GERARD'S SCHOOL
For further details see p. 98
Ffriddoedd Road, Bangor,
Gwynedd LL57 2EL
Tel: 01248 351656
Email: sgadmin@st-gerards.org
Website: www.st-gerards.org
Head Teacher: Mr
Campbell Harrison
Age range: 4–18 years
No. of pupils: 100
Fees: Day £11,652–£17,808

Treffos School
Llansadwrn, Nr. Menai Bridge, Isle
of Anglesey, Gwynedd LL59 5SD
Tel: 01248 712322
Headmaster: Dr S. Humphreys
Age range: 3–11 years

Monmouthshire

Llangattock School Monmouth
Llangattock-Vibon-Avel, Monmouth,
Monmouthshire NP25 5NG
Tel: 01600 772 213
Principal: Ms Rosemary Whaley
Age range: 2–19 years

Monmouth Prep School
Hadnock Road, Monmouth,
Monmouthshire NP25 3NG
Tel: 01600 715930
Age range: 3–11 years
(boarding from 7)

Monmouth School for Boys
Almshouse Street, Monmouth,
Monmouthshire NP25 3XP
Tel: 01600 713143
Head: Dr Andrew Daniel
BSc, MEd, PhD
Age range: B7–18 years
No. of pupils: 645
Fees: Day £11,415–£16,275
FB £20,868–£33,498

Monmouth School for Girls
Hereford Road, Monmouth,
Monmouthshire NP25 5XT
Tel: 01600 711100
Head: Mrs Jessica Miles
MA (Oxon), PGCE
Age range: G7–18 years
No. of pupils: 600
Fees: Day £11,415–£16,275
FB £20,868–£33,498

Rougemont School
Llantarnam Hall, Malpas Road,
Newport, Monmouthshire NP20 6QB
Tel: 01633 820800
Headmaster: Mr Robert Carnevale
Age range: 3–18 years

Pembrokeshire

Nant-y-Cwm Steiner School
Llanycefn, Clunderwen,
Pembrokeshire SA66 7QJ
Tel: +44 (0)1437 563640
Age range: 3–14 years

Redhill Preparatory School
The Garth, St David's
Road, Haverfordwest,
Pembrokeshire SA61 2UR
Tel: 01437 762472
Head Teacher: Mr Adrian Thomas
Age range: 0–11 years

Powys

OneSchool Global UK Newtown Campus
Sarn, Newtown, Powys SY16 4EJ
Tel: 01686 670152
Age range: 7–18 years

Index

Index

A

Abbey Gate College **Cheshire**	D136
Abbey School **Devon**	D153
Abbot's Hill School **Hertfordshire**	D112
Abbotsford Preparatory School **Greater Manchester**	D137
Abbotsholme School **Staffordshire**	D156
Aberdour School **Surrey**	66, D146
Abingdon Preparatory School **Oxfordshire**	D107
Abu Bakr Boys School **West Midlands**	D157
Abu Bakr Girls School **West Midlands**	D157
Ackworth School **West Yorkshire**	89, D161
ACS Cobham International School **Surrey**	D146
ACS Egham International School **Surrey**	D146
ACS Hillingdon International School **Middlesex**	D121
Adcote School for Girls **Shropshire**	D156
Afifah School **Greater Manchester**	D137
Akeley Wood School **Buckinghamshire**	D106
AKS Lytham **Lancashire**	D138
Al Ameen Primary School **West Midlands**	D157
Al Mu'min Primary School **West Yorkshire**	D161
Al-Aqsa Schools Trust **Leicestershire**	D116
Al-Ashraf Primary School **Gloucestershire**	D106
Al-Falah Primary School **London**	D126
Al-Furqaan Preparatory School **West Yorkshire**	D161
Al-Furqan Primary School **West Midlands**	D157
Al-Huda Primary School **Greater Manchester**	D137
Al-Khair School **Surrey**	D122
Al-Mizan School **London**	D126
Al-Qalam Primary & High School **Renfrewshire**	D167
Al-Sadiq & Al-Zahra Schools **London**	D127
Albyn School **Aberdeen**	D166
Aldenham School **Hertfordshire**	D112
Alderley Edge School for Girls **Cheshire**	D136
Aldro School **Surrey**	D146
Aldwickbury School **Hertfordshire**	D112
All Hallows Preparatory School **Somerset**	D154
All Saints School **Norfolk**	D113
Alleyn Court School **Essex**	D111
Alleyn's School **London**	D128
Alpha Preparatory School **Middlesex**	D121
Altrincham Preparatory School **Greater Manchester**	D137
Amesbury School **Surrey**	D147
Annan The Froebel School **East Sussex**	D143
Annemount School **London**	D126
Apex Primary School **Essex**	D120
Ardingly College Preparatory School **West Sussex**	D149
Ardvreck School **Perth & Kinross**	D167
Argyle House School **Tyne & Wear**	D134
Arnold House School **London**	D127
Arnold Lodge School **Warwickshire**	D157
Ashbridge Independent School **Lancashire**	D138
Ashfold School **Buckinghamshire**	D106
Ashton House School **Middlesex**	D121
Ashville College **North Yorkshire**	D160
Ateres Elisheva **Greater Manchester**	D137
Auckland College **Merseyside**	D139
Austin Friars School **Cumbria**	D136
Avalon School **Merseyside**	D139
Avenue House School **London**	D131
Avenue Pre-Prep & Nursery School **London**	D126
Avon House Preparatory School **Essex**	D120
Avondale Preparatory School **Wiltshire**	D108
Ayscoughfee Hall School **Lincolnshire**	D117
Aysgarth School **North Yorkshire**	D160
AZBUKA Russian-English Bilingual School **London**	D131
Azhar Academy Primary School **London**	D126

B

Babington House School **Kent**	D121
Bablake Junior School **West Midlands**	D157
Bablake Pre-Prep **West Midlands**	D157
Badminton Junior School **Bristol**	D152
Ballard School **Hampshire**	68, D144
Ballymoney Independent Christian School **County Antrim**	D164
Bancroft's School **Essex**	D120
Bangor Independent Christian School **County Down**	D164
Banstead Preparatory School **Surrey**	D147
Barfield School **Surrey**	D147
Barlborough Hall School **Derbyshire**	D116
Barnard Castle Preparatory School **Durham**	D134
Barnardiston Hall Preparatory School **Suffolk**	D114
Barnet Hill Academy **London**	D127
Barrow Hills School **Surrey**	67, D147
Bassett House School **London**	D131
Battle Abbey School **East Sussex**	D143
Beachborough School **Northamptonshire**	D117
Beaudesert Park School **Gloucestershire**	D106
Beaulieu Convent School **Jersey**	D104
Bedales Prep, Dunhurst & Pre-Prep, Dunannie **Hampshire**	D144
Bede's Prep School **East Sussex**	D143
Bedford Girls' School **Bedfordshire**	D110
Bedford Greenacre Independent School **Bedfordshire**	D110
Bedford Modern School **Bedfordshire**	D110
Bedford Preparatory School **Bedfordshire**	D110
Bedstone College **Shropshire**	D156
Beech Grove School **Kent**	D145
Beech Hall School **Cheshire**	D136
Beech House School **Greater Manchester**	D137
Beechwood Park School **Hertfordshire**	D112
Beechwood School **Kent**	D145
Beehive Preparatory School **Essex**	D120
Beeston Hall School **Norfolk**	D113
Beis Chinuch Lebonos Girls School **London**	D126
Beis Malka Girls school **Greater Manchester**	D137
Beis Malka Girls School **London**	D126
Beis Rochel D'Satmar Girls School **London**	D126
Beis Rochel Mcr Girls School **Greater Manchester**	D137
Beis Ruchel Girls School **Greater Manchester**	D137
Beis Soroh Schneirer **London**	D127
Beis Trana Girls' School **London**	D126
Belhaven Hill School **East Lothian**	D166
Belmont Grosvenor School **North Yorkshire**	D160
Belmont House School **Glasgow**	D166
Belmont, Mill Hill Preparatory School **London**	D127
Benedict House Preparatory School **Kent**	D121
Berkhampstead School **Gloucestershire**	D106
Berkhamsted School **Hertfordshire**	D112
Bertrum House Nursery **London**	D129
Bethany School **South Yorkshire**	D161
Bickley Park School **Kent**	D121
Bilton Grange Preparatory School **Warwickshire**	D157
Birchfield School **Shropshire**	D156
Birkdale School **South Yorkshire**	D161
Birkenhead School **Merseyside**	D139
Bishop Challoner School **Kent**	D121
Bishop's Stortford College Prep School **Hertfordshire**	D112
Bishopsgate School **Surrey**	D147
Blackheath High School GDST **London**	D128
Blackheath Prep **London**	61, D128
Blanchelande College **Guernsey**	D104
Blundell's Preparatory School **Devon**	D153
Bnois Jerusalem School **London**	D126
Bnos Margulis Viznitz Girls' School **Greater Manchester**	D137
Bnos Yisroel School **Greater Manchester**	D137
Bobov Primary School **London**	D126
Bolton School **Greater Manchester**	D137
Bootham Junior School **North Yorkshire**	D160
Boundary Oak School **Hampshire**	D144
Bournemouth Collegiate (BCS Prep) **Dorset**	D154
Bowbrook House School **Worcestershire**	D158
Bowdon Preparatory School for Girls **Cheshire**	D136
Brabyns Preparatory School **Cheshire**	D136
Brackenfield School **North Yorkshire**	D160
Bradford Christian School **West Yorkshire**	D161
Bradford Grammar School **West Yorkshire**	D161
Braeside School **Essex**	D120
Brambletye **West Sussex**	D149
Branwood Preparatory School **Greater Manchester**	D137
Breaside Preparatory School **Kent**	D121
Bredon School **Gloucestershire**	D106
Brentwood Preparatory School **Essex**	44, D111
Bridgewater School **Greater Manchester**	63, D137
Brighton & Hove Montessori School **East Sussex**	D143

Index

Brighton College Prep Kensington **London** ...D129
Brighton College Prep School **East Sussex**...D143
Brighton Girls GDST **East Sussex** ...D143
Bristol Grammar School **Bristol**...D152
Bristol Steiner School **Bristol**...D152
Broadhurst School **London** ...D127
Brockhurst & Marlston House Schools **West Berkshire**... D108
Bromley High School GDST **Kent**...D121
Bromsgrove Pre-preparatory & Nursery School **Worcestershire** ...D158
Bromsgrove Preparatory School **Worcestershire** ...D158
Brontë House School **West Yorkshire**...D161
Bronte School **Kent** ...D145
Brooke House School **Leicestershire** ...D116
Brooke Priory School **Rutland**...D118
Brookes UK **Suffolk**...D114
Broomfield House School **Surrey** ...D122
Broomwood Pre-Prep and Little Broomwood **London**...D129
Broomwood Prep - Boys **London** ...D129
Broomwood Prep - Girls **London**...D129
Broughton Manor Preparatory School **Buckinghamshire** ...D106
Bryanston Prep **Dorset** ...D154
Bryony School **Kent**...D145
Buckingham Preparatory School **Middlesex**...D121
Burgess Hill Girls **West Sussex** ...D149
Burton Hathow Preparatory School **Lincolnshire**... D117
Bury Grammar Schools **Greater Manchester** ...D137
Bute House Preparatory School for Girls **London** ...D131
Buttercup Primary School **London**...D126
Buxlow Preparatory School **Middlesex**...D121

C

Caldicott **Buckinghamshire**...D106
Cambridge International School **Cambridgeshire**...D110
Cambridge Steiner School **Cambridgeshire**...D110
Cameron Vale School **London** ...D129
Campbell College Junior School **County Antrim**...D164
Cardiff Montessori School **Glamorgan**...D170
Cardiff Muslim Primary School **Glamorgan**...D170
Cardiff Steiner School **Glamorgan** ...D170
Cargilfield School **Edinburgh** ...D166
Carleton House Preparatory School **Merseyside** ...D139
Carrdus School **Oxfordshire** ...D107
Casterton, Sedbergh Preparatory School **Cumbria** ...D136
Castle Court School **Dorset**...D154
Castle House School **Shropshire** ...D156
Caterham School **Surrey**...D147
Caversham Preparatory School **Berkshire** ...D142
Chafyn Grove School **Wiltshire** ... D108
Chandlings **Oxfordshire** ...D107
Channing School **London**...D126
Chapter House Preparatory School **North Yorkshire** ...D160
Chard School **Somerset** ...D154
Charlotte House Preparatory School **Hertfordshire** ... D112
Charlton House Independent School **Hampshire**...D144
Charterhouse Square School **London** ...D126
Chartfield School **Kent** ...D145
Chase Grammar School **Staffordshire** ...D156
Cheadle Hulme School **Greater Manchester** ...D137
Cheam School **West Berkshire** ... D108
Cheltenham College Preparatory School **Gloucestershire** ...D106
Chepstow House School **London**...D131
Chesham Preparatory School **Buckinghamshire**...D106
Chetham's School of Music **Greater Manchester** ...D137
Chigwell School **Essex** ... 54, D120
Child First Aylesbury Pre-School **Buckinghamshire** ...D106
Chingford House Nursery **London**...D126
Chinthurst School **Surrey** ...D147
Chiswick & Bedford Park Prep School **London**...D131
Chorister School (Bow) **Durham** ...D134
Chorister School (Cathedral) **Durham**...D134
Christ Church Cathedral School **Oxfordshire** ...D107
Christian Fellowship School **Merseyside** ...D139
Churcher's College **Hampshire** ...D144
City Junior School **London** ...D126
City of London Freemen's School **Surrey** ...D147
Claires Court Junior Boys **Berkshire** ...D142
Claires Court Nursery, Girls and Sixth Form **Berkshire** ...D142
Claremont Fan Court School **Surrey** ...D147
Claremont Nursery & Prep School **East Sussex**...D143
Clarendon Cottage School **Greater Manchester**...D137
Clayesmore Preparatory School **Dorset**...D154
Cleve House School **Bristol** ...D152
Clevelands Preparatory School **Greater Manchester**...D137
Clifton College Preparatory School **Bristol**...D152
Clifton Hall School **Edinburgh** ...D166
Clifton High School **Bristol** ...D152
Clifton Lodge School **London** ...D131
Clogher Valley Independent Christian School **County Tyrone** ...D164
Cokethorpe School **Oxfordshire**...D107
Colchester High School **Essex**... D111
Colfe's Junior School **London**...D128
Collège Français Bilingue de Londres (CFBL) **London** ...D127
Collegiate School, Bristol **Bristol** ...D152
Collingwood School **Surrey**...D122
Colston Bassett Preparatory School **Nottinghamshire** ...D118
Connaught House School **London** ...D131
Coopersale Hall School **Essex** ... D111
Copthill School **Lincolnshire**... D117
Copthorne Prep School **West Sussex**...D149
Cornerstone Academy **Cheshire** ...D136
Coteswood House Pre-school & Day Nursery **Nottinghamshire**... D118
Cothill House **Oxfordshire** ...D107
Cottesmore School **West Sussex** ...D149
Covenant Christian School **Greater Manchester**...D137
Coworth Flexlands School **Surrey** ...70, D147
Crackley Hall School **Warwickshire**...D157
Craigclowan School & Nursery **Perth & Kinross**...D167
Cranford School **Oxfordshire**... 40, D107
Cranleigh Preparatory School **Surrey**...D147
Cranmore School **Surrey**...D147
Cransley School **Cheshire**...D136
Cricklade Manor Prep **Wiltshire** ... D108
Crosfields School **Berkshire** ...D142
Crown House Preparatory School **Buckinghamshire** ...D106
Croydon High School GDST **Surrey** ...D122
Crystal Gardens Primary School **West Yorkshire** ... D161
Culford Pre-Preparatory School **Suffolk** ... D114
Culford Preparatory School **Suffolk**... D114
Cumnor House School for Boys **Surrey**...D122
Cumnor House School for Girls **Surrey** ...D122
Cumnor House Sussex **West Sussex**...D149
Cundall Manor School **North Yorkshire**...D160

D

Daffodil Preparatory School **London** ...D126
Daiglen School **Essex**...D120
Dair House School **Buckinghamshire** ...41, D106
Dallington School **London** ...D126
Dame Allan's Junior School & Nursery **Tyne & Wear** ...D134
Dame Catherine Harpur's School **Derbyshire**... D116
Danes Hill School **Surrey**...71, D147
Danesfield Manor School **Surrey** ...D147
Dania Scandinavian School **London**...D126
Darul Madinah Slough **Berkshire**...D142
Darvell School **East Sussex**...D143
Date Valley School Trust **Surrey** ...D122
Davenies **Buckinghamshire**...D143
De La Salle College **Jersey**... D104
Dean Close Airthrie **Gloucestershire** ...D106
Dean Close Pre-Preparatory & Preparatory School **Gloucestershire**...D106
Dean Close St John's **Gloucestershire**...D106
Deenway Montessori School & Unicity College **Berkshire** ...D142
Denstone College Preparatory School **Staffordshire** ...D156
Derby Grammar School **Derbyshire**... D116
Derby High School **Derbyshire**... D116
Devonshire House Preparatory School **London**...D127
Ditcham Park School **Hampshire**...D144
Dollar Academy **Clackmannanshire** ...D166
Dolphin School **London** ...D129
Dolphin School **Berkshire**...D142
Donhead Preparatory School **London**...D129
Dorset House School **West Sussex**...D149
Dover College **Kent**...D145
Downsend School **Surrey**...D147

Index

Dragon School **Oxfordshire** ...D107
Drumduan School **Moray** ...D167
Dudley House School **Lincolnshire** ...D117
Duke of Kent School **Surrey** ...D147
Dulwich College **London** ...D128
Dulwich College Kindergarten & Infants School **London** ...D128
Dulwich Cranbrook **Kent** ...D145
Dulwich Prep London **London** ...D128
Dumpton School **Dorset** ...D154
Duncombe School **Hertfordshire** ...D112
Durham High School for Girls **Durham** ...D134
Durlston School **Hampshire** ...D144
Durston House **London** ...D131
Dwight School London **London** ...D126

E

Eastcourt Independent School **Essex** ...D120
Eaton House Belgravia **London** ...D129
Eaton House The Manor Boys' School **London** ...D129
Eaton House The Manor Girls' School **London** ...D129
Eaton Square Prep School **London** ...D129
École Française de Londres Jacques Prévert **London** ...D131
École Jeannine Manuel - London **London** ...D126
Edenhurst Preparatory School **Staffordshire** ...D156
Edgbaston High School for Girls **West Midlands** ...D157
Edge Grove School **Hertfordshire** ...45, D112
Edgeborough **Surrey** ...72, D147
Edgware Jewish Girls - Beis Chinuch **Middlesex** ...D121
Edinburgh Montessori Arts School **Edinburgh** ...D166
Edinburgh Steiner School **Edinburgh** ...D166
Educare Small School **Surrey** ...D122
Edward Jenner School **Gloucestershire** ...D106
Egerton Rothesay School **Hertfordshire** ...D112
Elizabeth College Junior School **Guernsey** ...D104
Ellesmere College **Shropshire** ...D156
Elm Green Preparatory School **Essex** ...D111
Elmfield Rudolf Steiner School **West Midlands** ...D157
Elmhurst School **Surrey** ...D122
Elstree School **Berkshire** ...D142
Eltham College Junior School **London** ...D128
Ely Presbyterian Church School **Glamorgan** ...D170
Embley **Hampshire** ...D144
Emmanuel Christian School **Oxfordshire** ...D107
Emmanuel Christian School, Leicester **Leicestershire** ...D116
Emmanuel School **Derbyshire** ...D116
Emmanuel School (Walsall) **West Midlands** ...D157
Emmaus School **Wiltshire** ...D108
ESMS Junior School **Edinburgh** ...D166
Essendene Lodge School **Surrey** ...D147
Eton End School **Berkshire** ...D142
Eveline Day School **London** ...D129
Evergreen Primary School **London** ...D129
Eversfield Preparatory School **West Midlands** ...D157
Ewell Castle School **Surrey** ...D147
Exeter Cathedral School **Devon** ...D153
Exeter Pre-Prep School **Devon** ...D153
Exeter School **Devon** ...D153

F

Fairfield Prep School **Leicestershire** ...D116
Fairfield School **Bristol** ...D152
Fairholme Preparatory School **Denbighshire** ...D170
Fairstead House School **Suffolk** ...46, D114
Fairview International School, Bridge of Allan **Stirling** ...D167
Falcons Pre-Preparatory Chiswick **London** ...D131
Falcons School **London** ...D129
Falkner House **London** ...D129
Faraday Prep School **London** ...D126
Farleigh School **Hampshire** ...D144
Farringtons Junior School **Kent** ...D121
Farrowdale House Preparatory School **Greater Manchester** ...D137
FCJ Primary School **Jersey** ...D104
Felsted Preparatory School **Essex** ...D111
Feltonfleet School **Surrey** ...73, D147
Fernhill School **Glasgow** ...D166

Fettes College Preparatory School **Edinburgh** ...D166
Fig Tree Primary School **Nottinghamshire** ...D118
Finborough School **Suffolk** ...D114
Finchley & Acton Yochien School **London** ...D126
Finton House School **London** ...D129
Fitrah SIPS **Hampshire** ...D144
Fletewood School **Devon** ...D153
Forest Park Preparatory School **Greater Manchester** ...D137
Forest Preparatory School & Nursery **Greater Manchester** ...D137
Forest School **London** ...D126
Forres Sandle Manor **Hampshire** ...D144
Framlingham College Prep School **Suffolk** ...D114
Francis Holland Preparatory School **London** ...D129
Francis Holland School, Sloane Square, SW1 **London** ...D129
Frensham Heights **Surrey** ...D147
Froebel House School **East Riding of Yorkshire** ...D160
Fulham School **London** ...D131
Fulneck School **West Yorkshire** ...D161
Fyling Hall School **North Yorkshire** ...D160

G

Gad's Hill School **Kent** ...D145
Garden House School **London** ...D129
Gatehouse School **London** ...D126
Gateshead Jewish Primary School **Tyne & Wear** ...D134
Gateway School **Buckinghamshire** ...D106
Gateways School **West Yorkshire** ...D161
Gayhurst School **Buckinghamshire** ...D143
George Heriot's School **Edinburgh** ...D166
George Watson's College **Edinburgh** ...D166
Ghyll Royd School and Pre-School **West Yorkshire** ...D161
Gidea Park Preparatory School & Nursery **Essex** ...D120
Giggleswick School **North Yorkshire** ...D160
Glendower Preparatory School **London** ...D129
Glenesk School **Surrey** ...D147
Glenhurst School **Hampshire** ...D144
Godolphin Preparatory School **Wiltshire** ...D108
Godstowe Preparatory School **Buckinghamshire** ...42, D106
Goodwyn School **London** ...D127
Gordonstoun **Moray** ...D167
Gosfield School **Essex** ...D111
Grange Park Preparatory School **London** ...D126
Grangewood Independent School **London** ...D126
Grantham Farm Montessori School & The Children's House **Hampshire** ...D144
Grantham Preparatory International School **Lincolnshire** ...D117
Great Ballard School **West Sussex** ...D149
Great Beginnings Montessori Nursery **London** ...D131
Great Walstead School **West Sussex** ...D149
Greek Primary School of London **London** ...D131
Green Meadow Independent School **Cheshire** ...D136
Greenbank Preparatory School **Cheshire** ...D136
Greenfield School **Surrey** ...D147
Greenfields Independent Day & Boarding School **East Sussex** ...D143
Greenfields Primary School **West Midlands** ...D157
Greenwich House Independent School **Lincolnshire** ...D117
Greenwich Steiner School **London** ...D128
Gresham's Nursery and Pre-Prep School **Norfolk** ...D113
Gresham's Prep School **Norfolk** ...D113
Griffin House Preparatory School **Buckinghamshire** ...D106
Grimsdell, Mill Hill Pre-Preparatory School **London** ...D127
Guildford High School **Surrey** ...D147
Guru Gobind Singh Khalsa College **Essex** ...D120
Gurukula - The Hare Krishna Primary School **Hertfordshire** ...D112

H

Haberdashers' Boys' School **Hertfordshire** ...D112
Haberdashers' Girls' School **Hertfordshire** ...D112
Haddon Dene School **Kent** ...D145
Hafs Academy **London** ...D126
Hale Preparatory School **Cheshire** ...D136
Hall Grove School **Surrey** ...D147
Hall School Wimbledon Junior School **London** ...D129
Hallfield School **West Midlands** ...D157
Halstead St Andrew's School (Lower) **Surrey** ...D147
Halstead St Andrew's School (Upper) **Surrey** ...D147

Index

Hamd House School **West Midlands** D157
Hamilton College **South Lanarkshire** D167
Hampstead Hill School **London** D127
Hampton Court House **Surrey** D122
Hampton Prep and Pre-Prep School **Middlesex** D121
Handcross Park School **West Sussex** D149
Handel House Preparatory School **Lincolnshire** D117
Hanford School **Dorset** 84, D154
Harmony Christian School **County Down** D164
Harrodian **London** D129
Harvington School **London** D131
Hatherop Castle School **Gloucestershire** D106
Hawkesdown House School Kensington **London** D131
Hazelwood School **Surrey** 74, D147
Hazlegrove Prep School **Somerset** 86, D154
Headington Preparatory School **Oxfordshire** D107
Heath House Preparatory School **London** D129
Heath Mount School **Hertfordshire** D112
Heathcote School **Essex** D111
Heatherton School **Buckinghamshire** D106
Heathfield House School **London** D131
Heathfield Knoll School **Worcestershire** D158
Heathfield Preparatory School **West Yorkshire** D161
Heathside School Hampstead **London** D127
Helvetia House School **Jersey** D104
Hendon Prep School **London** D127
Hereford Cathedral Junior School **Herefordshire** D156
Hereward House School **London** D127
Heritage School **Cambridgeshire** D110
Herne Hill School **London** D129
Herries Preparatory School **Berkshire** 75, D142
Hessle Mount School **East Riding of Yorkshire** D160
Heywood Prep **Wiltshire** D108
High March **Buckinghamshire** D106
High School of Dundee **Dundee** D166
Highclare School **West Midlands** D157
Highfield and Brookham Schools **Hampshire** 76, D144
Highfield Prep School **North Yorkshire** D160
Highfield Preparatory School **Berkshire** D142
Highfield Priory School **Lancashire** D138
Highfields School **Nottinghamshire** D118
Highgate Junior School **London** D126
Highgate Pre-Preparatory School **London** D127
Hilden Grange School **Kent** D145
Hilden Oaks Preparatory School & Nursery **Kent** D145
Hill House **London** D129
Hill House School **South Yorkshire** D161
Hoe Bridge School **Surrey** D147
Holland House School **Middlesex** D121
Holland Park Pre Prep School and Day Nursery **London** ..D131
Hollygirt School **Nottinghamshire** D118
Holme Grange School **Berkshire** D142
Holmewood House School **Kent** D145
Holmwood House School **Essex** D111
Holy Cross Preparatory School **Surrey** 56, D122
Holywood Steiner School **County Down** D164
Homefield Preparatory School **Surrey** D122
Hopelands Preparatory School **Gloucestershire** D106
Hornsby House School **London** D130
Horris Hill **West Berkshire** D108
Howe Green House School **Hertfordshire** D112
Howell's School, Llandaff GDST **Glamorgan** D170
Huddersfield Grammar School **West Yorkshire** D161
Hulme Hall Grammar School **Greater Manchester** D137
Hunter Hall School **Cumbria** D136
Hurlingham School **London** D130
Hurst College Prep School **West Sussex** D149
Hurst Lodge School **Hampshire** D144
Hutchesons' Grammar School **Glasgow** D166
Hydesville Tower School **West Midlands** D157
Hyland House School **London** D127
Hymers College **East Riding of Yorkshire** D160

I

Ibstock Place School **London** D130
ICS London **London** D131
Immanuel Christian School **Gloucestershire** D107
Immanuel School **Essex** D120
Inchmarlo **County Antrim** D164
Instituto Español Vicente Cañada Blanch **London** D131
International School of Aberdeen **Aberdeen** D166
International School of London (ISL) **London** D131
Inwoods Small School **Hampshire** D144
Ipswich High School **Suffolk** D114
Ipswich Prep School **Suffolk** 47, D114
IRIS School **London** D127
Islamic Tarbiyah Preparatory School **West Yorkshire** ..D161
Ivy House School **London** D127

J

Jack & Jill Family of Schools **Middlesex** D121
Jameah Boys Academy **Leicestershire** D116
Jameah Girls Academy **Leicestershire** D116
James Allen's Girls' School **London** D129
Jamia Al-Hudaa Residential College **Nottinghamshire** ..D118
Jasper City School **London** D126

K

Keble Prep **London** D127
Kelvinside Academy **Glasgow** D166
Kensington Prep School **London** D130
Kensington Wade School **London** D131
Kent College Junior School **Kent** 77, D145
Kent College Pembury **Kent** D145
Kerem School **London** D127
Kerem Shloime **Greater Manchester** D137
Kew College Prep **Surrey** D122
Kew Green Preparatory School **Surrey** D122
Kilskeery Independent Christian School **County Tyrone** ..D164
Kimbolton School **Cambridgeshire** D110
King Edward VI Preparatory School **Hampshire** D144
King Edward's Junior School **Bath & North-East Somerset** ..D152
King Edward's Pre-Prep & Nursery School **Bath & North-East Somerset** ..D152
King Henry VIII Preparatory School **West Midlands** ..D157
King of Kings School **Greater Manchester** D137
King's College Prep School **Somerset** D154
King's College School **Cambridgeshire** D110
King's Ely Acremont & Nursery **Cambridgeshire** D110
King's Ely Prep **Cambridgeshire** 48, D110
King's Hawford **Worcestershire** D158
King's House School **Bedfordshire** D110
King's House School **Surrey** D122
King's School **Devon** D153
King's School Rochester Pre-Preparatory & Nursery **Kent** ..D145
King's School Rochester Preparatory **Kent** D145
King's St Alban's **Worcestershire** D158
Kings Kids Christian School **London** D129
Kings Monkton School **Glamorgan** D170
Kingscourt School **Hampshire** D144
Kingshott **Hertfordshire** D112
Kingsley School **Devon** D153
Kingswood House School **Surrey** D147
Kingswood School **West Midlands** D157
Kingswood School **Bath & North-East Somerset** D152
Kirkham Grammar School **Lancashire** D138
Kirkstone House School **Lincolnshire** D117
Kitebrook Preparatory School **Gloucestershire** D107
Knightsbridge School **London** D130

L

L'Ecole Bilingue **London** D131
L'Ecole de Battersea **London** D130
L'Ecole des Petits **London** D130
La Chouette School **London** D131
La Petite Ecole Bilingue Londres Kentish Town **London** ..D127
La Petite Ecole Française **London** D131
Lady Barn House School **Cheshire** D136
Lady Eleanor Holles (Junior Department) **Middlesex** ..D121
Lady Lane Park School **West Yorkshire** D161
Laleham Lea School **Surrey** D122
Lambrook School **Berkshire** D142

Index

Lambs Christian School **West Midlands** D157
Lancaster Steiner School **Lancashire** D138
Lancing Prep Hove **East Sussex** D143
Lancing Prep Worthing **West Sussex** D149
Langley Pre-Prep & Prep School **Norfolk** D113
Lathallan School **Angus** D166
Latymer Prep School **London** D131
Laxton Junior School **Northamptonshire** D117
Le Herisson **London** D131
Leeds Menorah School **West Yorkshire** D161
Leehurst Swan School **Wiltshire** D108
Leicester Grammar Junior School **Leicestershire** D116
Leicester High School for Girls **Leicestershire** D116
Leicester Islamic Academy **Leicestershire** D116
Leicester Preparatory School **Leicestershire** D116
Lewes Old Grammar School **East Sussex** D143
Leweston Prep School **Dorset** D154
LGS Stoneygate **Leicestershire** D116
Lichfield Cathedral School **Staffordshire** D156
Lime House School **Cumbria** D136
Lincoln Minster School **Lincolnshire** D117
Lingfield College **Surrey** D147
Little Acorns Montessori School **Hertfordshire** D112
Little Downsend Ashtead **Surrey** D147
Little Downsend Epsom **Surrey** D147
Little Downsend Leatherhead **Surrey** D148
Littlegarth School **Essex** D111
Llandovery College **Carmarthenshire** D170
Llangattock School Monmouth **Monmouthshire** D170
Lloyd Williamson School Foundation **London** D131
Lochinver House School **Hertfordshire** D112
Lockers Park **Hertfordshire** D112
Lomond School **Argyll & Bute** D166
London Christian School **London** D129
London Welsh School Ysgol Gymraeg Llundain **London** D131
Long Close School **Berkshire** D142
Longacre School **Surrey** D148
Longridge Towers School **Northumberland** D134
Longwood School **Hertfordshire** D112
Lord's School **Greater Manchester** D137
Lorenden Preparatory School **Kent** D145
Loretto Junior School **East Lothian** D166
Lote Tree Primary **West Midlands** D157
Loughborough Amherst School **Leicestershire** D116
Loyola Preparatory School **Essex** D120
Lubavitch House School (Junior Boys) **London** D126
Lucton School **Herefordshire** D156
Ludgrove **Berkshire** 78, D142
LVS Ascot **Berkshire** D142
Lycée Français Charles de Gaulle de Londres **London** D130
Lyndhurst House Prep School **London** D127
Lyndhurst School **Surrey** D148
Lyonsdown School **Hertfordshire** D120

M

Madani Academy **Portsmouth** D146
Madni Academy **West Yorkshire** D161
Magdalen College School **Oxfordshire** D107
Magdalene House Preparatory School **Cambridgeshire** D110
Maldon Court Preparatory School **Essex** D111
Maltman's Green School **Buckinghamshire** D143
Malvern St James Girls' School **Worcestershire** D158
Manchester High School for Girls **Greater Manchester** D137
Manchester Junior Girls School **Greater Manchester** D137
Manchester Muslim Preparatory School **Greater Manchester** D137
Mannafields Christian School **Edinburgh** D166
Manor House School, Bookham **Surrey** D148
Manor Lodge School **Hertfordshire** D112
Maple Tree Primary School **Kent** D145
Maple Walk Prep School **London** D128
Maranatha Christian School **Wiltshire** D108
Maria Montessori School - Bayswater **London** D131
Maria Montessori School - Hampstead **London** D128
Marlborough House School **Kent** D145
Mayfield Preparatory School **West Midlands** D157
Mayville High School **Hampshire** D144
Mehria Primary School **Bedfordshire** D110
Meoncross School **Hampshire** D144
Merchant Taylors' Prep **Hertfordshire** D112
Merchiston Castle School **Edinburgh** 94, D166
Merton Court Preparatory School **Kent** 57, D121
Methodist College **County Antrim** D164
Michael Hall School **East Sussex** D143
Micklefield School **Surrey** D148
Milbourne Lodge School **Surrey** 79, D148
Millfield Preparatory School **Somerset** 87, D154
Milton Keynes Preparatory School **Buckinghamshire** D106
Monkton Prep School **Bath & North-East Somerset** D152
Monmouth Prep School **Monmouthshire** D170
Monmouth School for Boys **Monmouthshire** D170
Monmouth School for Girls **Monmouthshire** D170
Moor Allerton Preparatory School **Greater Manchester** D137
Moor Park **Shropshire** 88, D156
Moorfield School **West Yorkshire** D161
Moorland School **Lancashire** D138
Moorlands School **West Yorkshire** D161
Moreton Hall Prep **Shropshire** D156
Morrison's Academy **Perth & Kinross** D167
Moulsford Preparatory School **Oxfordshire** 43, D107
Mount Kelly **Devon** D153
Mourne Independent Christian School **County Down** D164
Mowden Hall School **Northumberland** D134
Moyles Court School **Hampshire** D144
Myddelton College **Denbighshire** D170
Mylnhurst Preparatory School & Nursery **South Yorkshire** D161

N

Naima Jewish Preparatory School **London** D128
Nancy Reuben Primary School **London** D128
Nant-y-Cwm Steiner School **Pembrokeshire** D170
New College School **Oxfordshire** D107
New Hall School **Essex** D111
Newbold School **Berkshire** D142
Newbridge Preparatory School **West Midlands** D157
Newcastle High School for Girls GDST **Tyne & Wear** D134
Newcastle Preparatory School **Tyne & Wear** D134
Newcastle School for Boys **Tyne & Wear** D134
Newcastle under Lyme School **Staffordshire** D156
Newland House School **Middlesex** D121
Newton Prep **London** D130
Newtownabbey Independent Christian school **County Antrim** D164
Noor ul Islam Primary School **London** D126
Norfolk House School **London** D127
Norfolk House School **West Midlands** D157
Norland Place School **London** D131
Normanhurst School **London** D126
Normanton House School **Derbyshire** D116
North Bridge House Nursery and Pre-Prep Hampstead **London** D128
North Bridge House Nursery and Pre-Prep West Hampstead **London** D128
North Bridge House Prep School Regent's Park **London** D128
North London Collegiate School **Middlesex** D121
North London Grammar School **London** D127
North London Rudolf Steiner School **London** D127
Northampton High School GDST **Northamptonshire** D117
Northbourne Park School **Kent** D145
Northwood College for Girls GDST **Middlesex** D121
Norwich High School for Girls GDST **Norfolk** D113
Norwich School **Norfolk** D113
Norwich Steiner School **Norfolk** D113
Notre Dame Preparatory School **Norfolk** 49, D113
Notre Dame School **Surrey** D148
Notting Hill & Ealing High School GDST **London** D131
Notting Hill Preparatory School **London** D132
Nottingham Girls' High School GDST **Nottinghamshire** D118
Nottingham High Infant and Junior School **Nottinghamshire** D118

O

Oakfield Preparatory School **London** D129
Oakfields Preparatory School **Essex** D120
Oakhill School & Nursery **Lancashire** D138
Oakhyrst Grange School **Surrey** D148
Oaklands School **Essex** D120

Index

Oakleigh House School **Glamorgan** D170
Oakwood Preparatory School **West Sussex** D149
Oakwood Primary School **Bedfordshire** D110
Oakwood School **Surrey** D122
Octavia House School, Great Baddow **Essex** D111
Octavia House School, Vauxhall **London** D129
Octavia House School, Walworth **London** D129
Oholei Yosef Yitzchok (OYY) Lubavitch Boys School **Greater Manchester** D137
Oholei Yosef Yitzchok (OYY) Lubavitch Girls School **Greater Manchester** D137
Ohr Emes **London** D126
Old Buckenham Hall School **Suffolk** D114
Old Palace of John Whitgift School **Surrey** D122
Old Vicarage School **Surrey** D122
Old Vicarage School **Derbyshire** D116
Oldham Hulme Grammar School **Greater Manchester** D137
Oliver House Preparatory School **London** D130
OneSchool Global UK Atherstone Campus **Warwickshire** D157
OneSchool Global UK Biggleswade Campus **Bedfordshire** D110
OneSchool Global UK Bristol Campus **Gloucestershire** D107
OneSchool Global UK Caledonia (North) Campus **Aberdeenshire** D166
OneSchool Global UK Caledonia (South) Campus **Clackmannanshire** D166
OneSchool Global UK Colchester Campus **Essex** D111
OneSchool Global UK Dunstable Campus **Bedfordshire** D110
OneSchool Global UK Gloucester Campus **Gloucestershire** D107
OneSchool Global UK Hindhead Campus **Surrey** D148
OneSchool Global UK Kenley Campus **Surrey** D148
OneSchool Global UK Knockloughrim Campus **County Londonderry** D164
OneSchool Global UK Lancaster Campus **Lancashire** D138
OneSchool Global UK Maidstone Campus **Kent** D146
OneSchool Global UK Newry Campus **County Down** D164
OneSchool Global UK Newtown Campus **Powys** D170
OneSchool Global UK Northampton Campus **Northamptonshire** D117
OneSchool Global UK Northwich Campus **Cheshire** D136
OneSchool Global UK Nottingham Campus **Nottinghamshire** D118
OneSchool Global UK Plymouth Campus **Devon** D153
OneSchool Global UK Reading Campus (Primary) **Berkshire** D142
OneSchool Global UK Ridgeway Campus **North-East Lincolnshire** D160
OneSchool Global UK Salisbury Campus **Wiltshire** D108
OneSchool Global UK Swaffham Campus **Norfolk** D113
OneSchool Global UK Swansea Campus **Glamorgan** D170
OneSchool Global UK York (Springwell) Campus **Tyne & Wear** D134
OneSchool Global UK York Campus **West Yorkshire** D161
Orchard House School **London** D132
Orchard School & Nursery **Bedfordshire** D110
Orley Farm School **Middlesex** D121
Orwell Park School **Suffolk** D114
Oswestry School **Shropshire** D156
Our Lady of Sion School **West Sussex** D149
Our Lady's Abingdon School **Oxfordshire** D107
Our Lady's Preparatory School **Berkshire** D142
Overstone Park School **Northamptonshire** D117
Oxford High School GDST **Oxfordshire** D107
Oxford House School **Essex** D111
Oxford Montessori School **Oxfordshire** D107

P

Packwood Haugh School **Shropshire** D156
Palmers Green High School **London** D127
Papplewick School **Berkshire** D142
Paradise Primary School **West Yorkshire** D161
Park Hill School **Surrey** D123
Park School **Dorset** D154
Park School **Devon** D153
Parkgate House School **London** D130
Parkside School **Surrey** D148
Parsons Green Prep School **London** D130
Pattison School **West Midlands** D157
Pembridge Hall School **London** D132
Pennthorpe School **West Sussex** D149
Perrott Hill **Somerset** D154
Phoenix Academy **London** D127
Pilgrims Pre-Preparatory School **Bedfordshire** D110
Pillar Box Montessori Nursery & Pre-Prep School **London** D126
Pinewood School **Wiltshire** D108
Pipers Corner School **Buckinghamshire** D106
Pitsford School **Northamptonshire** D117
Plumtree School **Nottinghamshire** D118
Plymouth College **Devon** D153
Pocklington School **North Yorkshire** D160
Polam School **Bedfordshire** D110
Polwhele House School **Cornwall** D153
Port Regis **Dorset** D154
Portadown Independent Christian School **County Armagh** D164
Portsmouth High School GDST **Hampshire** D144
Pownall Hall School **Cheshire** D136
Prenton Preparatory School **Merseyside** D139
Prestfelde Preparatory School **Shropshire** D156
Prestwich Preparatory School **Greater Manchester** D137
Prince's Mead School **Hampshire** D144
Priory School **West Midlands** D157
Priory School of Our Lady of Walsingham **Isle of Wight** D145
Prospect House School **London** D130
Putney High School GDST **London** D130

Q

Quainton Hall School & Nursery **Middlesex** D121
Queen Elizabeth Grammar School (Junior Section) **West Yorkshire** D161
Queen Elizabeth's Hospital **Bristol** D152
Queen Ethelburga's Collegiate **North Yorkshire** D160
Queen Mary's School **North Yorkshire** D160
Queen's College **Somerset** D154
Queen's College Preparatory School **London** D132
Queen's Gate School **London** D130
Queenswood School **West Yorkshire** D161
Quinton House School **Northamptonshire** D117
Quwwat-ul-Islam Girls' School **London** D126

R

Radlett Preparatory School **Hertfordshire** D112
Radnor House **Middlesex** D121
Radnor House, Sevenoaks **Kent** D146
Rainbow Montessori School **London** D128
Ratcliffe College **Leicestershire** D116
Ravenscourt Park Preparatory School **London** D132
Red House School **Stockton-on-Tees** D134
Redcliffe Gardens School **London** D130
Reddam House Berkshire **Berkshire** D142
Reddiford School **Middlesex** D121
Redhill Preparatory School **Pembrokeshire** D170
Redmaids' High Junior School **Bristol** D152
Regius School **Edinburgh** D166
Reigate St Mary's Prep & Choir School **Surrey** D148
Rendcomb College **Gloucestershire** D107
Repton Prep **Derbyshire** D116
RGS Dodderhill **Worcestershire** D158
RGS Guildford Prep **Surrey** D148
RGS Springfield **Worcestershire** D158
RGS The Grange **Worcestershire** D158
Richmond House School **West Yorkshire** D161
Ringwood Waldorf School **Hampshire** D144
Ripley Court School **Surrey** D148
Riverston School **London** D129
Robert Gordon's College **Aberdeen** D166
Rockport School **County Down** D164
Rokeby School **Surrey** D123
Rookwood School **Hampshire** D144
Rose Hill School **Kent** D146
Rosemary Works Independent School **London** D127
Rosemead Preparatory School & Nursery, Dulwich **London** D129
Rossall School **Lancashire** D138
Rougemont School **Monmouthshire** D170
Rowan Preparatory School **Surrey** D148
Roxeth Mead School **Middlesex** D121
Royal Grammar School **Tyne & Wear** D134
Royal High Bath **Bath & North-East Somerset** D152
Royal Russell Junior School **Surrey** D123
Ruckleigh School **West Midlands** D158
Rupert House School **Oxfordshire** D107
Russell House School **Kent** D146
Rydal Penrhos Preparatory School **Clwyd** D170
Ryde School with Upper Chine **Isle of Wight** D145
Rydes Hill Preparatory School **Surrey** D148

Index

S

S. Anselm's School **Derbyshire** D116
Sacred Heart School **East Sussex** D143
Saint Christina's School **London** D128
Saint Felix School **Suffolk** D114
Saint Nicholas School **Essex** D111
Saint Pierre School **Essex** D111
Saint Ronan's School **Kent** D146
Salcombe Preparatory School **London** D127
Salisbury Cathedral School **Wiltshire** D108
Salterford House School **Nottinghamshire** D118
Sancton Wood School **Cambridgeshire** D110
Sandroyd School **Wiltshire** D108
Sarum Hall School **London** D128
Saville House School **Nottinghamshire** D118
Scarborough College **North Yorkshire** D160
Scarisbrick Hall School **Lancashire** D138
Seaford College **West Sussex** D149
Seaton House School **Surrey** D123
Sedbergh School **Cumbria** D136
Sevenoaks Preparatory School **Kent** D146
Shakhsiyah School, London **London** D127
Shakhsiyah School, Slough **Berkshire** D142
Shebbear College **Devon** D153
Sheffield Girls' GDST **South Yorkshire** D161
Sherborne House School **Hampshire** D144
Sherborne Preparatory School **Dorset** D154
Sherfield School **Hampshire** D144
Sherrardswood School **Hertfordshire** D112
Shoreham College **West Sussex** D149
Shrewsbury High School GDST **Shropshire** D156
Shrewsbury House Pre-Preparatory School **Surrey** D148
Shrewsbury House School **Surrey** D123
Sibford School **Oxfordshire** D107
Sidcot School **Somerset** D154
Silcoates School **West Yorkshire** D161
Sinclair House Montessori Nursery **London** D130
Sinclair House Preparatory School **London** D130
Skippers Hill Manor Preparatory School **East Sussex** D143
Slindon College **West Sussex** D149
Snaresbrook Preparatory School **London** D126
Solefield School **Kent** D146
Solihull Preparatory School **West Midlands** D158
Somerhill **Kent** D146
Sompting Abbotts Preparatory School **West Sussex** D149
South Devon Steiner School **Devon** D153
South Hampstead High School GDST **London** D128
South Lee Preparatory School **Suffolk** D114
Southbank International School - Hampstead **London** ...D128
Southbank International School - Kensington **London** ...D132
Spratton Hall **Northamptonshire** 53, D117
Spring Grove School **Kent** 80, D146
Springmead Preparatory School & Nursery **Somerset** D154
St Albans High School for Girls **Hertfordshire** D112
St Aloysius' College **Glasgow** D167
St Ambrose Preparatory School **Greater Manchester** ...D138
St Andrew's Prep **East Sussex** D143
St Andrew's School **Berkshire** D142
St Andrew's School **Kent** D146
St Aubyn's School **Essex** D120
St Augustine's Priory **London** D132
St Benedict's Junior School **London** D132
St Benedict's School **London** 62, D132
St Bernard's Preparatory School **Berkshire** D142
St Catherine's Prep **Middlesex** D121
St Catherine's School **Middlesex** 58, D121
St Catherine's, Bramley **Surrey** D148
St Cedd's School **Essex** 52, D111
St Christopher School **Hertfordshire** D112
St Christopher's Prep School & Nursery **Devon** D153
St Christopher's School **East Sussex** D143
St Christopher's School **Middlesex** D122
St Christopher's School **Surrey** D148
St Christopher's School **London** D128
St Christopher's The Hall School **Kent** D121
St Clare's School **Glamorgan** D170
St Columba's College Prep School **Hertfordshire** D112

St Columba's School **Renfrewshire** D167
St Crispin's School **Leicestershire** D116
St David's Prep **Kent** D121
St David's School **Surrey** D123
St Dunstan's College **London** D129
St Edmund's College & Prep School **Hertfordshire** D112
St Edmund's Junior School **Kent** D146
St Edward's Prep **Berkshire** D142
St Edward's Preparatory School **Gloucestershire** D107
St Faith's **Cambridgeshire** D110
St Faith's Prep **Kent** D146
St Francis School **Wiltshire** D108
St Francis' College **Hertfordshire** D112
St Gabriel's **West Berkshire** D108
St George's Junior School **Surrey** D148
St George's Preparatory School **Jersey** D104
St George's Preparatory School & Little Dragons Nursery **Lincolnshire** D117
St George's School for Girls **Edinburgh** D166
St George's School Windsor Castle **Berkshire** D142
St George's School, Edgbaston **West Midlands** D158
St Gerard's School **Gwynedd** 98, D170
St Helen and St Katharine **Oxfordshire** D107
St Helen's College **Middlesex** D122
St Helen's School **Middlesex** D122
St Helens Montessori School **Kent** D146
St Hilary's School **Surrey** D148
St Hilda's School **Hertfordshire** D112
St Hilda's School, Bushey **Hertfordshire** D112
St Hugh's School **Lincolnshire** D117
St Hugh's School **Oxfordshire** D107
St Ives School **Surrey** D148
St James Preparatory School **London** D132
St John's Beaumont Preparatory School **Berkshire** D142
St John's College School **Cambridgeshire** 50, D110
St John's College, Cardiff **Glamorgan** D170
St John's Priory School **Oxfordshire** D107
St John's School **Middlesex** D122
St John's School **Devon** D153
St John's School **Essex** D111
St Joseph's College **Suffolk** D114
St Joseph's College **Berkshire** D142
St Joseph's In The Park **Hertfordshire** D113
St Joseph's Park Hill School **Lancashire** D138
St Joseph's School **Nottinghamshire** D118
St Joseph's School **Cornwall** D153
St Lawrence College **Kent** D146
St Leonards School **Fife** D166
St Margaret's Preparatory School **Wiltshire** D108
St Margaret's Preparatory School **Essex** D111
St Margaret's School **London** D128
St Margaret's School for Girls **Aberdeen** D166
St Margaret's School, Bushey **Hertfordshire** D113
St Martin's Preparatory School **North-East Lincolnshire** ...D160
St Martin's School **Middlesex** D122
St Martin's School **London** D128
St Martin's School **Dorset** D154
St Mary's Hare Park School & Nursery **Essex** D120
St Mary's Music School **Edinburgh** D166
St Mary's Preparatory School **Oxfordshire** D107
St Mary's School **Buckinghamshire** D143
St Mary's School **Essex** D111
St Mary's School, Cambridge **Cambridgeshire** D110
St Mary's School, Hampstead **London** D128
St Michael's Church Of England Preparatory School **Essex** D111
St Michael's Preparatory School **Kent** D146
St Michael's Preparatory School **Jersey** D104
St Neot's School **Hampshire** D144
St Nicholas School **London** D128
St Nicholas' School **Hampshire** D144
St Olave's Preparatory School **London** D129
St Paul's Cathedral School **London** D126
St Paul's Juniors **London** D130
St Paul's Steiner School **London** D127
St Peter & St Paul School **Derbyshire** D116
St Peter's 2-8 **North Yorkshire** D160
St Peter's 8-13 **North Yorkshire** D160
St Peter's Preparatory School **Devon** D153
St Peter's School **Northamptonshire** D117

178

Index

St Philip's School **London** D130
St Philomena's Catholic School **Essex** D111
St Piran's School **Berkshire** D142
St Pius X Catholic Preparatory School **Lancashire** D138
St Swithun's Prep **Hampshire** 81, D144
St Teresa's Effingham (Preparatory School) **Surrey** D148
St Wilfrid's School **Devon** D153
St Winefride's RC Independent School **Shropshire** D156
St Wystan's School **Derbyshire** D116
St. Anne's Preparatory School **Essex** D111
St. Annes College Grammar School **Lancashire** D138
St. Anthony's School for Boys **London** D128
St. Bede's College **Greater Manchester** D138
St. Christopher's School **Jersey** D104
St. Dominic's Grammar School **Staffordshire** D156
St. Dominic's Priory School Stone **Staffordshire** D156
St. Edmund's School **Surrey** D148
St. John's Prep School **Hertfordshire** D113
St. Mary's College **Merseyside** D139
St. Mary's School **Borders** D166
St. Michael's School **Carmarthenshire** D170
St. Michael's School **West Berkshire** D108
Stafford Grammar School **Staffordshire** D156
Staines Preparatory School **Surrey** D123
Stamford Junior School **Lincolnshire** D117
Stanborough Primary School **Hertfordshire** D113
Stanfield Preparatory School **Merseyside** D139
Steephill School **Kent** D146
Stella Maris School **Greater Manchester** D138
Stephen Perse Junior School, Dame Bradbury's School **Essex** D111
Stephen Perse Junior School, Fitzwilliam Building **Cambridgeshire** D110
Stephen Perse Nurseries & Early Years **Cambridgeshire** D110
Stockport Grammar School **Greater Manchester** D138
Stockton House School **Hampshire** D144
Stoke College **Suffolk** D114
Stonar School **Wiltshire** D108
Stonyhurst St Mary's Hall **Lancashire** D138
Stormont **Hertfordshire** D113
Stover School **Devon** D153
Stratford Preparatory School **Warwickshire** D157
Streatham & Clapham High School GDST **London** D130
Summer Fields **Oxfordshire** D108
Summerhill School **Suffolk** D114
Sunningdale School **Berkshire** D142
Sunninghill Preparatory School **Dorset** D154
Sunrise Nursery Stoke Newington **London** D127
Surbiton Preparatory School **Surrey** D148
Sussex House School **London** D130
Sutton High School GDST **Surrey** D123
Sutton Valence Preparatory School **Kent** D146
Swanbourne House School **Buckinghamshire** D106
Swedish School in London **London** D130
Sycamore Hall Preparatory School **South Yorkshire** D161
Sydenham High School GDST **London** D129

T

Talbot Heath **Dorset** D154
Talbot House Preparatory School **Dorset** D154
Talmud Torah Chaim Meirim School **London** D127
Talmud Torah Machzikei Hadass School **London** D126
Talmud Torah Yetev Lev School **London** D127
Tashbar of Manchester **Greater Manchester** D138
TASIS England **Surrey** D148
Taunton School **Somerset** D154
Tayyibah Girls School **London** D127
Teesside High School **Stockton-on-Tees** D134
Terra Nova School **Cheshire** D136
Terrington Hall **North Yorkshire** D160
Tettenhall College **West Midlands** D158
The Abbey School **Berkshire** D142
The Academy School **London** D128
The Acorn School **Gloucestershire** D107
The Alternative School **Lancashire** D138
The American School in London **London** D128
The Annex School **Kent** D146
The Beacon School **Buckinghamshire** D106
The Belvedere Preparatory School **Merseyside** D139

The Blue Coat School **West Midlands** D158
The Branch Christian School **West Yorkshire** D162
The Brighton Waldorf School **East Sussex** D143
The Buchan School **Isle of Man** D138
The Cathedral School, Llandaff **Glamorgan** D170
The Cavendish School **London** D128
The Chadderton Preparatory Grammar School **Greater Manchester** D138
The Children's House **North-East Lincolnshire** D160
The Children's House Upper School **London** D127
The Compass School **East Lothian** D166
The Cornwall Independent School **Cornwall** D153
The Crescent School **Warwickshire** D157
The Croft Preparatory School **Warwickshire** D157
The Dixie Grammar School **Leicestershire** D116
The Downs Malvern **Worcestershire** D158
The Downs Preparatory School **Bristol** D152
The Drive Prep School **East Sussex** D143
The Eden SDA School **Middlesex** D122
The Edinburgh Academy **Edinburgh** D166
The Elms **Worcestershire** D158
The Firs School **Cheshire** D136
The Froebelian School **West Yorkshire** 90, D162
The Glasgow Academy, Kelvinbridge **Glasgow** D167
The Glasgow Academy, Milngavie **Glasgow** D167
The Glasgow Academy, Newlands **Glasgow** D167
The Gleddings School **West Yorkshire** D162
The Gower School Nursery **London** D127
The Gower School Primary **London** D127
The Grammar School at Leeds **West Yorkshire** D162
The Grange School **Cheshire** D136
The Granville School **Kent** D146
The Gregg Prep School **Hampshire** D144
The Hall Pre-Preparatory School & Nursery **Middlesex** D122
The Hall School **London** D128
The Hawthorns School **Surrey** D148
The High School of Glasgow **Glasgow** D167
The Independent Grammar School: Durham **Durham** D134
The Japanese School in London **London** D132
The Junior King's School, Canterbury **Kent** D146
The King Alfred School **London** D128
The King's House School, Windsor **Berkshire** D142
The King's School **Gloucestershire** D107
The King's School **Hampshire** D144
The King's School **Hertfordshire** D113
The King's School in Macclesfield **Cheshire** D136
The King's School, Chester **Cheshire** D136
The King's School, Witney **Oxfordshire** D108
The Kingsley School **Warwickshire** D157
The Ladies' College **Guernsey** D104
The Lyceum School **London** D126
The Mall School **Middlesex** D122
The Manchester Grammar School **Greater Manchester** D138
The Manor Preparatory School **Oxfordshire** D108
The Marist Preparatory School **Berkshire** D142
The Maynard School **Devon** D153
The Mead School **Kent** D146
The Meadows Montessori School **Suffolk** D114
The Merlin School **London** D130
The Montessori Pavilion - The Kindergarten School **London** D130
The Montessori Place **East Sussex** D143
The Mount Junior School **North Yorkshire** D160
The Mount School **West Yorkshire** D162
The Mulberry House School **London** D128
The New Beacon School **Kent** D146
The New Forest Small School **Hampshire** D144
The New School London **London** D129
The Norwegian School in London **London** D130
The Old Hall School **Shropshire** D156
The Old School Henstead **Suffolk** D114
The Oratory Prep School **Berkshire** D142
The Orchard School **Nottinghamshire** D118
The Paragon School **Bath & North-East Somerset** D152
The Perse Pelican Pre-Prep & Nursery **Cambridgeshire** D110
The Perse Prep School **Cambridgeshire** D110
The Peterborough School **Cambridgeshire** D110
The Pilgrims' School **Hampshire** D145
The Pointer School **London** D129
The Portsmouth Grammar Junior School **Hampshire** D145

179

Index

The Prebendal School **West Sussex** ... D149
The Purcell School, London **Hertfordshire** ... D113
The Queen's School **Cheshire** ... 64, D136
The Read School **North Yorkshire** ... D160
The Richard Pate School **Gloucestershire** ... D107
The River School **Worcestershire** ... D158
The Roche School **London** ... D130
The Rowans School **London** ... D130
The Royal Junior School **Surrey** ... D148
The Royal Masonic School for Girls **Hertfordshire** ... D120
The Royal School, Armagh **County Armagh** ... D164
The Royal School, Wolverhampton **West Midlands** ... D158
The Ryleys School **Cheshire** ... D136
The Shrubbery School **West Midlands** ... D158
The St Michael Steiner School **Middlesex** ... D122
The Study Preparatory School **London** ... D130
The Study School **Surrey** ... D123
The Ursuline Preparatory School Ilford **Essex** ... D120
The Villa School & Nursery **London** ... D129
The Village Prep School **London** ... D128
The Vine Christian School **Berkshire** ... D142
The Webber Independent School **Buckinghamshire** ... D106
The White House Preparatory School & Woodentops Kindergarten **London** D130
Thetford Grammar School **Norfolk** ... D113
Thomas's Academy **London** ... D130
Thomas's Battersea **London** ... D130
Thomas's Clapham **London** ... D130
Thomas's Fulham **London** ... D130
Thomas's Kensington **London** ... D132
Thomas's Outdoors **London** ... D130
Thorngrove School **Hampshire** ... D145
Thornton College **Buckinghamshire** ... D106
Thorpe Hall School **Essex** ... D111
Thorpe House School **Buckinghamshire** ... D143
Tockington Manor School **Bristol** ... D152
Torah Vodaas **London** ... D128
Tormead School **Surrey** ... D148
Torwood House School **Bristol** ... D152
Tower College **Merseyside** ... D139
Tower House School **London** ... D130
Town Close School **Norfolk** ... D113
Tranby **East Riding of Yorkshire** ... D160
Treffos School **Gwynedd** ... D170
Trent College and The Elms **Nottinghamshire** ... D118
Trevor-Roberts School **London** ... D128
Tring Park School for the Performing Arts **Hertfordshire** ... D113
Trinity Christian School **Berkshire** ... D143
Trinity Christian School **Greater Manchester** ... D138
Trinity School **Devon** ... D153
Truro High School for Girls **Cornwall** ... D153
Truro School **Cornwall** ... D153
TTTYY School **London** ... D127
Twickenham Preparatory School **Middlesex** ... D122
Twycross House Pre-Preparatory School (The Hollies) **Warwickshire** ... D157
Twycross House School **Warwickshire** ... D157
Twyford School **Hampshire** ... D145

U

Ummul Mumineen Academy **Glamorgan** ... D170
Unicorn School **Surrey** ... D123
University College School Hampstead (UCS) Junior **London** ... D128
University College School Hampstead (UCS) Pre-Prep **London** ... D128
Upton House School **Berkshire** ... D143
Ursuline Preparatory School **Essex** ... D111

V

Victoria College Belfast **County Antrim** ... D164
Victoria College Preparatory School **Jersey** ... D104
Vinehall **East Sussex** ... D143
Vita et Pax School **London** ... D127

W

Wakefield Girls' High School (Junior Section) **West Yorkshire** ... D162
Wakefield Grammar Pre-Preparatory School **West Yorkshire** ... D162
Wakefield Independent School **West Yorkshire** ... D162
Walhampton **Hampshire** ... D145
Walthamstow Hall Pre-Prep and Junior School **Kent** ... D146
Walthamstow Montessori School **London** ... D126
Walton Pre-Preparatory School & Nursery **Buckinghamshire** ... D106
Wandsworth Preparatory School **London** ... D130
Warlingham Park School **Surrey** ... D148
Warminster School **Wiltshire** ... D108
Warwick Preparatory School **Warwickshire** ... D157
Warwick School **Warwickshire** ... D157
Watchorn Christian School **Derbyshire** ... D116
Waverley Preparatory School & Day Nursery **Berkshire** ... D143
Wellesley House **Kent** ... D146
Wellesley Prep School **Hampshire** ... D145
Wellingborough School **Northamptonshire** ... D117
Wellington College Prep **Berkshire** ... 82, D143
Wellington Prep School **Somerset** ... D154
Wellington School **South Ayrshire** ... D167
Wellow House School **Nottinghamshire** ... D118
Wells Cathedral School **Somerset** ... D154
West Buckland School **Devon** ... D153
West Hill Park School **Hampshire** ... D145
West House School **West Midlands** ... D158
West Lodge School **Kent** ... D121
Westbourne House School **West Sussex** ... D149
Westbourne School **South Yorkshire** ... D161
Westbourne School **Glamorgan** ... D170
Westbrook Hay Prep School **Hertfordshire** ... D113
Westbury House **Surrey** ... D123
Westfield School **Tyne & Wear** ... D134
Westholme School **Lancashire** ... D138
Westminster Abbey Choir School **London** ... D130
Westminster Cathedral Choir School **London** ... D130
Westminster Under School **London** ... D131
Weston Green School **Surrey** ... D148
Westonbirt Prep School **Gloucestershire** ... D107
Westville House School **West Yorkshire** ... D162
Wetherby Kensington **London** ... D131
Wetherby Notting Hill **London** ... D132
Wetherby Preparatory School **London** ... D132
Wharfedale Montessori School **North Yorkshire** ... D160
Whitehall School **Cambridgeshire** ... D110
Widford Lodge Preparatory School **Essex** ... D111
Willington Independent Preparatory School **London** ... D131
Wilmslow Preparatory School **Cheshire** ... D136
Wimbledon Common Preparatory School **London** ... D131
Wimbledon High School GDST **London** ... D131
Winchester House School **Northamptonshire** ... D117
Windermere School, Infant & Junior School **Cumbria** ... 65, D136
Windlesham House School **West Sussex** ... D149
Windlesham School **East Sussex** ... D143
Windrush Valley School **Oxfordshire** ... D108
Winston House Preparatory School **London** ... D126
Winterfold House School **Worcestershire** ... D158
Witham Hall Preparatory School **Lincolnshire** ... D117
Withington Girls' School **Greater Manchester** ... D138
Wolverhampton Grammar School **West Midlands** ... D158
Woodbridge School Prep **Suffolk** ... D114
Woodcote House School **Surrey** ... D148
Woodford Green Preparatory School **Essex** ... 60, D120
Woodhouse Grove School **West Yorkshire** ... 91, D162
Woodlands School, Great Warley **Essex** ... D111
Woodlands School, Hutton Manor **Essex** ... D111
Worksop College, Ranby House **Nottinghamshire** ... D118
Wycliffe College **Gloucestershire** ... D107
Wymondham College Prep School **Norfolk** ... D113

Y

Yarlet School **Staffordshire** ... D156
Yarm Preparatory School **Stockton-on-Tees** ... D134
Yarrells School & Nursery **Dorset** ... D154
Yateley Manor School **Hampshire** ... D145
Yehudi Menuhin School **Surrey** ... D148
Yesodey Hatorah Senior Girls' School **London** ... D127
York House School **Hertfordshire** ... D113
York Steiner School **North Yorkshire** ... D160